MW00454726

'Ian Garner has produced a brilliant and chilling investigation. He meticulously details how extraordinary levels of hate permeate a large section of the under-30s, who came of age under Putin's tutelage. No one can finish this book and still believe the invasion of Ukraine was just the fault of one bad guy in the Kremlin. As Garner so expertly shows, whatever happens in the war, we will be dealing with the consequences of Russian fascism for years to come.'

Nick Cohen, *Observer columnist and author*

'A forensic and grippingly-told examination of the descent of Russian youth into state-encouraged violent fascism. Garner makes the reader understand both the scale of the problem, and that it is one we will be facing for decades to come.'

David Patrikarakos, author of *War in 140 Characters: How Social Media Is Reshaping Conflict in the Twenty-First Century*, which draws from his reporting on the Russia-Ukraine conflict

'An unflinching and essential portrayal of the Putler Jugend with all its paradoxes and sadism.'

Peter Pomerantsev, author of *Nothing is True and Everything is Possible: Adventures in Modern Russia*

'If you thought Putin's Russia was an ideology-free kleptocracy and most Russians are ashamed of or opposed to the invasion of Ukraine, read Ian Garner's gripping historical-cultural analysis of the descent of a portion of Russia's youth into fascist euphoria in support of their country's illegal invasion of Ukraine.'

Maria Popova, Associate Professor of Political Science and Jean Monnet Chair, McGill University

'What do young Russians think about their country, Putin and the world? Why do many tech-savvy, successful and well-educated young Russians support their country's invasion of Ukraine? Combining personal observations and academic research, this provocative book addresses questions crucial for understanding Russia's past, present and future.'

Eugene Finkel, Kenneth H. Keller Associate Professor of International Affairs, Johns Hopkins School of Advanced International Studies, and editor of *Coloured Revolutions and Authoritarian Reactions*

'Ian Garner's exceptional book deals with its subject matter—the growth of Russian fascism—in a way that is multifaceted and nuanced, but also clear-sighted about the threat it poses to Russia's neighbours, the liberal international order and Russia itself.'

Mart Kuldkepp, Associate Professor of Scandinavian History and Politics, University College London

Z GENERATION

NEW PERSPECTIVES ON EASTERN EUROPE AND EURASIA

The states of Eastern Europe and Eurasia are once again at the centre of global attention, particularly following Russia's 2022 full-scale invasion of Ukraine. But media coverage can only do so much in providing the necessary context to make sense of fast-moving developments. The books in this series provide original, engaging and timely perspectives on Eastern Europe and Eurasia for a general readership. Written by experts on—and from—these states, the books in the series cover an eclectic range of cutting-edge topics relating to politics, history, culture, economics and society. The series is originated by Hurst, with titles co-published or distributed in North America by Oxford University Press, New York.

Series editor: Dr Ben Noble—Associate Professor of Russian Politics at University College London and Associate Fellow at Chatham House

IAN GARNER

Z Generation

Into the Heart of Russia's Fascist Youth

HURST & COMPANY, LONDON

First published in the United Kingdom in 2023 by
C. Hurst & Co. (Publishers) Ltd.,
New Wing, Somerset House, Strand, London, WC2R 1LA
© Ian Garner, 2023
All rights reserved.

Distributed in the United States, Canada and Latin America by
Oxford University Press, 198 Madison Avenue, New York, NY 10016,
United States of America.

The right of Ian Garner to be identified as the author of this publication
is asserted by him in accordance with the Copyright, Designs and
Patents Act, 1988.

A Cataloguing-in-Publication data record for this book
is available from the British Library.

ISBN: 9781787389281

This book is printed using paper from registered, sustainable
and managed sources.

www.hurstpublishers.com

Printed in Great Britain by Bell and Bain Ltd, Glasgow

CONTENTS

ACKNOWLEDGMENTS

I'm immensely grateful for the patience, insights, and generosity of those who've helped me magic this book into existence at lightning speed.

Above all, to Masha and Varya. The moral support. The patience. The cups of tea. The concerts and compositions. All fabulous.

Michael Dwyer, Lara Weisweiller-Wu, Tim Page, and the rest of the team at Hurst who've made this project a reality. You're all superstars.

Dozens of wonderful people have answered questions, made suggestions, and provided their insights for me. They are too many to mention, but special thanks to: Emma Burrows, Robert Dale, Allyson Edwards, Aleksandr Fokin, Matthew Ford, Maximilian Hess, Greg Hicks, Francine Hirsch, Stephen Ivie, Jade McGlynn, Alison Meek, Ben Noble, Francis Scarr, Ivana Stradner, Jonny Tickle, and Josh Wright.

And to those who've given time for interviews and other commentary from or on the inside: Anton Barbashin, Toomas Ilves, Sokeel Park, Bob Rae, Oleksandra Tsekhanovska, and Bruce White.

Finally, my thanks go to my interviewees and subjects, both named and anonymous. I hope I have been fair in the ways I have portrayed you. We may always disagree on politics, but I hope we can find peace.

1

GOD IS WITH OUR BOYS

"Fuck those Ukronazi scum."

"God is with our boys, kill the f*gs."

"Don't sell out the motherland, bitch."

"Treacherous scum die."

Nineteen-year-old Alina is from Nizhny Tagil, a rather unwelcoming and rapidly shrinking post-Soviet city best known for its iron-ore industry and for producing Soviet tanks.[1] By Russian standards, she's had a fortunate upbringing. Her father is a senior accountant in a local business making good money, so she's been able to travel widely. She covets her iPhone and her MacBook, and she loves to get her hands on the latest designer clothes on her annual 2,000-mile round-trip to Moscow.

When she's not studying for her degree in graphic design, Alina does all the things anyone else of her age might. She hangs out with her boyfriend, Sergey, who works in a local mechanic shop. They and their friends watch the latest Hollywood blockbusters at the local cinema, which are today being pirated into the Russian market or played as second billing after a cheap domestic production (Anna's friends are, they say, "sick of" the "boring" domestic productions, which are usually cheap romance and state-funded World War II epics).

They down fearsome quantities of alcohol in local bars—but, inspired by the minimalist aesthetic of Instagram influencers, they also wish they drank less and are perpetually on the brink of embracing a "clean living" lifestyle. They love to go on long walks—the great Russian *progulki*—fueled by beer and cigarettes galore in the short summer months when temperatures are known to reach into the scorching high 30s. When she graduates, Alina dreams of ditching Nizhny Tagil's disintegrating Soviet-era architecture for the bright lights of Moscow with Sergey. She has her sights set on a job in the capital's up-and-coming high-tech industry.

Alina, like most young people in Russia, is addicted to her smartphone. She has uploaded all the trappings of ordinary millennial life to her page on VK, the "Russian Facebook" used regularly by over 70 million Russian citizens. She shows off photos of trips to Egypt—relaxing on the beach; taking dips in soothing, still pools—and to Sochi, the Black Sea resort that hosted the Winter Olympics in 2014 just before Vladimir Putin's army seized Crimea from Ukraine. She shares videos about nail design, fashion, and movies and TV. Alina's a big fan of Maisie Williams' *Game of Thrones* character, who is in her words a "fierce" role model of modern womanhood.

But since 24 February 2022, when Russia unfroze the conflict in Eastern Ukraine it had started in 2014 by sending an invasion force into the country, Alina's VK page has become a different world. The fripperies of consumerist life have been submerged. Like hundreds of thousands of other Russians, Alina has joined dozens of government-run and promoted (or "astroturfed") groups with names like "REAL Ukraine," "Antiterror Z," "Z for Victory," "The Russian Spring," and "Ztrength in Truth." Whether holed up in a bedroom still adorned with the accoutrements of teen life—gaudy posters plastered over drab flowery wallpaper, cosmetics tubs scattered over the table, framed photos of friends lining bookshelves—or whether posting from class, from the back seat of a bus, or from a bar while chatting with her friends, Alina's thirst for liking, commenting on, and sharing the world of Russia's war against Ukraine seems unquenchable.

Alina began by sharing posts direct from the groups she had joined. In this conspiracy-fueled world, new "truths" about depraved Ukrainian neo-Nazis are uncovered every day, Russia is under constant threat from shadowy forces led by NATO and the American government, and Ukraine has to be destroyed to save itself—and Russians—from a spectral Nazi threat. Alina's VK wall is packed with apocalyptic images of a burning White House in "Fashington, DC," of the Ukrainian flag (the "Devil's Swastika"), of Orthodox priests and saints blessing the troops at the Ukrainian front, and of Putin as a "savior." In this reality, a sacred Russia is surrounded by enemies bent on its total obliteration.

As the war in Ukraine has unfolded, Alina has begun to improvise. She riffs on the themes and language of these frightening social media communities in skittish, tempestuous remarks: "*Khokhols* [a derogatory term for Ukrainians] are assholes"; "The white of our Russian flag means cleanliness"; "Ukrofascists, you're RABID DOGS"; "If I was [in charge] you fuckers would get what you deserve"; "Ukrainians, better not talk in Ukrainian, it just sounds stupid, like fucked up Russian." Putin, Alina posts, is "a gift from God. We are all Putin." Alina's life before the invasion could have belonged to any American or European teenager who loved their phone and fancied big-city life over provincial tedium. No longer.

The talk of cleanliness, the language of dehumanization, the mockery. Alina is not merely parroting the propaganda of her own government and the social media groups she has joined. She has learned to speak a language of violence—a language of Russian fascism.

Alina is not alone. Thousands of Russians are today participating in this public display of hatred and warmongering on the Runet— the Russian-language internet, which has its own social networks; search engines; blogging sites; and food-delivery, ride-hailing, and shopping apps. Young Russian internet users flaunt their rage and drive each other into an anti-Ukrainian frenzy as news of (or, rather, conspiracies about) the war consumes every part of Russian society. Ukrainians are attacked as subhuman, the latest government conspiracy about Western evil is repeated ad nauseam to millions of social media users, Putin and God are praised for leading Russia into Ukraine to drive out and destroy the fascist threat, and dead young troops are lauded as saintly martyrs.[2]

How did Alina, a seemingly Westernized, Hollywood-loving, and carefree teen with dreams of a modern career in the buzzing and cosmopolitan hub of Moscow turn into an online fascist, seemingly overnight? Does she believe a word of what she writes, or is it all for show? Who is she writing for? And what next for Russia and for the world if a generation of furious, fascist Alinas grows up to take charge of the world's biggest nuclear power?

Invasion and purification

By early 2022, Russia had amassed almost 200,000 soldiers on its border with Eastern Ukraine, over 1,000 miles from Alina's home in Nizhny Tagil. The government was ready to dramatically intervene in a conflict that had roiled away since 2014, when Moscow seized Crimea and established separatist regimes in Donetsk and Luhansk in the east of Ukraine.

During the night of 24 February, Putin addressed the nation.[3] Speaking from a regal, wood-paneled office deep in the Kremlin, he claimed that Russia was obliged to launch a "special military operation"—a phrase that sounds as hollow in Russian as in English— in Ukraine.

The president reeled off a series of ahistorical and illogical justifications for his decision. The operation would defend Ukrainians from the "humiliation and genocide perpetrated by the Kiev regime."[4] Russia would not "impose anything ... by force"; it only sought to ensure "freedom" from a supposedly "Nazi" regime in Kyiv. Putin called on the Russian people to recognize their ancestors' sacrifices in World War II, when 25 million Soviets died fighting Hitler's armies, and to fight for their "ancestors' culture, values, experiences, and traditions." Putin concluded on a spiritually infused note of hope: "I believe in your support and in the invincible force that gives us our love for the fatherland." This was a war of belief, of faith: in Russian, the two words share a single root.

The invading forces were beset by logistical disasters, mass casualties, and a failure to reach their goal of rapidly overwhelming Kyiv. Nonetheless, infantry and artillery set about brutalizing the enemy. Bustling cities like Mariupol were razed. Civilians were deliberately targeted with rocket fire and bombing raids. In early April, when Ukrainian troops drove the occupiers away from Kyiv, they began to unearth evidence of the most shocking atrocities seen on European soil since the Yugoslav wars. Russian soldiers had run riot, torturing, murdering, and raping innocent civilians. Since then, the discoveries of mass graves and torture sites have kept coming.

At home, the government's allies in the media and the Orthodox Church went on their own 24/7 offensive. Foghorn opinion makers advocated for nuclear attacks on the West, invading the Baltic states, and claimed that Ukrainian "Nazis" were responsible for historical crimes from World War II to the present. Images of children supposedly killed by Ukrainian armed forces and rescued by Russia's "Allied Forces"—the allies being the occupied territories of Donetsk and Luhansk—flooded social media. Everyone from Ukraine to Britain; Canada; the United States Poland; Japan; Sweden; Finland; NGOs; and, most absurdly of all, Israel was labeled a Nazi-loving terror supporter.

Calls to commit genocide and descriptions of threats to Russia were delivered in a language of macho, misogynistic, and homophobic hatred. Russia's enemies are "f***ots," "women," "pussies," or "blacks" and "n****rs." Ukrainians are subjected to torrents of abuse that echo the language of Nazism: they are "diseased," "beasts," "monsters," "animals," and—worst of all—*nelyudi*, "unpeople."[5] "Why poison a handful of cockroaches with sarin when there are a host of simpler and cheaper ways to do it?" asked one popular journalist and blogger after Russia was accused of using chemical weapons in Ukraine.

Ever un-Christian, the Russian Orthodox Church does nothing to discourage violent behavior. Its leader, Patriarch Kirill, instead blesses the army from the pulpit of the Cathedral of the Armed Forces in Moscow, a state-funded megachurch that hosts military exhibitions and opened on Victory Day in 2020, the state's annual pageant in memory of the end of World War II. Religion is so totally at one with the state of 2022 that commentators assert that "the Russian Patriarch believes in Putin instead of believing in God."[6]

Users on the social media network Telegram—a WhatsApp-like messaging app favored for the news and discussion channels its users can join—and on Alina's beloved VK were hooked. Rape, torture, and violent fantasies encouraged by the state, the media, and the Church—the unholy trinity of power in today's Russia—were in turn made reality at the front.

The regime simultaneously moved to close off the Russian public's access to outside information—and to shut them up when they dared to deviate from the state's propaganda lines. The few remaining independent news outlets, like the liberal radio station Echo of Moscow and the independent TV Rain, were shut down. Journalists—

even the Nobel Prize-winning Dmitry Muratov—were publicly assaulted by heavies and hooligans. The hugely popular Instagram and Facebook were blocked, even if tech-savvy young Russians easily skirted the government's restrictions. A draconian new law forbade spreading "fake news" about the Russian army, threatening citizens with up to fifteen years in jail or up to 1.5 million rubles (over twenty times the monthly average salary of just under 58,000 rubles) in fines.

Russian audiences were enraptured and shocked. Some young Russians took to the streets in protest, leading to the arrest of 15,000 citizens by Putin's security forces in the three weeks after the declaration of war. Isolated, absurdist demonstrations against the government's policies—students covered in fake blood popping up outside universities or holding blank protest signs on Moscow's Red Square—went viral in the West but were mostly ignored in Russia.

A trickle of celebrities spoke out. Unexpected voices of reason like Ivan Urgant, the host of a long-running and hugely popular Jimmy Kimmel-esque late-night chat show on state TV, rapidly found themselves out of a job—and out of the country, fleeing to Israel, Cyprus, and beyond. Familiar thorns in the regime's side—young celebrities like the outspoken rapper Alisher Morgenshtern and YouTubers like Yury Dud, who makes confrontational documentaries about state corruption and authoritarianism for his millions of subscribers—rapidly found themselves classed as "foreign agents," a tag that comes with sweeping legal restrictions.[7] These famous "enemies of the state" were castigated by politicians, propagandists, and priests in a blaze of public criticism.

And it wasn't just famous Russians voting with their feet. An estimated 200,000 Russians left the country within weeks, taking advantage of favorable visa regimes to decamp to former Soviet countries with large Russian-speaking populations like Georgia, Armenia, and Kazakhstan. The lucky few with connections, money, and the right visas made it to the Baltic states or further afield in Europe.

But the protest movement fizzled out as quickly as it flared up. By late March, its public face was effectively dead. A handful of celebrities slowly announced their anti-war views and a trickle of Russians continued to leave the country, which turned into a brief flood when the state announced mandatory recruitment in late

September, but the opposition overall retreated and fell silent. Russia may be famed for centuries of dissidents—from the poet Aleksandr Pushkin to Lenin, Andrey Sakharov, and Aleksey Navalny—but its opposition has never been so browbeaten.

Something alarming had cracked open in Russian society. Putin's justification for the invasion may have been flimsy—and the propaganda flood of "discoveries" of Ukrainian COVID biolabs, plots to build nuclear weapons, and conspiracies spanning everything from rural American colleges to Kyiv veterinary clinics absurd— but most Russians to some extent professed support for the war. According to opinion polls, albeit of shaky reliability, up to 70–80 percent—and over half of the eighteen to twenty-five demographic—supported the "special operation."[8]

Indeed, for all the celebrities who left, there were equal numbers promoting the war. Aleksandr Ovechkin, the national sporting hero and Washington Capitals hockey captain, traveled to Moscow to meet a pro-Putin youth leader. The rap mogul Timati, Russia's answer to Jay-Z, who owns everything from record labels to burger joints and who has close ties to the Kremlin, claimed that "the world wants another Gorbachev or Yeltsin"—supposedly weak, anti-Russian leaders—"but history has other plans." Roma Zhelud, a photogenic young YouTube singer turned all-purpose celebrity, railed against Western support for Ukraine on his Instagram feed: "Go Russia! I'm for world peace, the hatred and calls to kill Russians made by those you support have shown us your true face!!"

A language of violence began to trample the shoots of anti-war protest. In April, Western publics were rocked by the discovery of mass murders in the Kyiv suburb of Bucha. Images of corpses, their hands tied and their eyes blindfolded, discarded in the streets, of mutilated bodies, of torture chambers in cellars and schools shocked the world. The Russian government went into overdrive to produce a narrative that promised the footage was faked, that it was a Western "provocation," that perhaps there were no bodies at all, or that Ukrainian and shadowy Western forces had committed mass murder to fit the good and honest Russian army up.[9]

Some Russians bought none of it. But plenty more found their voice on nationalist social media channels, where they almost chided their country's army for showing mercy to the enemy.

Hundreds of users left comments: these "*unpeople*," "vermin," and "diseased" Ukrainians "deserved to die." "We've got to kill these fuckers," said one user.[10]

Alina joined in the frenzy: "Bucha. I'll create another Bucha. I'll teach them." She does not merely deny atrocities committed by Russia; she embraces them. Alina even promises that she would like to take part in a genocide against two of the state's enemies— Ukrainians and homosexuals—at home: "Ukies, come have a gay pride parade in Tigil, we'll turn it into a meatgrinder." "Meatgrinder" is a favorite Russian synonym for a trial by torture, a bloodbath of the sort the Soviets had to live through in World War II. Now, supposedly, "ethnic Russians"—Russian speakers Putin's state claims to defend—are fed through another meatgrinder by their enemies. Alina lumps all of Russia's "enemies" into one basket: Ukrainians, homosexuals, and Nazis are all synonymously not Russian. Therefore, they are both evil and undesirable.

Prompted by the state, its propagandists, a whole host of famous faces, and a vast web of social media groups, Russians like Alina encouraged Russian troops to behave in the most abhorrent ways as they rampaged through occupied Ukrainian towns. The soldiers transgressed, and swathes—not all, but at least a sizable minority— of the public didn't just applaud. Like Alina, they egged them on, relishing their status as the Western media's bad guys. The worse the atrocity, the more the public proclaimed that *#WeArentAshamed* (*NamNeStydno*). They believed in their crusade. They believed they were purifying Russia—a country that exists wherever Moscow has once reigned and wherever Russian is spoken.

* * *

Alina's path is not the only one today's Russians are taking. Yet young Russians on the other side of the divide are more afraid than ever before to speak out. I sent dozens of emails to contacts and old friends. Even my most trusted contacts don't want to open up:

> Sveta, hey. Long time no speak, but I hope you're doing well. Listen up, I'm writing about young people in Russia. I know you're probably busy, but can I chat to you about it? I'd love to get your thoughts on what it's like teaching kids right now.

The ping is almost instantaneous. Sveta writes back with the same response I've seen so many times already: "That's so cool. It's lovely to hear from you. Everything in our country is complicated right now, so I can't help. Best, Sveta."

"Complicated": a word that said more than any lengthy political discussion. Sveta, who's now a schoolteacher in her early thirties, was never one to keep quiet. We used to hang out in a more hopeful St Petersburg, the canal-filled northern Venice that for many Russians embodies the nation's links to European culture and power, in the late 2000s.

Sveta loved the West, but she also loved her country. She spoke great English, but she always wanted to show off the "real Russia." She'd take me on tours of the city's baroque architecture, lead me through its canals and boulevards, shepherd me off on the subway to its far-flung modern outskirts, and invite me to family gatherings. Sveta loved hot indie bands from Britain and the States, but she never thought of leaving the country. For Sveta and many of her generation, St Petersburg, and Russia with it, had been drifting inexorably towards its European destiny in the 2000s. That meant cultural belonging, political calm, liberal values, and economic prosperity.

But in 2022, even Sveta didn't want to talk about what was going on. Something in her curt response—she'd totally brushed me off—was new. A curtain is again descending between Russia and the West. The old, Europeanizing values of Russian's young people seem to be disappearing as the revanchism, paranoia, and aggression of Alina's VK feed and Putin's speeches come to the fore.

On 16 March, Putin appeared again on television to address the nation. Russia, he claimed, was threatened not just by forces from the outside but by "fifth columnists" who had to be "cleansed."[11] The state media claimed spies and enemies were everywhere and always working on behalf of a shadowy cabal of forces that included "globalists," America, and Ukraine. Television depicted these so-called spies being violently arrested. Front doors were shattered with battering rams, car doors torn open, and bodies thrown onto sidewalks and stairwells. The faces of confused young men were smashed into the ground as thuggish security personnel screamed abuse into their ears. Images of supposed traitors' front doors daubed with graffiti—

9

"TRAITOR TO THE MOTHERLAND," "DON'T SELL OUT YOUR COUNTRY, BITCH"—spread widely online. They were celebrated in nationalist groups and received with funereal silence by stunned liberals.

A few days after she knocked me back, Sveta cracked. She and her colleagues at the public school in St Petersburg where she had worked for the last half decade uploaded images of themselves fanned out in the shape of a "Z"—the symbol of support for the war—to VK. Clad in dark gray overcoats that shielded them from the gloomy damp of Petersburg's early spring, the group in the photograph was almost imperceptible against the disintegrating gray asphalt of the Soviet-era schoolyard. Sveta was on the edge of the shot, limply waving a Russian flag.

* * *

Many average Russians with average salaries, regular dreams and ambitions, and no funding or special incentive from the government have been persuaded that Ukraine is such a great threat that the nation and its population may have to be sacrificed in order to cleanse Russia. They participate in the state's propaganda projects, offering up the limpest of protestations before caving in. This phenomenon is not new in Russia. In the Soviet Union, the most ordinary people were frequently the regime's most enthusiastic supporters, embracing its symbolism and language to construct their own identity.[12] Not every Russian today is following Alina's path to extremism, but even those who claim apathy are being constantly exposed to the extremists' world.

Young Russian zealots like Alina are, however, something new in the post-Soviet space. For Alina, publicly performing aggressive nationalist language, sharing conspiratorial memes, and demonstrating support for the Ukraine war is heartfelt. For her, Russia deserves to be a great nation. It is surrounded by threats. Western movies and TV are rapidly losing their appeal as she spots ever more terrifying conspiracies hidden within the Trojan horse of American culture. She, and everyone younger than her, may only ever know a Russia almost completely cut off from the West—a Russia driven by messianic, apocalyptic, and spiritual goals of Eurasian domination. This is a Russia they want to immerse themselves in, a Russia that promises more profound, spiritual rewards than the superficial but dangerous lifestyle of the "woke" West. This is a fascist Russia.

Fascism in the social media age

Two months before the dissolution of the USSR in December 1991, the former Soviet Foreign Minister Eduard Shevardnadze met a German delegation in Moscow. A perceptive reformer who had often clashed with hardliners in the Communist Party, Shevardnadze warned his German counterparts that in the wake of the USSR's imminent collapse it would be all too easy for a "fascist leader" to seize power in Russia and seek Crimea's return to the country's territory.[13] Even Shevardnadze, who would go on to become president of Georgia, could hardly have predicted the pernicious and all-embracing fascist vision that has come to dominate much of Russian public discourse in the first quarter of the twenty-first century. But what does "fascism," a contested term that at its most basic means running an ethnonationalist state which controls every part of society, really mean—especially in a country that claims to be fighting against that very ideology?

Putin's supporters would say the fascist comparison is absurd. After all, they have anointed themselves the leading "antifascists" of the twenty-first century. They claim that the invasions of Ukraine in both 2014 and 2022 are defensive acts that echo the USSR's defense against Nazi invasion in 1941. Russia was morally obliged to step in and play the role of "antifascist" defender in Ukraine. Motormouth primetime TV host Vladimir Solovyov even claims that Russians were the victims of a Nazi attack, not an invading force at all, in 2022. Nazism, he bawls on his nightly political discussion show, can be "anti-Slavic, anti-Russian" just as much as it is "antisemitic."[14]

Solovyov's words echo Soviet propaganda, which seized the mantle of "antifascism" for the USSR. Soviets were told that everything that threatened the communist state and ideology—a cabal of enemies that included the capitalist powers of Western Europe and North America—was "fascist." Then the real fascists did attack. During World War II, Russia faced down an apocalyptic threat from the invading Axis powers. In four years of brutal fighting, over 25 million soldiers and civilians lost their lives before the Red Army arrived in Berlin.

Antifascist themes dominated the post-war Soviet Union, when the mass sacrifice of World War II gave the ruling class a justification for their continued hold on power: they were the victors in the war, therefore only they knew how to keep the USSR safe. The Cold War enemy was just as likely as Hitler's Germany to be described as "fascist." "Fascism" for Russians has historically thus meant the outside, the bad, the non-Russian. The state and its propagandists today are re-establishing that simplistic binary of Russian and non-Russian. Russia's Foreign Minister Sergey Lavrov has even insinuated that Ukraine's Jewish president, Volodymyr Zelenskyy, is a Nazi, stating: "I believe that Hitler also had Jewish blood. Some of the worst antisemites are Jews." Russia's young are once more being readied to re-enact the sacrifice of their "grandfathers"—or, more realistically, their great- or great-great-grandfathers—at the behest of their leaders. By laying down their lives in a war against "fascism," they can ascend to the pantheon of the saintly forefathers.

Russia in 2022 seems to embody the darkest elements of twentieth-century fascism. Led by a supposedly miraculous leader, it is a place where an array of ahistorical and quasi-religious thinking, imagery, and myths support a total militarization of the state and a mission to wipe out a racial enemy—the Ukrainian people—and reconquer a lost empire. Denunciations and free-speech crackdowns are becoming more public and more violent. The last independent media are gone, and everybody is afraid to speak their mind on what is still not officially called a "war." Government supporters and opponents alike live in fear of arbitrary arrest and beatings. One acquaintance tells me his elderly, decrepit mother was arrested by the FSB—today's KGB—for sharing a post merely reporting on an anti-war protest in the first week of the Ukraine war, despite not attending the event or even encouraging others to do so.

The nation is fighting a war of colonial aggression to control what has become known as *russky mir*—the "Russian world"—an illusory sphere of control over all things culturally, linguistically, or otherwise deemed to be Russian.[15] That means eliminating Ukraine. The linguistic culture of multiethnicity and humanism that at least superficially governed even Soviet life has disappeared. Former President

Dmitry Medvedev makes public calls for the erasure of Ukraine and Ukrainians: "I hate them. They're bastards and freaks. They wish death on us Russians. For as long as I live I'll do everything I can to make sure they disappear." Medvedev's words are echoed by state propagandists online and in broadcast media: "Military success … won't be the final solution. Denazification of Ukraine is achievable only by erasing the history of its last thirty years." A cultural genocide—the erasure of Ukrainian language, culture, and tradition—is already mirroring the physical genocide being carried out in places like Bucha.[16]

Visions of territorial expansion are fueled by sweeping allusions to grand historical empires. Just as Hitler dreamed of *Lebensraum* for Teutonic Germans, so Putin and his propagandists speak of recreating the lost empires of the past. On occasion, they even promise to conquer Europe militarily and China and the United States economically. The historical visions of conquest, sacrifice, and nationhood that drive this project are inconsistent, illogical, and ahistorical. They are more fairy tale than reality.

Russia is awash with images of uniform masculinity, religiosity, and nationality conjured up ad hoc as the war has spun out of the Russian military's control. Images drawn from the nation's Soviet, religious, and tsarist pasts are embroidered on soldiers' jackets, flown from cars, and daubed on classroom windows. "Z," the government's symbol of war, is everywhere. Military parades and "spontaneous" pro-war demonstrations are on television. Endless memes, videos, and slogans that hail Russia's military past and present—tsarist, Soviet, holy, Putinist—are plastered all over the internet. The bricolage is as ahistorically eclectic as the imperial and religious posturing that underpins Putin's public justification for the Ukraine invasion.

Meanwhile, in paramilitary youth groups for children, in compulsory training in schools and universities, in the constant diet of new films and shows about wars past and present, and in military parades and through conscription, young Russians are being prepared to play out the nation's historically fated role as the savior of humanity. Anybody younger than nineteen-year-old Alina will grow up with the oxymoronic phrase *borba za mir*—the "battle for peace," a Soviet-era slogan now making an unironic comeback—ringing in their ears. In today's Russia, war is not a last resort. It is an essential part of life, and it is paradoxically essential for peace.

Fascism may be a term with a vexed history, but this paradox—war is peace—is central to its political philosophy.[17] Umberto Eco, the Italian philosopher, noted that one of the key facets of fascism was the constant war that had to be waged to prove that the nation was always on the path towards a cleansing regeneration: "Pacifism is ... collusion with the enemy," he wrote in the mid-1990s; "pacifism is bad; life is permanent warfare."[18] But why should Putin, a twenty-first-century autocrat seemingly without real internal security threats and ruling a country fueled by income from abundant natural resources, be attached to such a vision?

The British scholar Roger Griffin argues that fascism seeks to regenerate the nation through war. It aims to destroy elements of modernity in order to create a new world order in response to the "degenerative forces of conservatism, individualistic liberalism, and materialist socialism."[19] The obliteration of morally degenerate enemies and moral orders by an ethnonationalist society totally dedicated to this goal is meant to bring about a new era in history. That new era, however, only ever recreates a supposedly lost past: a time of mythical, wondrous harmony when a nation and its subjects were culturally and military powerful. For Russia, this fantasy era tears up and reassembles chunks of the medieval, the tsarist, and the Soviet. Symbol and myth transcend the reality of the past. The longed-for utopia can only ever exist as fictional spectacle, performed for and by the public. It is pure fairy tale.

Fascism, Griffin tells us, thus perpetually promises to replace "gerontocracy, mediocrity, and national weakness with youth, heroism, and national greatness." The fascist project of regeneration is to be embodied in the creation of a new order of beings—an ascendant generation of young national flag-bearers. Hitler's Aryan Übermensch was meant to represent an ordered, purified ideal free of disease, weakness, anarchy, and decadence. The fascist project focuses all its military, religious, and cultural energy on achieving this regeneration—even if that means sacrificing its own people, destroying its economic resources, or acting in any other way irrationally. The fascist, after all, perceives the world in mythical terms. Reality need not get in the way of chasing fantasy.

Yet as rulers and generations age, fascist regimes have to perpetuate violence so that they can drag society into a constant cleansing—the constant perpetuation of violence against an enemy of choice. If we are to understand Russian fascism, we must look to how the state has fed this ideology to its youngest generations, and how they engage with and spread dangerous, mythical visions of global turmoil and national regeneration. Putin's Russia is a flimsy, Potemkin state. His people have seen few gains after twenty-two years of his rule. With no real achievements bar the perpetuation of their own wealth and position, Russia's rulers have to look beyond mass material gain to satiate a population hungry for self-esteem and respect.

Putin's Russia has bolted the fascist dream onto a distinctly modern popular culture. In the last two decades, the world has seen the rise of a new caste of fascists that hijack democratic systems, paint them as failed or useless, then viciously attack a chosen "Other."[20] The modern fascist's images of degeneracy are, the Danish scholar Mikkel Bolt Rasmussen explains, "subjects that threaten the naturalness of the patriarchal order. Migrants, people of colour, Muslims, Jews, women, sexual minorities and communists are perceived as the causes of a historical and moral decline."[21] The tropes of 1930s fascism as a group project are married to the language of twenty-first-century identity politics to conjure up a sense of a better, lost past destroyed by the West's globalization. Attacking the Other becomes a means to reconstruct that past.

Modern fascist culture, Bolt Rasmussen argues, spreads itself not in formal parties and institutions—twenty-first-century Nazi parties or Brownshirts—but through popular and internet culture.[22] Today, there are no more closed doors beyond which fascist ideology cannot reach. Parties are not required to create mass movements when social media groups can be created, joined, and eviscerated at the click of a mouse. Fascist governments and their subjects continually construct and reconstruct themselves—and do the opposite to their enemies—online and in "real life." In online spaces where performance and public display easily overpower empirical reality, fascism has, explains Bolt Rasmussen, found itself "apt at staging a simulacrum of society."[23] To take any part in society means belonging to the fascist society. Even the apathetic and the resistant are inevitably drawn in.

In 2022, there is no real distinction between the "online" and the "real world," between the "real" Alina in Nizhny Tagil and the "online" Alina on VK. At any time, night or day, Alina can dip her toes into the warmth of collective belonging and the glamour of the fascist spectacle. The fascist rally—glittering, alluring, ordering—is always accessible with the stroke of a thumb across a smartphone screen.

The theatrical, always-on spectacle of social media forces individuals to constantly engage with, and define themselves in relation to, political performance. The self, and society writ large, is constructed through public and private ritual, engaging with others, and producing and reproducing elements of culture. The world and the individual are built through aesthetics and language—what academics would term "performativity."[24]

Online comments or memes that support war crimes are not merely throwaway ideas. Even those made by government-created bots shape a world in which those crimes are normalized and encouraged, making their real perpetration more likely. An atomized, individualized population amped up by media clickbait and social media pizzazz gives way to a snowballing torrent of fascist resentment and utopianism. In turn, the "synthetic worlds" of narratives constructed on social media and in popular culture inform real policy decisions: the fictional, the peripheral, the ephemeral, and the chaotic are made reality.[25] Idle online chatter of genocide and Ukrainian-baiting memes become real.

It is in an often contradictory, pantomimic, and ghoulish popular and youth culture that Russia's young people have spent over twenty years encountering and re-encountering the state's ideological urges. Within this space, mythical thinking easily elides with snippets of external reality to produce a distinctly modern, Russian fascism. Weak in ideology and inconsistent to the extreme it may be, but Russian fascism is in there—detectable in the ambitions of the state and in the minds of many of its subjects.[26]

And it's there on social media. If there is anything that modern politics in the West—the phenomena of Donald Trump, Brexit, the anti-vax movement—has taught us, it's that reality is shaped on social media. Social media is real life. Alina's online self is her real self.

Putin's fascism: fragmentation and identity

Putin has rarely appeared to be a consistent ideologist. He often rifles through Russian nationalist philosophical writings, slapping together ideas and contextless quotes in his speeches, making definitive claims then dropping them in favor of striking a deal to make some quick cash or humiliate his Western opponents.[27] He—along with a nostalgic population—waxes lyrical about the Soviet era's stability, security, and culture. Soviet banners mingle with Russian flags everywhere from the Kremlin to schools and online communities. But the USSR isn't being recreated. There are no Gulags, few learn about Marx, and nobody talks of a communist future. Putin's Russia sometimes seems more like a state for kleptocratic pragmatists than one with ideological convictions.

In a nuanced treatment of the question of Russia's fascism published the year before its invasion of Ukraine, Marlène Laruelle asserted that "Russia has no ideology of racial destruction or domination that would allow for a parallel with Nazism. Nor does it display an ideological doctrine forcibly inculcated in the population, successful mass mobilisation around a project of utopian regeneration, a high level of repression, or dictatorial functioning."[28] In 2022, none of that holds true. Russian society, especially online, has been suffused with an ideology of destructive war motivated by racial and misogynistic animus and by Russian exceptionalism. The ideology is contradictory, weak, and illogical, but it is constantly transmitted in popular culture.

Between Putin's election to the presidency in 2000 and Russia's invasion of Ukraine in 2022, pushed by ideologues who have found themselves drawn from the margins of the Kremlin and society toward the country's center, the fascistic narratives in Russian society have grown more prominent.[29] Russian society, prompted by the state, has responded to various economic, political, and cultural challenges by excluding the Other—which in Putin's Russia can be just about anything that doesn't fit into a narrow definition of Russianness. Being "Russian" means being masculine, Orthodox Christian, strong, and aggressive. Being "Russian" means accepting the nation's historical status as a messianic savior of the world. Anyone who doesn't fit in—a "fifth column" of liberals and progressives, homosexuals, and people of color—is a traitor. But anyone today can become Russian by drawing on (or, of course, being forced to draw on) a visual and verbal toolkit, recreating their identity online and in person to meet their own and their peers' expectations.

A shocking discourse of nationalism, genocide, and rage has been brought in from the cold. The language of liberal values that flared up in the Russia of the 1990s has been squeezed out by the torrent of animus that Alina and her online peers dispense. They might lust after Soviet aesthetics and everyday life, they might consume old TV shows and join "Sovietcore" nostalgia groups online, but they—like the state's propagandists—roundly mock Marxist ideology.[30] Instead, they dream of a new sort of ordered, martial life arising from the wreckage of the post-Soviet years.

The goals relate to morality and psychology, to inner transformation, as much as to geopolitics. To achieve them requires the internalization of a paranoid ultranationalist worldview: the old self must be rewritten by the state's political culture as society is cleansed of everything non-Russian. This internal battle is reflected externally in a racist, imperialist war against the ethnic Other in Ukraine. Russian messianism—an old historical trope that suggests that the nation has a special role in dragging the world toward utopian ends by means of destruction, martyrdom, and sacrifice—is married to the fascist process of self and societal cleansing.

Today, these fascist ideas are being raised openly not just in the dark corners of the Runet but at the center of national political discourse. Not every Russian might be rushing to open the state's newspapers or switch on the non-stop propaganda that's dominated state television channels since the start of the Ukraine war, but in the maelstrom of the Runet ideas quickly filter from the center to the periphery and back again.[31] Fascist thinking radiates outward from the Kremlin's army of mouthpieces and fellow travelers, a group of media pundits dressed up in the garb of the Western expert—smart suits, neat spectacles, impeccable educational background—who express extreme ideologies in bitesize chunks for a social media generation.

Three recent articles published in the state media capture some of the extreme thinking that informs Alina's sophomoric online outpourings.

The first article, "What Russia Should Do with Ukraine," appeared in April 2022 on the state RIA Novosti agency after news of Bucha broke. The article lays bare the government's intention to destroy the very idea of Ukraine. Timofey Sergeytsev, its author, was hitherto a little-known "political technologist"—a Russian term for a spin doctor with no aversion to extra-legal methods and corruption to achieve their ends—who had worked in Ukraine and Russia since 2014.[32] "Ukrainism," Sergeytsev writes, "has never existed in history, and it does not exist today." The only way to fix the "mass of the population [which is] Nazi" is to have a "generation born, grow up, and mature under the conditions of denazification." "Denazification," Sergeytsev explains, means "ideological repression," mass tribunals, lustration, and the "liquidation" of Nazis. Any trace of Ukraine and Ukrainianness would be wiped out through judicial and capital reprisals. This is a program of aggressive ultra-nationalism: a blueprint for the destruction of the state's Other, physically and culturally. The very idea of Ukraine, proposes Sergeytsev, is to be eliminated through violence.

However, the program isn't just about destruction. In an article entitled "From Constructive Destruction to Gathering," Sergey Karaganov, a historian and advisor who once enjoyed a positive reputation in the West, suggests that war with Ukraine is an opportunity for "constructive destruction." War, Karaganov argues, could remake the world itself by sweeping away the old order. NATO and the United States are labeled "aggressors" that constantly try to trick Russia as they advance their own interests in Moscow's territory (which include, of course, "aggressive LGBT and ultra-feminist movements"). "History demands we take action," thunders Karaganov, to destroy the Western alliance and move beyond the capitalist, globalized model of economics and global affairs.[33] Karaganov has long been calling for the destruction of the existing "world order" led by a collapsing West and the rise of a new, transcendent Russia.[34] But the Ukraine war gives new luster to his old ideas. The real war anchors utopian dreams of "constructive destruction" and the creation of a new world in reality. In this reality, embracing apocalypse and risking nuclear war (which Karaganov admits is a possibility, and which legions of other Kremlin advisors blithely encourage) is a good thing. Thank God for messianic Russia, argues Karaganov, which alone can be responsible for destroying the old and creating the new world order.[35]

Finally, in an article from late April 2022, also published by RIA Novosti, the arch-nationalist Petr Akopov lays out a philosophy of fascist renewal of the self for Russians themselves. In "The Russia of the Future: Forward to the USSR," Akopov imagines the internal battles that Russians would have to wage to cleanse themselves of Western immorality. Akopov rails against globalization, the West, Ukraine, the rich, and those of "weak" morality. All of them, he cries, must be swept away: "We shall live in the USSR again. But not the USSR the anti-Soviets fear or the Communists dream of. No, we shall build a strong, just, and sovereign Russia."[36] For Akopov, "the USSR" is a metaphor for a mythical Russia with total control over its own affairs, a Russia free of LGBTQ, feminist, democratic, and liberal tendencies. It is a synonym for an imagined era when the Kremlin will be at the height of its power to reject apparently deleterious outside influences according to its own nationalist, Orthodox whims.

Akopov turns his attention from Ukrainians to Russians. He aggressively advocates for the exclusion of the "stupid" and "greedy" rich, liberal elites who "despise their own people." Akopov builds towards an angry conclusion, wherein he insists that the real fight must take place inside the mind: "The most important sovereignty is in our heads, in our minds, in our thinking. Our thinking must become more Russocentric." It is here we find the internal, spiritual cleansing typically asked of the fascist subject. Akopov demands not just the driving out of the Other or a blind trust in authority but the total reconstruction of the reader from the inside out.

These articles, and dozens more like them, tore through the Runet. Bloggers, influencers, and their followers re-shared, recreated, and regurgitated their content, adding their own comments and splicing in new material. For example, the pro-Kremlin blogger Anton Korobkov-Zemlyansky, a Muscovite hipster with a young family who works for the state media and posts non-stop lifestyle and propaganda updates for his large Instagram and Telegram following, managed to dig up a video from the 1990s showing Karaganov discussing Ukraine with then President Leonid Kravchuk on Russian television.

In the clip, the TV panelists imagine a war instigated by a NATO-sponsored Ukraine against Russia "sometime around 2025." "Turns out Russian TV predicted today's conflict twenty-five years ago," explained Korobkov-Zemlyansky, suggesting that Karaganov was some sort of seer. One of his followers chimed in admiringly: "Fu-uck me. They've got the whole thing planned out a hundred years in advance." Re-shared by fellow travelers, posts like Korobkov-Zemlyansky's can easily reach a million and more accounts on Telegram.

At the bottom of the pile, young Russians like Alina won't bother to log onto Russia's rather staid official media to read Karaganov's, Sergeytsev's, or Akopov's Putinist catechesis. They imbibe it sip by sip, in re-shared clips, comments made by friends, and in group posts scrolled by and liked with barely a second thought. They learn that Russia is fighting against the West in an apocalyptic, ahistorical battle. By eliminating their enemies and transforming themselves, Russians can somehow regenerate their nation. And they can see their peers buying into this language on social media feeds and groups.

Fascism has broken free of parties, institutions, and places. It exists everywhere, constantly restated as citizens perpetually reassemble themselves in dialogue with trumped-up tales of heroism, nightmare visions of the future, and outrageous soundbites that burst into life and melt away again in an instant.

This is how the state can whisper meaning into empty symbols like the letters "Z" and "V," which have come to symbolize the war. Concocted by the Kremlin's PR teams on the fly to bring the public together after the failure to rapidly overwhelm Kyiv in February 2022, the symbols have no root in Russian culture. "Z" first appeared in a rash of online videos clearly produced by the state. Footage of young men in matching black "Z" shirts waving flags and chanting their fealty to the state and clips of students wearing white "Z" tops while leading pro-war chanting in shopping malls meant nothing to Russian audiences. But, when bolted onto the familiar images of fascism and war we'll explore in the coming pages, Russians could find meaning in this emptiness. "Z" could be rewritten as Orthodox scripture or as a symbol of World War II.[37] "Z" could mean the defense of children, carried to safety by Russian soldiers in Ukraine.

"Z" could mean "For Peace" or "For the Future" (the Russian *za* means "for"). "Z," pumped through the social media sphere, could mean anything—so long as it was accompanied by familiar symbols, familiar rage, and familiar language. So long as it was *Russian*.

Endless streams of movies, television shows, musical acts, and public demonstrations feed this social media maelstrom. The startlingly modern—reality shows and Jerry Springer-style talk shows, slick TV news discussions—crashes into remnants of the Soviet era—parades, "volunteer" events for students and state employees, military service, and the raft of Soviet symbolism on display on everything from clothes to tanks.

It's unavoidable. If you choose not to consume it, your friends and family will drip the content into your smartphone through their own social media feeds. To oppose is to fail to be sufficiently Russian—and therefore, by default, to be a traitor. I send Alina a news report about a thirty-something doctor who has left Russia to assist Ukrainian refugees in Poland: "What do you think about this? Isn't she just helping people out?" Alina's reply is unequivocal: "She's a traitor. Don't come back." The semantic and visual world she has created for herself permits no nuance, flexibility, or comprehension of alternate points of view.

But transforming the self is not always so straightforward as it has been for Alina. While Russians are often described as apathetic or passive political subjects, those positions are becoming ever harder to sustain. Totalitarian regimes like Putin's—those that seek to completely subjugate the individual to the state's ideology and thus create a new collective society—operate by smashing the individual's psyche apart, exerting greater and greater pressure on them until their minds buckle under the weight of the government's assault.[38] Vasily Grossman, the Soviet propagandist turned dissident novelist, described the phenomenon eloquently in his 1961 novel *Life and Fate*. In the work, set during World War II, the protagonists find freedom wherever they can escape the language of Stalin's regime: in parlors, in private laboratories, and in encircled bunkers at the front. Whenever a newspaper or letter arrives, a telephone rings, or a military messenger turns up, Grossman's characters find themselves choking, asphyxiating, unable to breathe, crushed by a burden of questioning and doubt as their selves come into conflict with the regime's version of reality.

In the novel's most important scene, Viktor Shtrum, a Jewish physicist whom the regime is pressuring to participate in the building of the atomic bomb, receives an official questionnaire. Shtrum, worn down by the regime's attacks, cannot answer the most basic question about himself, his name and his patronymic, which ought to be derived from his father's forename:

> Surname, name and patronymic … Who was he, who was this man filling in a questionnaire in the dead of night? Shtrum, Viktor Pavlovich? His mother and father had never been properly married, they had been separated when Viktor was only two; and on his father's papers he had seen the name Pinkhus—not Pavel. So why was he Viktor *Pavlovich*? Did he know himself? Perhaps he was someone quite different—Goldman … or Sagaydachny? Or was he the Frenchman Desforges, alias Dubrovsky?[39]

His identity split into pieces, Shtrum no longer knows who he is. He cannot identify either as Russian or Jewish (here, the Soviets' detested "Other"). He does not know where he comes from. All Shtrum can do is tick boxes. And even then he is beset by crippling doubts. The state has snatched the power of self-creation away from him and replaced it with its own boxes, forms, and descriptors.

The power of the state to break apart and reassemble Russians like Shtrum today, when there are fewer private spaces than ever before, exceeds anything the totalitarian leaders of the twentieth century could have dreamed of. In a hyper-connected online world, the language of fascism is unavoidable. There are no more closed doors. The mind is always being broken and put back together again. War on the inside mirrors war on the outside.

* * *

In mid-April 2022, Alina re-shared a video of a group of Russians in Kursk cheering their troops off to the front.[40] In the video, several dozen vehicles are parked alongside a dusty road in the city of Kursk, just a few miles from the Russia–Ukraine border. Some of the vehicles are marked with the Latin "Z" and "V" letters that depict support for the war. The vehicles' owners stand by the roadside, waving Russian flags and cheering, as a convoy of Russian trucks and military materiel rolls past. The military equipment is, of course, also marked with "Z" and "V." People and military are drawn into a shared symbolic space, united around the military markings. So what? We might say the same about any group of citizens cheering their boys off to the front: the RAF roundel or the Stars and Stripes might as well stand in for the "Z" and the Russian flag.

A few seconds into the video, a thirty-something man wearing a retro USSR sports jacket is captured in the camera's gaze. He throws up his right arm. Unlike his neighbors, this man is not waving. He is performing a Nazi salute. Forward another few seconds, and a small boy of no more than five or six in combat fatigues a few places further down the crowd appears, clinging with his left arm to his father. Up his father's arm goes in another Nazi salute. The boy reaches his right arm outwards in imitation of his father. Like Alina's improvised social media posts, these figures are doing something more than merely displaying patriotism or turning up at a rally to save face. They are embracing a collage of symbolism that denotes their allegiance to the Soviet past (the USSR jacket), the militaristic present (the combat fatigues and markings), and an ideology of racial superiority (the Nazi salute and Z/V markings that symbolize a war of ethnic destruction). The older generations are encouraging their children to perform themselves into this mash-up reality.

Russian audiences lapped it up, expressing their support for the video by leaving comments on Telegram channels with hundreds of thousands of users:[41] "Guys, just you keep holding firm!"; "Death to the UkroNazis"; "May God save you." The troops' performance—the parade of waving soldiers has an element of the theatrical—the crowd's performance of salutes and public fealty, the original poster's performance of recording and sharing the video, the Telegram channels' further performance of good citizenhood by re-sharing it, and users' comments on those re-shares: the symbols and behaviors of Russian fascism are amplified again and again by repetition. Each invocation is unprompted, or only covertly prompted, by the state. In this small visual excerpt, then, we can glimpse the whole performative enactment of modern Russian fascism.

Like its predecessors, Russian fascism draws on "a rag bag of thirdhand ideas and specious rationalizations."[42] It's a nonsensical ideology that combines contradictory elements of the Soviet past, apocalyptical spirituality, material spread directly by propagandists, and a fast-paced postmodern culture.

That's fascism today. It churns up and spits out memes, tropes, and other transitory ideas. It tries to imbue meaning in empty letters. Russian fascism is as likely to be embedded in a grammatically incoherent comment on a picture of children dressed up in dollar-store World War II-era dress or a cartoon character re-imagined as a soldier in Ukraine as it is in immaculately tailored army uniforms and grand military parades.

But don't mistake what Russians might call the *poshlost'*—the almost vulgar banality—of such second-hand content for a lack of meaning. This is a culture that is preoccupied with death. Whether killing off the "non-Russian" inside the country, sending its young to die in wars abroad, or butchering civilians in genocidal military campaigns, death is glorified. And that glorification isn't confined to state institutions, state politicians' speeches, or state media. The state has spent twenty years, abetted by eager radical nationalists, forming a national identity fixated on death. Today, Alina and her fellow believers are bubbling over with revolutionary zeal. They are ready to "cleanse" themselves, their children, and their neighbors through acts of violence—and death.

In the following chapters, we'll journey deep into the heart of Putin's fascist project. We'll trace the stories of Russians who have grown up under Putin's rule, following their experiences of remaking, failing to remake, or refusing to remake themselves as fascist youths. I interacted with dozens of Russians from a range of backgrounds, sending hundreds of messages and speaking through countless hours of video and phone calls, through the spring, summer, and fall of 2022. I sought out those who had shaped themselves, or been shaped, using the language and culture of Putinism: average Russians—teachers, artists, writers, community leaders—who had sought to turn themselves and others into ideal subjects by performing a language of state power. Naturally, that meant cataloguing too the thoughts of those who would not or could not remake themselves: the apathetic, the marginalized, the excluded. I asked them to relate their life stories and explain how they felt about political events in the country as the public was seized by discussion of the "special operation." I charted how they have used social media to find places of belonging over the past two decades as the state has played out its constant pantomime of violent purification.

The interview pool skews heavily toward the male and the white. That's no surprise, given the racial and misogynistic dimensions of Russia's fascism, but I was still struck by how hard it has been to find young, non-ethnic Russian and/or female supporters of the war. I intersperse these life stories with profiles of some of the leading figures in youth movements and with the stories of how politicians, propagandists, and media manipulators shaped individual perceptions of the government's increasingly revanchist nationalism. The lives and languages of my subjects seem to embody trends academic research suggests exist in wider society and the ways in which identities are shaped by analogue and digital political cultures. Unfortunately, I could not include every story I charted, and there are many nuances that are ironed out by my approach.

My tales and interviews are jarring, circling, contradictory, and fragmentary. I often found myself flummoxed by the non-sequiturs and illogicalities of the fascist world I had entered, a world in which waging war and carrying out violence is perceived as an entirely logical way to end war and stop violence.

We'll see how the Putin regime cultivated the idea of "war as peace." It sold itself to the young as the creator of a fairy-tale utopianism while cultivating the imagery, language, and ideology of a violent fascism everywhere from schools to social media platforms, cinemas, and the stands of Moscow's football stadiums. We'll meet plenty of Russians who've encountered this world: the fascist social media stars and rock bands belting out tunes for young admirers, young journalists and queer activists who've been sucked in and spat out by the regime, and teachers wrestling with their consciences as they are asked to preach sermons of apocalyptic messianism in the classroom.

In the second part of the book, we'll explore how the invasion of Ukraine in February 2022 has been a turning point in the life of the country's young. While the opposition seems lost for words, a new generation of militarized youth, disconnected from outside influences, is being indoctrinated into an ever more extreme version of the state's language of martial utopianism. The Z Generation, short on opportunities to discover what it means to be "non-Russian," is growing up militarized and zealous. Isolated from the world, they are told that there is no greater good than to cleanse themselves, their communities, and the world of the state's enemies.

Although this work is not an academic study, I aim through writing it to bring to life work by academics from a range of fields spanning politics, history, and cultural studies. It's a catalogue of thoughts, opinions, and reflections on the turning point that Russia finds itself at as the nation seems to be descending into a bleak, hateful form of twenty-first-century fascism. It's a call to action for citizens across the world who are seeing many of the same dangerous identity-forming processes unfold in their own societies.

When I speak with Alina, I am reminded of the years I spent studying in Russia and working with Russian students. Many of the children I taught are Alina's age. They grew up, middle class and privileged, with every opportunity to receive a quality, international, liberal education. I think back to their innocence. I look again at Alina's increasingly disturbing social media reality. I wonder: how many young Russians—the younger brothers and sisters, the children of my former students—will follow her over the precipice and into this amoral void? Is there anything we can do to stop them? And, once Putin's regime ends, what can we do to bring them back into the light?

2

A FAIRY-TALE REBIRTH

We were born to make a fairy tale come true.

Soviet Aviators' March, 1923

In 1996, seven-year-old Ilya Fedotov-Fedorov is suddenly taken ill in gym class with a searing pain in his stomach. Despite his parents' best efforts, nothing soothes the agony. The doctor he sees is mystified. Why should a small boy be in such crippling pain? "Nobody," recalls Ilya today, "really got what was going on with me." And nobody expected that Ilya was about to exchange his rather ordinary Moscow life for a descent into the bowels of the post-Soviet healthcare system.

Ilya was dragged on a Dantean journey from doctor to doctor and hospital to hospital. Rickety doors led into corridors caked in drab, flaking paint and onward to dirty, overcrowded wards. The acrid odor of cheap sanitizer bit into the nostrils as orderlies scrubbed down the peeling linoleum floors. Flickering lights and burned-out bulbs left consultation rooms and lobbies in perpetual twilight. After months of testing in these festering hulks, which had been left to rot into disrepair since the Soviet system's economy slowly collapsed through the 1980s, a diagnosis was finally reached. Ilya had a rare kidney problem so severe that he ought to have been dead.

Ilya was encountering the sharp end of the post-Soviet economic and cultural collapse. The economy was on its knees. The healthcare that Ilya was trying to access suffered too. Equipment failures, supply shortages, and decaying buildings made access to quality healthcare a difficult business.[1] In 1998, the country defaulted on its debt, wiping out life savings, hobbling fledgling private businesses, and crippling the government overnight.

The chaos told across every aspect of family life. Alcoholism grew to such an extent that in some parts of Russia, half of deaths in the decade after the USSR fell were linked to consumption of spirits. Young men and women dropped out of the economy as they failed to find jobs—or didn't even bother trying. Educational standards dipped as teachers left under-equipped classrooms for work in the black market and shadow economies. The poor and underemployed abandoned their children to a state that was ill-equipped and unwilling to look after them. By 2001, there were 2.5 million homeless children in Russia—250,000 in Moscow alone. Between 1 and 2 million girls and young women were forced into prostitution by mafia gangs who operated with impunity. Rates of chronic disease, drug usage, and domestic abuse skyrocketed among the young. The deep stigmatization attached to homelessness, poverty, disease, and abuse caused devastating psychological damage to a generation of young people.[2] These problems were only compounded by a disastrous war against breakaway Chechnya, where the Russian army lost up to 14,000 young conscripts and effectively relinquished control of the region by the late 1990s.

The promises of post-Soviet democratization gave way to an inexorable sense of hopelessness. A generation of youth seemed to have lost out on its future. All communities need stories, myths, and narratives of the future to make sense of the world. When they're traumatized, people look for ways to bind together fragmented memories of strife into bundles of sense.[3] Young Russians had no way to do so. Living in a disordered present, they were futureless.

Ilya became an object of fascination:

> I was in the hospital every three months; three or four times a year. Doctors and students would hold conferences while I was on the table, half-naked. They would queue up to touch me. The chief doctor even wrote a dissertation about me and my disease. It was like a circus.

Trapped in a collapsing system, this small boy experienced life as a clash between an anarchic carnival and an academic study—an attempt at bringing order to the chaos.

The effect was psychologically crippling: "I developed a very big dissociation from my body," Ilya tells me. "You start to think of yourself not as a person but as a body. A problem. A disease. It was strange. And constant. My dissociation with myself developed even further; I started to think of myself as a creature, a strange person, even not a human." Ilya, like Russia itself, was ailing. He was losing hope and the sense of himself as a person at all. As the doctors queued up to prod and poke the sick boy, so Western political consultants, economic experts, and diplomats lined up to poke the struggling Russia. Money and help poured in, but it never seemed to do much good.

The psychological effects on the nation echoed Ilya's feelings of dissociation. While many young people were excited by dreams of moving to the West, reading formerly forbidden literature, listening to music from abroad, and consuming Western films, few felt attached to Boris Yeltsin's Russia. Dreams of Western lifestyles born as the USSR collapsed seemed to drift ever further away. Much of the population met this crisis with a shrug or a typically dark Russian joke: "Today"—the joke-teller would attempt to imitate the voice of Soviet-era radio announcer Yury Levitan—"At the age of seventy-two, after a long and difficult illness, and after failing to recover consciousness, Boris Nikolaevich Yeltsin has ... decided to run for a third term." Others were drawn to extreme nationalist and neo-fascist mobs and political parties.[4] The national prognosis was bleak.

Traumatized, unable to articulate a sense of community, identity, or the future, Russia's young had little to look forward to. Yet thanks to a masterfully staged government PR campaign, by the end of the 2000s, Ilya and many of his young compatriots would be bursting with a new sense of life. The government would provide the young with all the narratives they needed to feel whole again—even if, in reality, the government was constantly, violently smashing apart the marginalized and the opposition to build that wholeness.

A fairy-tale millennium

On 31 December 1999, the ailing Boris Yeltsin announced his resignation and made the forty-seven-year-old Vladimir Putin, a former KGB agent who had come from almost nowhere to be appointed prime minister a mere four months earlier, acting president.

Russians caught their first glimpse of President Putin on television that night as he gave the traditional New Year's presidential address. The softly spoken, athletic Putin cut quite the contrast with his elderly, alcoholic, and overweight predecessor. The contrast was intentional: Putin's spin doctor, Gleb Pavlovsky, explained that it was "all part of a script. Putin played the part to perfection."[5]

The new president read from the script for the TV audience: "Freedom of speech, of conscience, and of the media, along with property rights. The state will duly protect these, the foundations of civil society." The state's police and security services, he promised, would "complete their work as normal. The state has been guarding, and will continue to guard, the safety of every one of our citizens."

Putin promised to bring individual and collective order and security through the promotion of Russian values.[6] To close, Putin hailed New Year—Russians' equivalent of Christmas, when families come together in celebration and Grandfather Frost brings gifts to children—as a time of miracles: "We all know that dreams come true at New Year. And that's only more true at this most unusual of New Years. All the good things you can dream of will most certainly come true."[7] Everything was possible: collective power and security, individual rights and dreams.

As the camera cut from Putin to reveal the Kremlin's clock tower tolling midnight, a new era of order and miracles had been announced to Russia's first post-Soviet generation. Putin would remain wildly popular for the next decade—his approval rating never dropped below 60 percent and reached almost 90 percent in 2008. Meanwhile, the state played out a merry televisual pantomime that sold Russia as a fairy-tale land of opportunity.

The state, however, rapidly moved to seize control of its fairy tale's script. Real news coverage and real politics disappeared as the state took over TV networks and staged a simulacrum, a pale imitation, of reality—a reality of invented traditions and myths around which to build a nation.[8] Directed by Vladislav Surkov, Vladimir Putin's PR guru, weekly meetings at Ostankino, the 1,700 ft TV tower that has needled the Moscow sky since the 1960s, scripted reality as if it were a movie or one of the melodramatic Mexican soaps beloved by Russian audiences.[9] Viewers guzzled down entertainment mixed with lashings of scripted political events: Putin appearing here to dispense wisdom or show off the latest state achievement, a "crook" being taken down by the new regime there. Everything—including voting and the anti-corruption campaigns that punctuated the public spectacle—was stage managed.[10] High on the excitement of a reality manipulated by state governors, politicians, and propagandists, Russians watched their new president bend reality to his—to their—will. Out with the shattered sufferings of the 1990s, in with the dizzying cocktail of the new Russia as the economy soared. Russia was going places. Who cared if real reform never came when the story of success seemed so tangible, so appealing?[11]

The story was built on two myths that danced around each other in constant counterpoint. In the first, a hyperbolized myth of the "wild 1990s"—as Yeltsin's decade in power became known—Russia had been betrayed by traitors at home (the last Soviet leader, Mikhail Gorbachev; Yeltsin and his administration; corrupt business leaders and politicians) and enemies abroad (America and its allies, who sought to take advantage of the country when it was on its knees).[12] The myth of the 1990s sold the idea that nefarious Western powers had sabotaged the Soviet Union and then the nascent Russian Federation. The government's new media networks sought every opportunity to denigrate American values as deleterious and traumatic. Everything Russian, however, was touched by virtue.

The government had, hand-in-hand with a traumatized population looking for the common language to describe and grow beyond their immediate post-Soviet experience, created a myth of a degenerating Russia under attack from the West that needed both fixing and defending. But to leave Russians trapped in what Serguei Oushakine terms "communities of loss," bonded only around the tragedy of the past, was never the Putin regime's intention.[13]

The myth of destruction required an opposite: a myth of the *future*.[14] Putin began to describe the 1990s as a period of *necessary* sacrifice that had to be endured before the country's rebirth in the 2000s. His annual address to the legislature from 2005 painted the previous decade as a time of national disease when "tens of millions of our co-citizens and compatriots found themselves outside Russian territory." This "epidemic of disintegration *infected Russia itself*." The idea of the nation's "infection" by a diseased Other could have been pulled from a mid-century fascist propaganda leaflet.

The "epidemic," however, seemed to have been the catalyst for a better, more *Russian* future:

> That was precisely the period when significant developments took place in Russia. Our society was generating not only the energy of self-preservation, but also the will for a new and free life. [The Russian people] had to accomplish the most difficult task: how to safeguard their own values, not to squander undeniable achievements, and confirm the viability of Russian democracy. We had to find our own path in order to build a democratic, free and just society and state.[15]

Russians had been living through a period of torment that generated "energy" and "will for a new and free life." "We had to find our own path," explained the president. It is as if the 1990s were a period of wandering in the desert, confronting sin and temptation, and surviving nevertheless. The present, though, was full of life and potency. The present was a time of moral restoration and national decadence in which life would not just get back to normal but become better than ever for the young so hard done by in the 1990s.

Ilya and his peers had been promised a world of fairy tales. And in the state's myth of the present, a fairy tale was what they got. Even as it was still happening, the 2000s was mythologized as a time of boundless opportunities for every young Russian.

Waves of extraordinary promises followed Putin's election in 2000. GDP would double. Life expectancy would go up. Children would be able to travel abroad on vacation or to study. All the bad experiences of the 1990s? Gone, already suffered through, already wished away.

The regime did begin to resolve some of the problems of the 1990s during its first decade in power. Crime and homelessness rates fell while healthcare slowly improved. The country's GDP grew on average by 7.1 percent annually between 2000 and 2007. Wealth didn't just accumulate at the top of the tree: the poverty rate fell from 35 percent in 2000 to under 10 percent by 2010, and a growing middle class had disposable income to spend on consumer goods, extracurricular activities for kids, and holidays abroad. The middle classes toured Europe, North America, Dubai, and (like Alina and her family) Egypt. The privileged could even send their children to receive world-class education at top universities and colleges in America and Europe, so that 35,000 Russians were studying outside the country by 2010 (compared with just 7,000 when Putin came to power).

Increased budgets saw schools and universities renovated. The high-school curriculum was standardized and modernized, and a new national standard school leaver's certificate, the Unified State Exam, was introduced. University courses were redeveloped so that degrees were internationally recognized. Students from Kamchatka to Kursk and Krasnodar found their educations and home lives steadily improving as the remnants of old Soviet classrooms were ushered out in favor of the new.

The country embodied young Russians' path to self-esteem. The regime cooked up a series of grandiose performances that asserted Russia's coming of age on the global stage too. These performances buttressed a new economic conception that defined the West not as a partner but as a "competitor."[16] Russia wasn't just going to keep up with the West. It was going to beat it everywhere from the stock market to the playing field.

Participation in competitions like the Eurovision Song Contest—masterminded and funded by the authorities—flaunted Russia's newfound cultural vitality to its European competitors. Between 2006 and 2008, Russia's three top-three finishes in the annual contest culminated with a win for the Muscovite superstar Dima Bilan. The hotshot American songwriter Jim Beanz was hired to write the winning song, "Believe," a mushy ballad about making dreams come true—just so long as you believe in yourself. Bilan's performance was a splashy demonstration of Russia's brilliance: he was flanked on the one side by Emmy-winning violinist Edvin Marton and on the other by Olympic-gold-medal skater Evgeny Plyushchenko, who pirouetted through three minutes of music on a tiny ice rink.[17]

As Bilan's silky voice carried through the auditorium on finals day, Russia's fairy tale was being broadcast to the world. What did Russia "believe" in? What was its fairy tale? It didn't matter. All things were possible, and everybody knew it. Young Russians could dream; the country could dream; every dream could come true.

In the sporting arena, the Kontinental Hockey League, founded in 2008, drew big-name players away from North America and back to the motherland. The league's popularity and financial clout opened up serious political links to boot: "hockey diplomacy" was a cheap means of growing soft and hard power in the former Soviet republics and in Scandinavia, and audiences at home suddenly had a league to rival America's.[18] However, while top athletes and clubs who could show off Russia's prowess received attention and funding, government money only trickled into youth sports on a national level. The number of local clubs, players, and quality of coaching in football and hockey alike slightly improved between 2000 and 2010, but the health benefits for the young population were limited.[19] In sports and music, it was more important to create the impression that Russia was a youthful, powerful nation than to create real reform. This wasn't managed democracy. It was stage-managed neo-authoritarianism.

The centerpiece of the Putin era's new myth of regeneration, however, was the transformation of Moscow from a crumbling, Soviet-era concrete behemoth into a glamorous, neo-imperial capital. Moscow has long been at the center of Russia's messianic dreams. After the fall of Constantinople in 1453, the city became known as the "Third Rome," representing the sole outpost of true—Orthodox—Christianity. Russia itself was, consequently, charged with leading the world in the defense of Christian belief against both Islamism and Catholicism. The idea of Moscow as the "Third Rome" was embodied in works of art and literature in centuries to come. It was then revived in the Soviet era to posit the city as what Katerina Clark calls the "Fourth Rome," the leader of world revolution and a site of civilizational progress.[20]

Moscow, like many capitals that attract incomers with shimmering chic, was long meant to be the place where fairy tales could come true.[21] How humiliating it was as a nation to see the city as Ilya Fedotov-Fedorov had experienced it in the 1990s, a world of crumbling and rusting buildings, institutions, and hopes.

Moscow—at least as it was presented on TV—was thus transformed into a miraculous symbol of the nation's progress towards both spiritual and financial health. Conveniently, the president's predecessors had left him the reconstructed Cathedral of Christ the

Savior, a vast symbol of imperial religion on the banks of the Moskva River in Moscow. The clean white tiers of the cathedral, topped with ornate gold cupolas, had been built to celebrate Russia's victory over Napoleon in 1812 and destroyed under Stalin in the 1930s. The cathedral re-opened in late 1999, and Putin duly attended a church service there just two weeks into his term as acting president. Russia as a religious nation was back; its president leading the way to the pews. The new government kept pouring money into constructing new palaces of religion. The capital even saw the construction of a chapel on the site of the FSB's notorious Lubyanka headquarters and jail. Church attendance, especially in Russia's cosmopolitan cities, actually fell through the 2000s, and Russians remained opposed to religious education in schools.[22] But travelling to a city like Moscow meant witnessing a sparkling resurrection of national pride embodied in the glittering domes of the city's new churches.

New temples of capitalism mingled with sites of religion. A range of commercial and business developments jointly masterminded by the state and private sector sprang up throughout the capital city.[23] By the decade's end, the city was home to malls hosting all the international brands Russians could imagine, and housing stock and public space in the city center had been transformed. Visually, Moscow had become a capital to match any of Russia's rivals: a slew of sparkling glass boxes towered over the wreckage of the old buildings, swept away in an epic act of destruction and recreation by central powers and Russia's money men. A vision of new life was birthed by the bulldozer and the wrecking ball. Russians, joined by economic immigrants from Central Asia, quit the stagnating provinces in search of the Moscow good life en masse.

The city's rapid growth culminated in the early 2010s, when its young population outnumbered that of Russia's next six largest cities put together.[24] Little matter that back home in the provinces, hulking skeletons of abandoned construction projects— really just vehicles for embezzlement and corruption—littered the downtowns of every city from Petrozavodsk to Petropavlovsk. And little matter that even in Moscow, ordinary homes were swept away in the orgy of construction and property prices rose much faster than average incomes.

New films, which the government funded to the tune of millions of dollars, hailed hip Moscow's vibrant status for an eager young viewership. The smash-hit 2008 musical comedy *Stilyagi* ("Hipsters"), for example, follows a group of teens in 1950s Moscow who dream of American lives, jazz music, and the outrageous fashions of Western youth. Re-imagining popular Soviet and post-Soviet rock, jazz, and pop songs as upbeat, sing-along swing numbers, the movie has its characters dancing through their rebellion against drab Soviet culture in Moscow's underground clubs, apartments, and houses. The city bubbles over with possibilities; the director whimsically mixes together time periods, musical genres, and shots.

But such works were often vehicles that perpetuated the conflict between the morally bankrupt, Western-influenced 1990s and the vibrant present. In *Stilyagi*'s climax, the heroes' American dream is smashed apart. The male protagonist, Mels ("Marx, Engels, Lenin, Stalin"—a briefly popular Soviet name), meets a friend who has returned from New York, where his diplomat father had been stationed. The American dream, it turns out, is fantasy: the country is just as lifeless and dull as the USSR. Mels walks out onto a Moscow boulevard, where he is joined in song by representatives of Moscow's youth subcultures from across the ages. Hippies, skinheads, punks, and skaters unite, marching in time and singing in harmony. Mels and his love interest sprint out into present-day Moscow and kiss as the music soars to its conclusion.

Worlds and systems collapse—Soviet values, underground culture, American music, the past, the present—in this fairy-tale Moscow. The film's vague opposition sentiment—rebellious youth overcome dastardly Komsomol members (the Soviet-era Communist Youth movement that was the path to Party membership and thus all sorts of career and educational benefits)—is outweighed by its links to this heroic, 2000s present, and by its total rejection of the West. Sure, the message goes, dance and dress *po-amerikanski*—"in the American way"—but real unity and happiness is only possible in the Moscow of 2008. As one raucous dance number, set to a cover of an old song, has it, "I don't need an American wife." Russia was younger than its peers abroad. Russia was better than its peers abroad. To be young in Russia was to live in a mythical reality.

Audiences lapped it up. Dozens of swing dancing clubs sprang up around the capital, and not a day went by without a school talent show featuring a dance to the film's most popular tune, the catchy "Bugi vugi" (a Russianized version of *boogie woogie*). Even today, users continue to post themselves covering the tune's songs, performing its dances, and recreating the iconic concluding scene in YouTube and social media clips.[25] While the film was directed and conceived by Valery Todorovsky, who has been an outspoken government critic in recent years, it was no product of capitalist markets. Leonid Lebedev, a member of Putin's United Russia Party and and then a member of the Federation Council, Russia's upper house of parliament, co-produced and funded the movie.[26] *Stilyagi* appeared to be the product of a forward-looking, resurgent culture, but it was actually funded by a Kremlin-linked businessman. The cultural production of glittering Moscow was thus something of a mirage conjured up by government-aligned actors.

And while *Stilyagi* seems so lightweight as to be almost totally superfluous, it encapsulates the 2000s simultaneous embrace and rejection of non-Russian elements in youth culture. Surkov and his spin doctors were creating, as Peter Pomerantsev puts it, a "world of masks and poses." Irony, appropriation, fun, the West. Everything was acceptable—but behind the curtain, something serious, something nationalistic, always drew these loose strands together.[27] Beyond the masks, a new culture of mash-ups and contradictions gave young Russians a means to imagine themselves—or, in this case, dance themselves—into a world of youthful harmony and unity based around an emergent national myth. The state didn't need mass youth movements to sell its myths when it had cheap DVDs and online video sharing.

* * *

The power of the Moscow myth was enormous. Ivan Kondakov spent his childhood in 1990s Arkhangelsk, a port city nestled on the shore of the White Sea some 600 miles north of Moscow. It's a brutal place. Although packed with natural resources, the region's climate was so severe and its location so remote that it was the ideal place for the notoriously harsh Soviet-era Solovetsky Island prison camp. Hushed-up industrial and nuclear accidents were a feature of life here in the Soviet years.

Local residents may have prided themselves on their work for the national submarine fleet, but that work dried up with the end of the USSR. Now rusting hulks littered the region's dry docks and coast-line, a constant reminder of the decaying fabric of life in Arkhangelsk. Brief flashes of progress, like a partnership between a local university and a Norwegian counterpart, made little impact on most people's daily experiences.[28] Sixty thousand residents—approximately 15 percent of the population—had left the city for good by the turn of the millennium.

Ivan remembers the 1990s in Arkhangelsk as full of "people committing theft everywhere, mafia turning up and stealing whole factories. There were criminals all over the place. The courtyards"—Soviet-era apartment blocks were usually built several stories high around a central, publicly accessible courtyard—"were full of all sorts of hooligans." He remembers difficulties acquiring basic goods and seeing the homeless, alcoholics, and otherwise marginalized occupying street corners and courtyards. Many died of overdoses, by suicide, or from the freezing conditions.

The situation was so tragic, Ivan explains, that "what was happening felt like—to use an English word—*fallout*." Ivan remembers the 1990s as a kind of post-apocalyptic nightmare. If Ilya Fedotov-Fedorov's early years in hospital drove him apart from society, then Ivan's forced him to confront the reality of life on the margins. "It truly was an awful time," Ivan, almost hoarse with the weight of memory, croaks: "There was no purpose to life. There was nothing to live for."

Ivan studied hard and arrived as a teen to study in Moscow in the early 2000s. Things were no better than back home: "People were falling about drinking on the streets, lying all over the place, playing guitar. There were alcoholics everywhere."

Twenty years later, when we meet, Ivan, who is today a father of three, swings on a comfortable leather office chair. Behind him I can glimpse a small but well-appointed apartment, kitted out with airy, Instagrammable, Ikea-style furniture. An aerospace engineer with a PhD and a fluent English speaker, Ivan is also a keen musician who splits his time between his home office and central Moscow.

Like many, he's enjoyed the discovery of a hybrid working life during the pandemic, even if he found himself at a loose end for several months when Moscow was placed under a strict lockdown in the spring of 2020. Ivan's life couldn't be further away from his experiences of the early post-Soviet years.

Ivan—educated, eloquent, multilingual—is far from the stereotypical image of a brutish, monosyllabic Putin supporter. Yet like many Russians who've seen their lives and the world around them transformed, Kondakov is an eager participant in the state's myth of regeneration.[29]

He can talk about the "wild 1990s" at the drop of a hat. Like many of his generation, Ivan can't name anything positive about the decade. Criminality, poverty, goods shortages, anarchy, and corruption reigned supreme.[30] Ivan lays the blame for the tragedies of the 1990s squarely at the feet of Boris Yeltsin—a "total disgrace, say no more," he chuckles wryly—and Mikhail Gorbachev, whom he describes as "a populist traitor" and a "dim man" in thrall to an impossible vision of the future that came directly from the American government's "propaganda agencies." The American dream of "a beautiful house, a beautiful lawn, a car (maybe even two!)," he believes, was never possible in a Russia that was raided by American and European capitalist bandits in the years after 1991. But, he sadly intones, "we—me, my parents—we all believed in it back then." Russia, thinks Ivan, was sold down the river.

In the 2000s, Ivan ravenously consumed the pop culture that sold this myth. His bookshelves today are still packed with cheap cod-history paperbacks he picked up from Moscow bookstalls. The books make elaborate and wild-eyed arguments about Russia's historical destiny and enmity with the West. He's a huge fan of the 1997 gangster film *Brother* and its sequel from the year 2000, which are cornerstones of Russian macho nationalist culture. In the first movie, the protagonist Danila, a young soldier returned from Chechnya, enters the lawless mafia world of 1990s St Petersburg as a hitman. In the second, the young hero travels to the United States. Ivan chuckles as he recalls how Danila travels to the US to shoot up his enemies in the American and Ukrainian mafias before returning home unscathed. American capitalism was just a mafia scam aimed at taking advantage of Russians. Danila's vague, mythical values—

"strength is in truth," not money, he explains—and violent acts of revenge are far superior.

"*Everybody*," Ivan says, started "to slowly see that we have been hoodwinked, that America didn't love us. We were all so disenchanted." Ivan is a modern-day Mels from *Stilyagi*. After an infatuation with an imagined, perfect America, he has discovered that it was all a lie. It's better to stay at home, in Russia.

For Ivan, the world is divided into two simple blocs: "creators" who build things and "traitors" who tear them apart. For example, Stalin and the Bolshevik Party, he explains, were the "creators" of their time. Indeed, he explains at length why Stalin wasn't a tyrant but a decent man, a "creator," who "did the right thing" under difficult historical circumstances. Using this simple moral compass, Ivan can divide the world into two camps: NATO and the West versus Russia; 1990s versus 2000s; destruction and regeneration; Putin as hero and his critics as enemies. This logic-resistant, conspiratorial approach to the world imposes order on the chaos of Ivan's youth.

The myth of the 1990s, which took off at the dawn of the internet age, was an early example of aggressive nationalism embedded in meme culture. Indeed, there are countless viral fragments circulating even today that depict drunk Yeltsin, ramshackle scenes from the decade, and heroic Danila of *Brother* fame. Alina and Ivan both share them on their social media feeds.

Graduating from university at the height of Russia's boom times in 2007, Ivan saw that "life had become radically better. There was still a lot of stuff wrong, but it was obvious that life was better. People had the opportunity not just to survive but to thrive." And it was all thanks to Putin, who was most definitely a "creator."

Wide-eyed at the speed of progress, young Russians like Ivan suddenly found they had the world at their feet. And, like Ivan, many would soon find themselves attracted to ever darker elements of Russian nationalism. Theirs would soon be a world in which office clothes and commuter life rub shoulder to shoulder with racism, genocide, and war.

Spectacles of violence and sacrifice

But underneath the spectacle of opportunity and happy-go-lucky spectacle, real change was limited. The wealth gap between rich and poor widened. Cities in European Russia like Moscow and St Petersburg benefited from investment and improving standards of living in newly constructed apartment blocks, while residents of provincial towns complained that the best they might hope for was new cladding to cover up the cracking facades of their aging buildings—cladding that might last for a few months before falling off at the first sign of the winter freeze. Clean tap water, indoor toilets, and reliable heating remained a distant dream for millions of Russians. If they managed to reach Putin at his annual televised "Direct Line" phone-in to complain, the leader might make a vague promise to have a local leader "look into it." If they were lucky, the leader himself might even "think about it" himself. But little action came out of such promises.[31]

Like millions of others, Zhanna and her family left Central Asia for Moscow in the early 2000s. Then just a schoolgirl, she knew what to expect from Russia's capital: "Lights. Action. Life." Sold on the heady cocktail of the dreamy imperial capital, coming to Moscow would mean endless opportunity. The reality was crushingly different. Zhanna was bullied by white children in school. The teachers scolded her Russian pronunciation, even though she was a fluent speaker. She and her family argued endlessly in the pressure cooker of their cheap tenement-block apartment.

Even the journey to school was a daily trial. As Zhanna slid up the interminably long escalators toward metro-station exits, she would often catch sight of a pair of policemen waiting to "inspect" her documents. The "fine" to pay would be trifling—just a couple of hundred rubles—but it was enough. She began to experience anxiety attacks. Zhanna would bury her head in a dark hoodie. Then she started avoiding the metro in favor of the privately run and rickety *marshrutka* minibus services, whose drivers were usually other immigrants from Central Asia. Zhanna and her Kazakh friends lived in fear of the police and, worse, the OMON—the heavily armed riot police who might attack or abuse them at any moment.

The effervescent culture of splashy Eurovision victories, sporting events, and glass palaces was always built on violence. Suffering might have been swept out of *your* life, but the average Russian endlessly consumed conflict through the media, through films, and through play-acting. The violent motifs of the 1990s were endlessly replayed in different tonalities: something, some scapegoat, was always being destroyed to solve all Russia's problems once and for all. Perhaps a media figure, a TV owner, an oligarch. Perhaps a local functionary. Perhaps the enemy in Chechnya. Or perhaps the West. To be a good Russian, you had to learn to play along by consuming the violence on TV and perpetuating it in state-led rituals in school and at work.

Turn back the clock to Putin's 2000 electoral campaign, which was in the works for months before the public knew Boris Yeltsin would be stepping down. Even then, when the youthful parvenu was promising fairy tales, macho violence was always on the table.

At the crack of dawn on 9 September 1999, a vast explosion ripped through a 9-story apartment block in Moscow. Four days later, another building suffered the same fate. Over 200 residents were killed. In response, then Prime Minister Putin declared: "We will pursue them everywhere. We'll get them in the toilet. We'll do them in on the shitter."[32] By the end of the month, Russian forces were mobilizing to launch an all-out assault on Chechnya. State media breathlessly followed this grotesque election ploy masquerading as defensive war, hardly bothering to report the deaths of dozens of Chechen civilians from Russian air and tank fire in the week after the invasion.[33]

As Russian forces were entering the Chechen capital, Grozny, in February 2000, Putin announced his manifesto to Russian voters in the national press. He would, he claimed, fix the economy, combat criminality, fight poverty, and defend "national interests." But the chief problem facing Russia, Putin asserted, was something inside—something spiritual. The experiences of the 1990s had caused, he said, "a weakening of the will." Defending the nation and attaining a "life of dignity," as Putin put it, meant casting off the mindset of the 1990s, defining oneself in opposition to the Western influences of the previous decade, and using extreme violence in the pursuit of "national interests" like re-attaching Chechen territory to the motherland. Creating the fairy tale, repudiating the trauma of the 1990s, would mean waging war.

Russia's Chechen venture dragged on in the dark wings of the public stage. The war barely even made sense: "What does Chechnya have to do with me for God's sake, and where is it anyway?" one frontline soldier remembered as he fought his way through a vicious conflict of mud, confusion, and looting.[34] Bored, underpaid, and poorly equipped, Russia's army of conscripts took to violence— attacking the enemy, each other, and civilians with abandon.[35]

And yet, even as the young troops on the ground descended into animalistic amorality, the state presented the Chechen war in increasingly megalomaniacal terms. After 9/11, Putin framed his war as part of a global battle against terrorism.[36] The regional conflict was no longer about hemming the edges of a fraying empire. It was about restoring stability to the entire world—and Putin saw that Russia's leading role in fighting the threat of Islamic terrorism was a means to restore its imperial greatness on the world stage.[37] Russian forces were fighting a tiny enemy—perhaps some 1,000 Chechen guerillas—but their control over the territory remained unstable. Stories of tragedies trickled into the Russian media: Russian military errors, equipment shortages, horrific discipline that saw conscripts killed by their superiors, and a spate of unpunished rapes and murders carried out by troops.

The "good things coming true" Putin spoke of on 31 December 1999 began by clamping down on dissent, speaking a language of violence, and launching military action to make Russia whole again. So much for the happy-go-lucky Moscow of youthful dreams. Across society, the process was repeated as journalists and regime opponents began to be increasingly targeted with harassment, violence, and even death. And young people would be taught to speak the regime's language of violence for themselves.

Performing war, fighting the self

It's 9 May 2000. Just two days after President Putin's inauguration. Trumpeters bedecked in shining regalia, their instruments adorned with gilded red banners, sound a fanfare. The new president steps up to a dais on Red Square to address the massed public and troops.

"Dear Frontliners," he intones, "through you we learned how to achieve victory." The new president explained that victory in World War II had, like the sacrifice of the 1990s, been a struggle to bring about new life: "It has helped us achieve much beyond the military. And it will continue to help us in civilian life, it will help our generation to build a strong, blossoming nation." The country's soldiers, remarked Putin, can "help us escape from every trial." "Victory," in Putin's conception, was a byword for sacrifice and regeneration—*blossoming*—in the present and the future. The throngs of spectators breathed in the joyous major-key militarism of the army's marching bands. Under the beaming sun of a late spring Moscow day, the event seemed proof of Russia's new blossoming.

When Putin concluded his speech by explaining that "we will pass on" the memory of the war "to our children," he was linking the past with the "blossoming" future of the nation. To observe, to remember, to recreate World War II would always mean sunny spring days. The parade of the year 2000 was not the grandiose affair the Victory Day celebration would become, but Putin had laid down a marker.[38] Reconstructing the nation meant paying symbolic tributes to the victories of the past and learning to imitate the mentality of the wartime generation.

Respect for a lost, mythical generation of fathers began to be built into the rituals of daily life from the top to the bottom of Russian culture. Putin would always attend Victory Day parades and visit the sites of important battles, treating these trips as ritualistic pilgrimages.[39] Speaking to veterans, telling stories of his family's wartime past in Leningrad (although Putin was born seven years after the war's end), and attending memorials in churches, the president engaged with the public and constructed a legend of himself as an ideal adherent of the religion of war—a religion that suggested that Russia had to continually relive its most tragic moment of sacrifice in order to stave off the trauma of the 1990s. The approach was openly masterminded by Putin's PR men, but older Russians didn't seem to mind.[40] They remembered the reverence with which the war had been publicly treated under the Soviet leadership, embraced the country's "only remaining sacrality," and admired Putin's piety.[41]

Everyone was encouraged to imitate the president. The somber memorials of the Soviet era were conjoined to a trashy, pop culture that turned Victory Day into both an object of reverence and an excuse to have a good time. At parades across the nation, *popsa*—Russia's low-rent, cheesy pop music—blasted from PA systems as families dressed up in cheap period costumes to enjoy a fun day out. Cars daubed with slogans—"Hitler *kaput!*"—blazed through the streets of Moscow and St Petersburg, bearing drunk drivers and drunker passengers raucously celebrating Soviet victory. Anyone could get on board with the state's love of war when it meant having a good time.

The young were led into this celebratory war culture at school. The state began to favor Soviet-style rote learning of sacred devotion to the motherland by paying respects to the memory of World War II.[42] A range of new picture books and young-adult novels celebrated the feats of the "generation of the grandfathers." Older Soviet works were republished in vast quantities and incorporated into school syllabuses. Patriotic history textbooks introduced in 2007 would, in Putin's words, inculcate an appropriate "sense of pride" in Russia. Zhanna remembers the tedium of being forced to rote learn poems by Konstantin Simonov, a wartime correspondent and fiction writer who was widely published in the Soviet years. "I had to memorize some lines from 'Wait for Me'"—Zhanna refers to Simonov's ubiquitous poem, a departing soldier's slushy appeal to his sweetheart—"and stand in front of the class to recite them. But I didn't understand what the poem meant, and I didn't really care."

Others who attended school in the early 2000s remember singing wartime songs at talent shows, usually to the banal backing of a tinny karaoke machine or the accompaniment of an untuned Soviet-era "Red October" piano. The really unfortunate were treated to dreary yarns told by aging veterans at assemblies. Most of the tales, lifted verbatim from old Soviet war movies and novels, were as tall as Moscow's new skyscrapers. Dressing up to perform the language of the World War II soldier in school or at a concert might still have been optional, but it was fast becoming central to young people's engagement with Victory Day.

Underneath the carnival of costumery and pop culture, the core of Russia's World War II story was frighteningly apocalyptic. In the story Russians were learning to recite, the advancing Wehrmacht in the 1940s had not merely sought to conquer and enslave Slavs. They had planned to totally obliterate Russians and every aspect of their civilization, enacting an anti-Russian genocide on a par with the Jewish genocide taking place in Europe. The Nazis planned, according to the story, to destroy humanity itself. Of course, that much was not far removed from the truth: the Germans murdered millions of Soviet citizens in a destructive orgy as they advanced across Ukraine, Belarus, and Western Russia before the tide of the war was turned in late 1942.

In this story, though, the deaths of millions of Soviets were not merely regrettable. They were essential. In the war, the nation had been murdered. Sent to die at the front, Russia's heroes had sacrificed themselves to resurrect their dead motherland. In this pastiche of the Passion of Christ, Russia's young had literally been sacrificed and resurrected to save humanity at the front—becoming saints in the process. Every descendant of the "grandfathers' generation" owed an unpayable debt to their saviors. A young Russian's most ideal self could only ever be a pale imitation of their grandfathers', since they could never make the ultimate sacrifice: self-sacrifice to save the world. The best that young Russians could do was to be pious like Putin, who cared for veterans, attended parades, and re-instituted Soviet and tsarist-era flags, uniforms, and anthems.

Indeed, for the young, developing military piety was like developing a religious faith. In the Orthodox Christian tradition, imitation is as important as questioning or understanding. To imitate the paths of the saintly is for the Orthodox faithful a means to "bravely face consequences like death."[43] Russia's young could learn to remember, learn to imitate language and behavior in cultural rituals that would ready them for war—a connection the Russian Orthodox Church was only too eager to encourage as its priests turned out for Victory Day parades and began blessing men and machines heading to war. Russia's war faithful would not learn the Western "never again." For them, it was Putin's "we can do it again."[44]

The Putinist rendition of Victory Day might have been dressed up as the festival of a confident, forward-looking nation, but it tied Russia's young to a militarized past and present. Nostalgia for the culture of the socialist past has been widespread across the former communist bloc, where the pop music, film, and iconography of the Soviet era seem to represent a warm, homely, and safe golden era. In most post-communist states, young people's nostalgic longing for a past they don't even remember—expressed by consuming the music and movies of their parents' generation—is linked to a desire for belonging in a time of rapid social change.[45]

In Russia, the state encouraged nostalgia for the most violent and dangerous time in the country's history: Russia's peak as a historical force was a time of heroism enabled by mass death. "Victory" really meant "martyrdom." The narrative that could truly repudiate the trauma of the 1990s was clear: the present is miraculous, Moscow is an imperial capital, Russia is great again, but it's all built on endless and unrepayable moral—and mortal—debt.

And, as the Chechen war dragged endlessly on, young Russians didn't have to look far for an opportunity to perform valiant, youthful Russian sacrifice. As one leader writer at the newspaper *Izvestiya* put it in 2007, "the main heroes of this war are its political leaders and also the several thousands of young lads—Chechens, Russians and others—who gave their lives for the territorial integrity of Russia, for the security of the citizens of Russia and for the reduction of the threat of terrorism."[46]

The historical parallels with World War II were hammered home in movies like *Breakthrough* (*Proryv*).[47] Released in 2006, *Breakthrough* turned a disastrous military engagement from the year 2000, in which over eighty Russian soldiers were killed as their positions were overrun, into a triumphant martyrdom.[48] What was an embarrassing catastrophe became a *podvig*—a spiritual, military feat—in which brave young Russian boys were slaughtered by hordes of "terrorists" for the greater good.[49] Savage barbarians were being subdued, civilized, by an enlightened imperial army.[50] Little matter that Chechnya was still part of Russia, and that Chechens were Russian citizens: they, and all other Caucasians, were always potential enemies. Only through the Chechen's eradication and the Russian's martial perfection was the empire made whole and peace attained.

Being an exemplary young man in 2000s Russia wasn't just about enjoying the new economic opportunities offered under Putin. It meant joining the army and being prepared to make the ultimate sacrifice.[51] It meant living out—through recitation; consumption; and engagement with dance, song, media, and language—the fantasy of World War II. The best of the young would sacrifice their ties with their own families, and with life itself, in favor of a macho dream.[52] The only way to eliminate the chaos and disorder of the fragmented 1990s—to bring about Ivan Kondakov's time of "creators"—was through murder and martyrdom.

Performance and identity were far more important than real reform. Performance, after all, could teach citizens to imitate their forebears' martyrdom in a war to defend Russia's existence. To most of the Russian public, the violence of the Chechen war seemed far off—restricted to Putin's vicious asides, to news clips, and to TV serials and movies like *Breakthrough*. Before long, though, violence broke back into the Russian homeland. And the state used the chance to violently wrap up the Chechen wars, further selling destructive victory as a path to heavenly rebirth.

Real and fake violence

When Ilya Fedotov-Fedorov hopped onto the Moscow Metro to travel to the Krylya rock festival at the old Tushino airfield in the city's northwest outskirts in the summer of 2003, he could hardly have imagined he was about to experience separatist violence first-hand. Queuing in the searing summer heat to enter the festival, he and his companions heard a loud bang. Like the rest of those attending, he was confused. There must have been an accident. A quarter of an hour ticked by. Another bang. Panic reigned, and Ilya and his friends were waved away by descending security forces. Chechen suicide bombers had killed fourteen music fans outside the festival's compound.

More bombings followed. Horrific sieges at a school in Beslan in North Ossetia and the Dubrovka theater in Moscow played out to an enraptured audience following every twist and turn on TV. Viewers were as entranced as they were horrified by the gruesome spectacle of Russia's fearsome security forces assaulting their opponents.[53] A harmonious resolution had to follow the violence, especially when the 2004 presidential election was fast approaching.[54] In a wave of violence and lawlessness, and with the help of a program of soft power to address cultural differences and a catastrophic local economy that had young male unemployment running as high as 40 percent, Putin's forces and their Chechen allies turned the tide against the separatists.[55]

The suicide bombings in Russia, and kidnappings and violence in Chechnya itself, slowed to a trickle; a background white noise of violence against the hubbub of the metropolis. Moscow poured money into reconstructing the destroyed Grozny, turning its downtown from a wasteland into a word of shining, glass-faced towers that projected a superficial Islamism on top of a hard-nosed Russian culture.[56] Tourists were encouraged to visit Grozny in marketing campaigns and hip travel documentaries.[57] The region's pacification and reconstruction paralleled the regeneration of Moscow. Not only was the capital booming, but so too were the far-off peripheries.

Soon, Ilya remembers, "things were good again. Moscow felt great. It was safe again." The fear of suicide bombers and terrorism in Moscow—after the horrors of Beslan, Dubrovka, and the Krylya festival—dissipated into a stream of calm confidence. Another perfect mythical script had played out: violence, threat, and fear was followed by relief, renewal, and joy—all thanks to the sacrifices made by young Russians at the front.

And it was thanks to these sacrifices that young Russians like Ilya, armed with higher degrees and—increasingly—better pay packets, were suddenly able to explore a cosmopolitan culture that seemed to offer endless diversity. Despite his lonely teen years, he managed to enroll in a degree program at RUDN, the "Peoples' Friendship University," a public college in Moscow. Two years into Ilya's program, the university shuttered—"destroyed," in Ilya's words—the degree program he was taking when funding was cut to renovate the old Soviet-era laboratories. Ilya's nascent career as a scientist was cut short by the march of Putinist progress. The old had to be swept away in favor of the new.

Yet for Ilya, the setback turned out to be a blessing in disguise. Turning to art, a hobby he had long nurtured, he decided to become a professional artist. Over the following years, he would slowly build a name for himself on the Moscow art scene.

Plugged back into human society, Ilya managed to take a huge leap forward. He reminisces nostalgically about his growing interest in camp idols like the singer Boris Moiseev, an over-the-top androgynous Europop idol whose public coming out in the early 2000s caused a tabloid scandal. The isolated teen Ilya had been all ears for Tatu, the bubble-gum pop duo who enjoyed global success after their management launched a salacious PR campaign claiming the singers were lesbians.[58] Soon, Ilya would come out as a gay man.

Being openly gay at the start of the 2000s would have been unthinkable, he says, even in his permissive family: "I remember watching a documentary about [Tatu] late one night. My mother came in and asked, 'Do you like it?' And I said, 'No, it's just interesting, no, no, no, I'm not gay. I'm just watching.'"

But by the late 2000s, as a young man in Moscow, Ilya found a circle of friends who welcomed him and his sexuality. The growth of the internet in Russia—43 percent of Russians had home internet by 2010, compared with 2 percent a decade earlier—made the discovery of culture, identity, and opportunity even easier. The wildly popular Russian social network Vkontakte ("In Contact," now known as VK), a carbon copy of Facebook founded by the thirty-one-year-old entrepreneur Pavel Durov, started a Runet boom on its launch in 2006. Anybody could find anybody else, and cultures and communities could thrive—all without the feeling that the state was watching. And for those in the big cities, networks of private bars and clubs even offered real meeting spaces for the marginalized.[59] Young, queer Russians—and anybody else, no matter their fancy—could find, as one of my interviewees explained, "a place that was my own, where my parents didn't bother me. I could say anything and be anything."

The myths of destruction and regeneration continued to play out their contrapuntal dance. Real violence once again seemed a distant threat. It happened to conscripts, to immigrants, to those on the peripheries. Young Russians like Ilya could choose to engage with the myths of the state seriously, or they could shrug them off, burying themselves in subcultures and communities as they saw fit. They could swing dance into the night as they played at being *stilyagi*, or they could hoover up stories of glittering Moscow and queer idols to their heart's content. The new Russia was an empire at ease with itself. The mirage of violence was just a spot in the corner of the eye: always there, but never quite in focus.

* * *

The state was, however, continually sowing the seeds of a violent youth politics, playing nationalist performance off against its myths of fairy-tale worlds in Ilya's and Ivan's Moscow backyard.

In the days leading up to the anniversary of the 1917 Revolution on 7 November 2000, Muscovite metro commuters were bemused by the appearance of thousands of stickers displaying the words "Walking Together." Where they came from, and what "walking together" meant, nobody was quite sure. But things became clearer on 7 November itself.

That morning, 3,000 young Russians turned up in one of Moscow's central squares. Wearing red T-shirts plastered with Putin's face and the slogan "We're on the way," they enthusiastically waved the Russian tricolor flag. "Who's on the way *to where?*" onlookers may have asked, but the spectacle linked the new president's political project to Soviet nostalgia—the October Revolution anniversary was always the most important holiday under the Communist Party—to Russian national symbolism, and, most importantly of all, to the potent image of youthful support for the new government. Little matter that most of the attendees were attracted only by the offer of free gadgets, train travel to the capital, and concert tickets in exchange for their time. The Kremlin had staged the first of its big youth rallies.

The perpetrators were "Walking Together," the first in a string of Kremlin-sponsored youth groups. Led by Vasily Yakemenko, a twenty-nine-year-old who had just joined the new president's administration, Walking Together was really yet another Surkov brainchild that had been personally approved by Putin as a "new Komsomol."

Using a combination of photogenic spectacle and confrontational violence, the Kremlin's youth groups would begin to blur the lines between genuine youth support and PR campaigns, between the fake and the real, and between the destructive and the constructive. And the Kremlin meant business. Walking Together was flush with cash and connections. By 2001, it had acquired a headquarters on Denisovsky pereulok, a charming old street just a few miles from the Kremlin. Sub-branches had sprung up in cities ranging from cosmopolitan St Petersburg to wartime Grozny, the capital of Chechnya.

The group's methods became more confrontational. Members protested a book signing for the postmodern author Vladimir Sorokin's 2003 novel *Blue Lard*, which they claimed contained "vile words and revolting scenes of perverted sexual contacts." They eviscerated Sorokin in public as a "literary hanger-on," reviving the language of Soviet-era literary criticism to, as their manifesto put it, "cleanse" Russian culture of "pornography."[60] Men like Sorokin were the degenerate and unwanted moral detritus of the 1990s, and movements like Walking Together were meant to scrub them from Russian public life.

Moscow's streets felt more like those of the European 1920s—when groups of ideological opponents would confront each other with public performances of art, poetry, and politics—than those of a modern democracy. The aesthetics of the show, though, were more Eurovision botox than Brown-shirted violence. After all, the aim was not just to intimidate. It was to get the message on television, onto the internet, to get photographed by the media. In the vast country that is Russia, anybody could drink in the togetherness, the power of this youth movement. And surely, if these young people supported Putin—the great "creator"—they must have been on to something?

Indeed, Walking Together wasn't just a front to organize glitzy rallies and PR stunts. It was a serious means to radicalize angry, disenchanted youths into a state-sponsored, aggressive vision of Russian life. The group actively recruited from skinhead and neo-Nazi gangs. Gang members were not averse to violence and would simply swap out their leathers and Swastika T-shirts for Putin shirts before they arrived at a rally.[61] At regular Walking Together meetings, these angry young men learned more about the Great Patriotic War, read nationalist literature, and listened to speakers lecture on Russia's imperial past and historical destiny.

The regime was beginning to tacitly encourage confrontation and aggression as ways to cleanse young minds and public life of supposedly non-Russian elements: Western values, perversion and queerness, and cosmopolitan readings of history.[62] The model young Russian was not a counterculture hero, like the American dreamers of *Stilyagi*, but somebody who could—as Zhanna was learning to do in school—recite a mythical, nationalist story of loss, embrace the Soviet and Russian past, and attack anybody and anything who was tarred with the arbitrary label of moral degeneracy. The present was a time of miraculous progress, but it could only be built by violently driving out the Other both internally and externally. Young Russians, like their peers who had fought in Chechnya, would have to fight and fight again to keep the country pure.

By 2005, Walking Together had collapsed in a series of scandals uncovered by the independent media, which labelled the group the "Putinjugend."[63] But more groups—some with grassroots origins and picked up by the Kremlin's PR men, others entirely a mirage—took its place. Residents of Moscow and other towns might find "flashmobs" of flag-waving youths pop up out of nowhere. At shopping malls, they might suddenly be surrounded by bands of glamorous young girls with provocative, pro-Putin slogans scrawled on their clothes.[64] On the internet, the pictures spread like wildfire: the liberal media was as entranced by this dizzying guerrilla youth fodder as the passers-by who stopped for selfies.

The youth projects grew in size. Walking Together was replaced by Nashi—"Ours"—led by the very same Vasily Yakemenko. Even though it was called an "anti-fascist movement," Nashi continued its predecessor's mix of confrontation and publicity stunt, harassing the British ambassador and even assembling 70,000 "members" to mark the sixtieth anniversary of the World War II Battle of Moscow in 2006.[65] But the work wasn't about stunts. In the group's manifesto, "liberal" society is attacked as "the worst advertisement for democracy," and Putin is hailed as a visionary who has "turned Russia into a global power."[66] In addition to regular meetings, Nashi organized summer training camps where members' patriotic education and physical training could take place.[67] Just like in the Soviet days, young Russians could spend their summers at camp, meeting like-minded peers and discovering how to be good citizens. Now, though, the content they learned was not Marxist, and not merely imperialistic. It was violent, misogynistic, and racist—and it meant that the powerless young of the 1990s were learning to take the fight to the West.

Nashi coordinated increasingly violent confrontations on Moscow's streets. Hundreds of members descended on the capital in 2011 to "seek out fascists" on the day of Hitler's birth.[68] Hunting down these fascists in fifty-strong vigilante groups, one member explained, "We can't arrest anyone ... but we can observe and report things to the militia." In reality, the day was marked by violent scuffles as members sought out anybody perceived as a *neformal*—an "informal," a Soviet-era word used to describe any young person from the counterculture, which was, of course, associated with Western influences. Walking Together's October Revolution march in 2000, all stickers and T-shirts, seems almost quaint in comparison with this public display of violence.

When I speak to two of the group's former members—both are today urban professionals in their thirties—they told me that they only joined Nashi because the group seemed like a good place to get ahead in life and to meet likeminded, aspirational young people.[69] They took part in all the "right" activities—attending "flashmobs," parades, political meetings, and handing out pro-government flyers—but just as important was the chance to attend after-hours social events. Waging mythical wars with the West or slavishly building up the demi-god Putin in the minds of the mostly blasé Muscovites they encountered during their travails was an afterthought.

But it doesn't matter what the "members" actually believed. The story was being created for TV cameras and photographers, ready to be shaped and spread by revanchist patriots. Violence was linked with Russian symbols. It seemed spontaneous. Anybody could watch and breathe in Russia's young "defending" the motherland. The *stilyagi*—the cool young hipsters—of the 2000s were fighting for Russia's fairy-tale future, not rebelling against the state.

Groups came and went, and education programs carried on, but genuine ideologues—"the real Putin types" as one of my interviewees put it—seemed few and far between. The membership of groups like Walking Together and Nashi never exceeded more than a couple of hundred thousand, and most members were older teens and students who were either keen to participate in some state-sanctioned violence or get their foot on the career ladder. Long-term members were outnumbered by those recruited ad hoc for big events. Nonetheless, even after Nashi went the way of Walking Together, collapsing in on its own corruption and contradictions in the early 2010s, some groups soldiered on.

Most of all, these groups' young leaders found all sorts of opportunities in the state apparatus. Indeed, some of the young leaders of Nashi and Walking Together—even those with openly neo-Nazi views—have gone on to occupy positions as state MPs, leading businesspeople, and journalists. And as the state was inviting extremists into organized youth groups and into the apparatus of government, it was also cultivating a far more extreme form of nationalist violence that spiraled from Moscow's streets onto the internet and back again.

Murder in the stands

Ivan Katanaev, a cheery, barrel-chested young man with dusty blonde hair and a perpetual half-smile on his square jaw, grew up in an intellectual Muscovite family. But like many young Russians in the late 1990s, he found himself adrift. Education and the world of work offered little when everything seemed to be collapsing. Bunking off school, he stumbled on a local football match. Katanaev was hooked on the "sense of freedom" and belonging as he latched onto Moscow's hooligan scene. Drawn into a world where "everyone was doing" violence, Katanaev enjoyed going to matches to celebrate patriotic markers like Victory Day and to "beat up the blacks and the CSKA [Moscow] fans." It was all okay, he explains, because war was everywhere: war in Chechnya, war in Yugoslavia, so why not war on the terraces?[70]

By July 2010, Katanaev was twenty-six years old. As leader of Moscow Spartak's notorious "Fratria" supporters' group, he became, as one leader writer put it, "Russia's most famous football fan." Fratria was a byword for uber-violent Russian nationalism, Orthodox Christianity, and neo-Nazism: Katanaev openly described himself as a fascist and even gave himself the nickname *Kombat*, inspired by the British neo-Nazi group Combat 18.[71] Its members were constantly embroiled in bloody match-day brawls. When Fratria members weren't stirring up trouble at matches, they were swapping footage of violent attacks, making plans to mob opposing gangs, and chatting about their "feats" in a language that mixed militarism, national patriotism, and extreme racism.[72] Online and on the terraces, these men found shared spaces of belonging.

The state looked on with approving eyes. These young men were soldiers of the motherland going into battle, just like the heroes of *Breakthrough* and Chechnya, against the state's enemies. Indeed, when the state began to provide tacit direction and material support, some members of football-hooligan groups started to call themselves "Putin's foot soldiers." People of color, homosexuals, and anybody else deemed too effete or liberal had to watch their back when big games took place in Moscow, lest they be targeted by angry young men as the police stood idly by.

In the summer of 2010, Spartak supporters—there's no suggestion that Katanaev was involved in events, but the perpetrators had followed his path from isolation to belonging in their macho group—caused a national stir.[73] In July 2010, Yury Volkov, a twenty-three-year-old ultranationalist Spartak Moscow fan, was knifed in a brawl outside the metro station in Chistye prudy. Three Chechens were arrested and blamed for the murder. Online supporters' groups were quickly filled with angry posts. Spartak fans spurred each other on with outpourings of racist bile against Chechens: "Chechens are killing Russians," "There's a war going on in our own home."[74] Within days, groups of supporters gathered to occupy Moscow's Manezh Square, where they shouted racist abuse, scuffled with Caucasians, and daubed the local streets in xenophobic graffiti. Online hate talk had quickly spilled over into reality.

That December, another Spartak fan, Egor Sviridov, was murdered in another brawl with a group of Caucasians. This time, the football fans' discussion boards and social media groups boiled over. Thousands of hooligans again took to Manezh Square, where they chanted "Russia forward! Russians first!" and hurled missiles at the riot police, who made some half-hearted attempts at crowd control before leaving them to it. Left-wing counter-protestors attempted to engage the hooligans but were beaten back. Twenty-nine people were hospitalized.

Events like the riots of 2010 gave young football hooligans a means to play out their aggressive fantasies as part of a lifestyle that offered a sense of belonging. Posting on bulletin boards, supporters' sites, and online fanzines, men like Katanaev were heroized by football fans as real Russian Orthodox heroes who were defending the nation through their incoherent and arbitrary violence. In their online lives, they imitated the state's increasingly violent performances. In December 2010, virtual performance led to real deaths.

The 2010 football violence got the attention of the national media. Yet most pundits suggested that Russia had a problem with Muslim "guests" who could not "respect their hosts."[75] State media could not accept the idea that uncontrollable, state-sponsored nationalists were seeking each other out and coordinating online to cause violent chaos.

Indeed, the state's elites staged their own spectacle around the football murders. Dmitry Medvedev, who had replaced Putin as president in 2008, wrote on Twitter that "we'll deal with everyone who stirred this up, have no doubt." But no hooligans were prosecuted—unlike the left-wing counter-protestors, whose case was criticized in the European Court of Human Rights. Vladislav Surkov chipped in too: "What happened on 11 December on Manezh Square? The 'liberals' are determined to make unsanctioned protests a thing, so the Nazis and the hicks follow on." The blame lay not with aggressive nationalists but with the young representatives of the non-Russian "liberalism." Indeed, Patriarch Kirill made the threat even clearer, calling the affair a "political provocation" that was intended to bring back "the chaos of the early 1990s."[76] Muslim criminals and liberal provocateurs threatened to undo the fairy tales that had supposedly come true in the past decade. Putin himself visited Sviridov's grave, calling for calm and mutual respect. He made no effort to reach out to or visit Moscow's Caucasian community.

The state had nurtured young football hooligans who committed real violence. In turn, the state used the violence those hooligans had performed to further its own pro-Russian, anti-Western, and anti-liberal performances. A cycle of discursive and physical violence between the state and bands of its young supporters was leading to trouble on the streets for anybody—LGBTQ, Caucasian, "liberal" youth—who found themselves in the way of this storm.

* * *

And just as violence always brewed in the language of Putin's speeches, in the performative demonstrations of youth groups, and the groups of football hooligans, so it was still perpetuated by the state on the battlefield. As the Chechen war was dying down, Moscow waged a second war against a former imperial subject, invading the north of Georgia. The media went on the offensive too, spinning 24/7 headlines about Georgia's nefarious ties with the United States and NATO and its plans to carry out a genocide against "ethnic Russians."[77] Moscow had to "keep the peace"—even though it had concocted the war, and even though the media reality of the war was a hyperbolized mirage of anti-Russian violence whisked out of the ether by employees in Ostankino Tower.

Indeed, the symbolic value of the Georgia war was far greater than its strategic potential. Russia, embarrassed by the disintegration of its Soviet empire and its military failures in the 1990s, was now supposed to be in the ascendant. Chechnya had been beaten back into the federation. The great military power could easily subjugate the non-Russians in its post-imperial hinterland. War, a chaotic and violent expression of masculine strength that reflected the country's buoyant internal mood, was a means to reinvigorate the nation internally. The reality, as it had been in Chechnya, was quite different from the images being projected. Moscow ultimately prevailed, but the brief conflict revealed gaping holes in its forces' battlefield readiness.

When we wish on Grandfather Frost

A decade of fairy-tale dreams and performative violence left youth trapped in the state's debt. They could have anything they wanted, but they knew they would have to fight for it; without doing so, they barely deserved what they were getting. Young Russians found themselves invited to wrap themselves up in the myth of constant war, sacrifice, and destruction that offered the key to renewal in the present. Thus, the state perpetuated conflict in a constant cycle, offering up opportunities for young Russians to consume and perform violence.

During the New Year's holiday in 2010, Russian audiences flocked to movie theaters to see *Christmas Trees*, a schmaltzy holiday film helmed by comedian and talk show host Ivan Urgant and made "largely" with state money. The movie's protagonist is a sparkly eyed, blonde-haired orphan girl, Varya, who boasts to her peers that she is the daughter of then President Dmitry Medvedev. Challenged to prove the claim, she and her equally photogenic friend Vova announce that they will have Medvedev declare, "You can wish on Grandfather Frost, but don't let yourself down"—a twist on an old Russian New Year's proverb—in his televised New Year's address.

Thanks to a series of chance encounters and family connections— the movie imitates the British Christmas film *Love Actually*, with a series of saccharine subplots linked by Varya's message—an ethnic Tajik street cleaner writes the phrase in the snow outside Medvedev's window. She beams in confusion as the president reads her message out. Varya's honor is upheld. Romantic connections and friendships are confirmed across the nation, and the orphans live happily ever after. It's all staged. It's all absurd. But there was the real president on screen, making fairy tales come true in Moscow.

Medvedev, exactly eleven years after Putin had promised a fairy-tale-make sure hyphenated reality in his first New Year's address, further blurred fiction and reality when he tweeted the magic line from the film on 31 December: "You can wish on Grandfather Frost, but don't let yourself down ..." The chaos of the 1990s seemed to be gone for good. Even the most hopeless, most marginalized children could look forward to a better future in this stage-managed reality.

Critics savaged *Christmas Trees* as a mawkish piece of holiday mush, but audiences loved it (just as they did the increasingly ropy eight sequels that followed). But did the boundaries between the fantasy of a benevolent, watchful state and the reality of a still chaotic, unstable, and violent existence end with the film? Or on Medvedev's social media account? Nobody much seemed to mind.

If children in the early 2000s were writing to President Putin to tell him that they refused to go to dangerous and underfunded orphanages,[78] now an avuncular state was always watching over them and granting their every wish. Only good things could happen in fairy-tale Russia—even as, mere days before *Christmas Trees* was released, racially motivated violence was breaking out just a few hundred feet from where Varya and Vova's dreams were supposedly made real. When images of a nation reborn after its traumatic 1990s—a nation that had great musicians and sportsmen and a glittering imperial capital—saturated the cultural miasma, the dissonance didn't matter.

* * *

By the decade's end, our two protagonists Ilya and Ivan had found their feet. Ilya's nascent artistic efforts were beginning to attract attention on the hip Moscow art scene, and he was, finally, comfortable in his own body. Ivan had finished his degree and started work as a technical expert working on domestic Sukhoi jets. His career took him from Moscow, all over Europe, and into a comfortable apartment. He was far away from the chaos of his childhood in 1990s Arkhangelsk. Ivan thanks Putin for all of that: "When he came along, we didn't hope for much. He was just some young politician, what could he possibly do?" For Ivan, Putin was a savior, and life really did seem like a fairy tale. And so long as they avoided bumping into football hooligans from Katanaev's Fratria or groups of Nashi members on parade days, even queer young men like Ilya could be themselves.

Within just a few short years, however, state-sponsored violence would spill over into conflicting protest and patriotism, wrenching young Russians apart inside and outside. Ivan would soon become a social media bard for the ultranationalist movement. Ilya would find his psyche and spirit crushed as the government, sated by its attacks on Chechens and Georgians but now under threat from economic chaos and disgruntled young democrats, trained its sights on the queer community.

3

THE ENEMY WITHIN

Victory Day, 9 May 2022. A bearded young Muscovite sits with a laptop balanced on the table in front of him. His carefully packed bag is beside him. He hasn't eaten for hours. He hasn't slept. His hand trembling, he reaches for the trackpad. Inhale. Click.

Thirty-year-old Egor Polyakov has just taken a sledgehammer to the state's big celebration day.

* * *

Two decades earlier, Polyakov was growing up in what he jokingly calls "the Moscow Bronx." Living just outside the dangerous Golyanovo district, Egor often witnessed thefts, drug deals, and street violence as a child. Just a few subway stops from the glamorous life of central Moscow and years after the 1990s era of *bespredel*—the Russian word, literally "without boundaries," that is often used to describe the decade's lawlessness and chaos—was meant to be over, the outskirts of the glittering neo-imperial capital seethed with ethnic resentment and petty criminality.

Putin's fairy-tale 2000s had not revolutionized life for many in places like Golyanovo.[1] Egor learned about Moscow's seedy underbelly firsthand, not from movies and TV shows about the bad old days of the 1990s: "I remember one incident when the police in Golyanovo and [the neighboring district] Metrogorodok were chucking a corpse back and forth across the district lines just because they each couldn't be bothered to investigate a murder!" He chuckles out of something between fear and helplessness at the memory of the police forces' indifference to human life.

Young Egor was always looking for ways to broaden his mind. But it was studying a second language that altered the way he looked at his own life: "I was lucky to study English for eight years in school … learning another language was a way to broaden my worldview." He used his English skills to delve into texts from abroad and internet communities. For Egor, exploring the world beyond Russia's state fairy tales and the rote learning of the Russian social studies curriculum unlocked new possibilities for constructing his identity.

Thanks to his self-education, Egor broke out of Moscow's crime-ridden suburbs. He coasted through the bureaucratic enrolment process to sign up for a politics major at Moscow's Higher School of Economics, a post-Soviet institution that had become known as a breeding ground for the country's elite. "It was one of the best decisions I've ever made" to study at "Vyshka," as the institution is colloquially known, recalls Egor: "I soaked up different sorts of knowledge like a sponge."

When Putin was handing over his presidential seat to Dmitry Medvedev for four years in 2008, the fifteen-year-old Egor already knew, he says, that "the country wasn't getting any better. It wasn't undertaking any reforms. I was under no illusions." But now, following the path of so many young Putinist subjects who had seen their fortunes made as they ascended to power in glittering 2000s Moscow, Egor thought he could change everything.

Sitting in renovated lecture halls listening to the country's top minds deliver courses on liberal arts, political science, and modern economics, he was full of zeal: "We were like young Decembrists." Egor refers to the army officers who attempted a palace coup after Tsar Alexander I's sudden death in December 1825. Like the Decembrists, Egor and his group didn't want to destroy the state.[2] "We planned," he said, "to go to university, receive a good education, and work for the good of the state, to transform the state and bring it into the civilized world and toward democracy. But none of that worked out." They thought they could imbue Russia with new, youthful energy without a revolution.

Many young Russians shared the same hopes for reform. Russia's fairy-tale coming of age had crashed into the reality of the global financial crisis at speed at the end of the 2000s, when the economy contracted as fast as it had ever expanded.[3] Unemployment was up. Disposable incomes were down. Anxiety crept in.

Smart young Russians who, like Egor, had access to Western media and could even interact with foreigners online saw their peers abroad getting ahead while Russia's development stalled. They didn't hesitate to make their discontent known. The carefully manicured public image of the then Prime Minister Putin took a beating. For example, the leader was drowned out by jeers during a speech after national hero Fedor Emelianenko's MMA (mixed martial arts) victory over an American challenger at the national Olympic Stadium in Moscow in the fall of 2011. The clip of Putin, flanked by the two mammoth sportsmen and almost lost for words, went viral. Young internet users piled in: "Fedor should have torn the useless dwarf apart!"; "So that's his real poll rating!!:D"; "The Tsar of All *Rus*. Piss off forever."[4] This was the sort of thing that happened to Western retail politicians, not masters of political performance like Vladimir Putin.

Putin's and Medvedev's approval ratings plummeted, hitting an all-time low in early 2013. With no wars to boost national pride, no obvious victims to blame for stalled economic growth, and no apparent direction beyond a failing fairy tale, the regime entered a new period of turmoil. The response was to slam the lid shut on the proliferation of diversity that had been tolerated in the 2000s. Young Russians would be encouraged to give in to the most violent nationalistic urges by fighting those who wouldn't toe the line—and then, when the rage in Russia began to die down, to make Ukraine the victim.

Young Egor would find himself forced to make a difficult decision. As unwilling as he was, he came down on the side of the state. The project of remaking the Russian young was in full swing. And he would be on the inside of it, working for the state media.

But first, the violence of the periphery was coming home to Moscow and into the mind's eye of every young Russian.

The anti-Putin youth comes of age

While Egor was settling into his studies, Anna Veduta was just finishing hers at the prestigious Moscow State University, a vast institution housed in a behemothic Stalinist skyscraper not far from the Higher School of Economics.

Anna graduated in the summer of 2011. When parliamentary elections were conducted that fall, pro-Kremlin parties waltzed their way to yet another whopping majority. Interning at the newspaper *Kommersant*, which was then a bastion of relative independence, Anna was closely following events. She, like thousands of others, was livid when smartphone recordings spreading online revealed the depthless fraud committed by the state. The elections may have been conducted according to the state's principles of "managed democracy," with "real" voting, campaigns, candidates, rallies, and media attention, but the government barely bothered to conceal its cheating.[5]

Anna was even more irate that the then Prime Minister Putin seemed certain to swap places with Medvedev, who had been keeping the top seat warm for four years, and return to the presidency the next spring. Casting around online to find an outlet for her frustration, she stumbled on a young opposition leader's blog on the popular LiveJournal platform. Aleksey Navalny had her hooked with the simple slogan "Anybody but Putin."

The biggest demonstrations since the 1990s were about to rock Moscow. As disquiet spread online, Yeltsin-era Deputy Prime Minister Boris Nemtsov and liberal former chess champion Garry Kasparov joined forces with young upstarts like Ilya Yashin and the charismatic Navalny to organize nationwide protests. Exploiting the relative freedom of the internet, the protest movement was able to use Facebook and LiveJournal to organize protests in central Moscow and across the country.[6]

"I was reading Navalny's blog very closely," says Anna:

He would say "Okay today, we have a rally—or not even *we*, just some kind of democratic force, but we shouldn't care who the organizer is, if it's communists, if it's someone who is pro-green, or something else. That doesn't matter at this point because the election was stolen from all of us. Please come."

Thousands poured onto the streets: "I am just a student who is tired of all these lies," one protesting student told the BBC at the time.[7] Tired of broken promises and drowning in a failing economy, ever expanding militarism, and the burdensome myth of World War II, the urban young had had enough. The ex-president's putative return to the Kremlin was too much.

Anna headed to her first protest the day after the Duma election. "It was 5 December 2011. That was the first major rally … for most of us it started on 5 December at Chistye prudy" in downtown Moscow. Despite the freezing Moscow weather, between 5,000 and 10,000 protestors turned out. As the crowd roared approval at bravado speeches attacking the state's naked corruption and waved placards—sometimes witty, sometimes crude, always damning—it felt like something entirely new had been created: "I saw a lot of people there and I saw the possibility of change." But first, the crowd had to contend with Putin's baton-wielding riot police, who dragged protestors into waiting paddy wagons at random.[8] Gangs of thugs—football hooligans, nationalists, and drunken louts—beat and kicked protestors as law enforcement looked the other way.

Anna made it out unscathed. But she turned up for the following protests. Even though Navalny was detained, a letter he had posted on his blog was read out at one demonstration: "The time has come to throw off the chains. We are not cattle or slaves. We have a voice and we have the strength to defend it."[9] These words had an enormous effect on Anna: "That's when I saw him as a leader of the opposition. Before that I didn't even think in terms of leader or not of the opposition. It started there, to me, it was very personal." Navalny, says Anna, had "emerged as a new *type* of politician with his humor, his manner of writing, his manner of joking. He was something really new, extraordinary. A change of scene." Indeed, Navalny's wit and eloquence make him unusual in the *chopornyi*— dull, gray, tedious—world of Russian statesmen.[10] Perhaps a rejuvenated future didn't rest on constant destruction.

Navalny's words were giving young Russians like Anna a way to see themselves outside of the state's diet of military myths and imperial fairy tales. Indeed, Navalny himself stressed the importance of speech in the blog post that summoned his supporters to the Chistye prudy rally that Anna attended, playing on the word *golos*, which means both "voice" and "vote" in Russian: "Nationalists, liberals, leftists, greens, vegetarians, martians. The Party of Crooks and Thieves [United Russia] has stolen everybody's *vote/voice*." And if they lacked a voice, Navalny gave his young supporters plenty of verbal ammunition. He regularly assailed the ruling clique as "thieves," mocked the police, and called out the flawed Duma election process as a "crime."[11]

The state couldn't stand idly by as the opposition captured the imagination of the nation's youth. Vladislav Surkov's PR men played out a vintage Kremlin charade by drumming up one of its youth "protests." Nashi packed the downtown Manezh Square to bursting with a 15,000-strong counter-protest. Columns of attendees corralled by leaders in branded jackets were led by drummers from metro stations to the square, where they sheltered from the cold by disappearing into bulky overcoats. Military-patriotic pop music— "Putin and Stalingrad are with us!" screamed one singer—blasted over the audience, who peeked from under toques and raised hoods at giant screens bearing Putin's and Medvedev's faces. Wielding flags and home-made placards declaring their support for the president ("Facebook sucks!"; "We put our trust in Putin!"), they made quite the impression on the nightly news, which of course neglected to mention the opposition protests.

As clips of the rally spread online, viewers could taste the surging excitement of the fascist rally over and again. It didn't matter that many state "protestors" were forced to attend by their employers, or that a police cordon made sure nothing spoiled the visual effect for the TV cameras.[12] The magic of television and rapid-fire repetition of social media ironed out all the difficult nuance. The pro-democracy protestors didn't have a monopoly on internet discussion when the state could seed its performances into growing networks of Kremlin supporters.

Surkov followed up with verbal attacks on the opposition protestors, suggesting they were being funded by shadowy Western powers who would undo all the good work of the last ten years at the first chance they got. In a rare interview granted to the newspaper *Izvestiya*, Surkov explained: "It is an incontrovertible fact that some wish to turn the protests into a color revolution. They are operating according to [American political scientist Gene] Sharp's books and the most up-to-date revolutionary methods."[13] The protestors, explained Surkov, were full of energy and might contain "future leaders"—the door was left open for youthful enthusiasm to join the Putinist cause—but their actions were a vehicle for dangerous Western influence. A pro-democracy "color revolution" like those that had occurred in the previous decade in Ukraine, Georgia, and Kyrgyzstan might threaten the "progress" made since the 1990s.

The mere idea of democratic protest was a threat to Russia's fairy-tale reality. Indeed, Putin's former KGB colleague, the Orthodox Patriarch Kirill, would soon chip in to attack the provocative riot grrl punk-cum-performance art group Pussy Riot, who had staged a brief protest against Putin's re-election in the Cathedral of Christ the Savior in Moscow on 21 February 2012. "Those people don't believe in the power of prayer," fulminated Kirill in an interview. "They believe in the power of propaganda, in the power of lies and slander, in the power of Internet and mass media, in the power of money and weapons. We believe in the power of prayer."[14] From now on, it was to be us—religious, faithful, national, ordered, Russian—versus them—young, democratic, liberal, naive, non-Russian. The real Russians were the pro-state "protestors" orchestrated by Nashi, not the feeble Navalny fans.

Nonetheless, the opposition returned fire by deploying a symbolic arsenal of its own online. The movement spread its message by sharing posts, videos, blogs—in particular those written by Navalny—and adding a new symbol of protest, the white ribbon, to their profile pictures. Musicians like the outspoken young rapper Noize MC joined the protests, appearing at Bolotnaya Square in person in mid-December and releasing a track entitled "A New Year without Putin" to YouTube. Thousands of young internet users from across the nation were able to access online spaces—blogs, VK groups, forums—where they could mimic the urban protestors in Moscow and Petersburg by sharing the symbols and language of opposition.

The state and opposition dueled with volleys of rhetorical and visual fire across online and physical landscapes, each slowly building up its own realities—free and fair elections and the threat of more degeneration versus corrupt elections and the threat of sociopolitical stagnation—for its own, walled-off audience.

Despite the size of the anti-government protests, the opposition didn't build up a head of steam. For young Russians like Ivan Kondakov, who was then relatively uninterested in day-to-day political discourse, the two sides seemed relatively evenly matched. Each side had placards, slogans, claims, and counterclaims. For every opposition claim that democracy had been corrupted in the election, performances like the one staged by Nashi created the impression that the opposite was true. For the Putinist believers, the protestors weren't "creators." They were traitors.

But a generation of young Russians frustrated by the stuttering promises of a stagnant regime had discovered they could use the disjointed nature of the internet to create alternative communities and alternative centers of power. A nascent opposition was born.

Anna was so fired up by the protest movement that she put on hold her plans to study abroad at Oxford, to which she would soon be offered a full scholarship. Three months later, she would respond to a job advert. Within the week, she was starting work as Aleksey Navalny's press secretary. Navalny's words of introduction on Anna's first day in the job? "Welcome to hell." The "vegetarian times," as Anna called them, were about to end. The nascent generation of protestors and malcontents would be targeted as the state's new anti-Russian Other.

Welcome to hell: rooting out the non-Russian

In early 2012, Putin marched back to center stage as the presidential elections approached. He had been shaken by the widespread protests. It was time to fire up the population.[15] The returning president—there was never any doubt who would win the election—dispensed with the talk of optimistic, all-things-possible futurism.[16] Now he preached ethnic Russian tribalism, myths of triumphant national history, and the militarization of life and culture. He promised to obliterate the threat of Western culture and remake young Russian minds and bodies to secure the future.[17] Through corruption, coercion, and violence, the state of Putin 2.0 would cajole its people into a new, *Russian* world.

Two months before election day, Putin set out a new ethnocentric politics in a lengthy essay, "Russia: The National Question," published in the newspaper *Nezavisimaya gazeta*.[18] At first glance, Putin appeared to embrace openness and multiculturalism. Bemoaning the problem of "internal animosity and strife" in Russia—protests, murders, poverty—he suggested that "nationalism and religious intolerance ... destroy and undermine states." Putin seemed to be offering an olive branch.

But the road to peace was paved with nationalist poison. Across the world, Putin argued, the modern nation-state was in an existential crisis. In Russia, though, that meant the state was under threat from young, Western-looking reformers like Anna Veduta and her boss Aleksey Navalny; Russian nationalists like the football hooligans and Nashi thugs carrying out violent attacks were perfectly acceptable. Willfully misquoting from medieval religious texts and throwing in some cod Soviet and Civil War history, Putin painted a dark picture of a future without ethnic Russian leadership. Bathed in darkness and threatened from all sides, Russia could all too easily collapse under the weight of external and internal fighting.

But Russia had hope: give Putin the reins of power for good and another great national rebirth was possible. The path to creating such a national rebirth? The "formation of a worldview that holds the nation together" by placing "the Russian people and Russian culture" in the nation's driving seat. The sorts of cultural experimentation that had proliferated in the previous decade were no longer to be tolerated.

Putin's piece meandered on, explaining that a "soft cultural therapy"—art, culture, schools, and history—disseminated in every nook and cranny of society would promote Russianness and rebirth. But "soft" wasn't synonymous with a light touch. Putin rounded off the piece with a reference to World War II: "Together we won the most terrible war. And we will continue to live together. And to those who want or try to divide us, I say one thing: just wait and see …" If voters wanted to rebirth society, to create a new sort of culture for children, and to end internal discord, they would have to fight. And now fighting didn't just mean in Chechnya, in Georgia, or on Nashi marches. It meant constantly battling the non-Russian, both in the community and in the mind.

Putin's PR machine launched a flotilla of shimmering, glittering performances into the social media sea to reinforce the message. On 23 February, the annual Day of the Defender of the Fatherland—yet another national holiday for troops and veterans, but chiefly an excuse for loutish young servicemen to get plastered in public—Putin's campaign managers staged a whole day of photo ops in Moscow. The events laid the aesthetic foundations of Putin 2.0 as the standard bearer for Russia's youth into the 2010s.

The soon-to-be president laid a wreath at the Tomb of the Unknown Soldier outside the Kremlin's walls, reminding audiences of his devotion to the cult of World War II. Then, he traveled to the Luzhniki Stadium for a grand, flag-waving performance. Thousands of attendees—some genuine fans, some enticed with rewards—bearing Russia flags and banners with Putin's face filed past placards reading, "We will defend our country!" Inside, the rhetoric of attack and defense continued. Putin told the listening crowd, "We really are the defenders of the fatherland ... we won't let anybody interfere in our business. Don't betray the motherland!"

Concluding his speech, Putin borrowed World War II-era phrases used by extreme nationalists in the 1990s in their clashes with Western "degradation." The leader cried, "The battle continues! We shall be victorious!" Who were the eager listeners defending the country against, and what were they battling? Putin didn't need to say. The answer was clear: the young opposition, who were freezing and fighting heavies and the police on the other side of town, and their putative Western backers.

Cameras zoomed in on the young audience members, clad in matching Putin T-shirts and feverishly waving campaign flags, as they applauded wildly. Svetlana, an eighteen-year-old attendee, was enraptured by Putin's vision. "Of course I want a bright future for Russia!" she squealed to a foreign interviewer who asked why she'd attended.[19] Voting Putin would mean voting for the future. He could still make it happen for Russia's young. The event played as well on television and social media as it did in person.

Beneath the fanfare, there was very little of substance. There were no policy promises. The threat from without and within was nothing more than a shadowy bogeyman. Yet young listeners like Svetlana knew that the fairy tale was under attack from within. Better to stick with Putin than to risk amoral degradation or total obliteration at the hands of a *liberast*—a "liberal pederast"—blogger like Navalny.

After coasting to victory in the presidential election, Putin strode out to speak at a gathering on Manezh Square in Moscow. Shedding a tear—a rare display of tenderness from a man who had cultivated an image of impeccable machismo—Putin declared, "We showed that no-one can impose their will on us ... We showed that our people know how to distinguish between the desire for change and renewal, and political provocations that pursue the sole objective of undermining Russia's statehood."

Russians' semantic world had been hacked up into *us* and *them*, *renewal* and *undermining*. And soon, the battle between the pro-Putin young and the young opposition would cascade into real attacks on everything deemed insufficiently "Russian."

Fragmenting the queer self

A thousand miles away from Moscow's political turbulence and street skirmishes, Alla Chikinda was at home in Yekaterinburg, a huge riverside city where the temperatures can plummet to below −40 degrees each winter. Alla, like Ilya Fedotov-Fedorov, had buried herself in queer culture online and on TV as a youth. Showbiz idols, online groups, and dubbed American movies like *Brokeback Mountain* and *Milk* (the 2008 biopic of US politician Harvey Milk) helped her understand her queerness. In the late 2000s, it was easy to be out: "I had some friends from the LGBT community. I didn't feel any hostility." From beneath a shock of feathered pink hair and thick-framed, hip glasses, Alla says, "I didn't have to hide, and I didn't know that I wasn't 'allowed' to talk about it."

In 2006, Alla left to study in France. By the time she returned four years later, everything had changed. Suddenly, "a couple of my friends were shocked by my behavior. They said, 'You're used to living in Europe. But here it's different.' I didn't understand." Things only got worse. "I was criticized for my openness. 'Why are you telling everybody? It's private. Why are you showing off?'"

Russia's LGBTQ community had become the first target in Putin's war against the enemy within. Russian political discourse had long been afflicted by a deep homophobia: staging gay pride parades was hugely controversial; Moscow's mayor Yury Luzhkov decried homosexual culture as "satanic"; even major cities were slow to embrace private queer community hubs.[20] And unlike the pro-democracy protestors, who Surkov suggested possessed the potential for future leadership, Russia's LGBTQ youth would be told that they were innately, irredeemably evil.

When the state was threatened by a serious opposition movement and its own economic failings, the queer community was a convenient target. Attacking the homosexual could reinforce an ill-defined sense of national wholeness.[21] Only the "traditional family"—whatever that was—could incubate the growing generation of *better*—straight, masculine, and "patriotic"—Russians. Anna Veduta remembers that being part of Navalny's team felt like belonging to an alternate, and therefore dangerous, sort of "family."[22] The fascist state simply had to wage war against the enemy of the patriarchy—against a family unit that rejected its demand for sacrifice in the name of national ideology.[23]

In the late 2000s and early 2010s, a series of domestic bans on LGBTQ "propaganda" were proposed as a means to reinforce "children's morality and health" in cities from Ivan Kondakov's hometown of Arkhangelsk all the way to Magadan in the distant Far East.[24] The charge was led by men like the rising political star Vitaly Milonov, a bearded zealot who resembles an Orthodox priest as much as a typical politician. For Milonov, all homosexuals were "pieces of shit" who wanted to stage an "invasion" of kindergartens with the support of the West.[25]

These early pieces of homophobic legislation linked homosexuality to two moral crimes: attacking young people, who embodied the future; and spreading a disease that would afflict both individuals and the wider, healthy body of the fascist society. The defense of Russia's young against an "epidemic" of Western disease had, of course, been Putin's watchword from the earliest days of his rule.

The anti-homosexual legislative pogrom reached the Duma in the summer of 2013. When a national law was passed, it was purposefully vague: "No positive description or information about so-called 'non-traditional sexual relationships'—understood as lesbianism, homosexuality, bisexuality, and transgenderism—can be disseminated in the presence of minors." What was a "positive description"? Did dissemination mean publicly, at home, on the media, on private social media accounts or groups? Nobody knew. The young and queer were seized by a state of uncertainty.

The state media didn't just kiss goodbye to queer role models for young Russians. It staged homophobic witch-hunts and incited extreme violence. In one scene from 2012, TV journalist Dmitry Kiselyov took to the podium on a political discussion show on the flagship Channel One. Surrounded by audience members and pundits scattered around a glitzy, modern stage set, the besuited Kiselyov clasps his hands together. He confidently declares that "imposing fines on gays for homosexual propaganda to minors is insufficient. They should be prohibited from donating blood, sperm and, in the case of a road accident, their hearts should be either buried or burned as unsuitable for the prolongation of life."[26] The audience applaud vigorously as Kiselyov's expert peers nod in agreement. Ritual violence to cleanse Russia of its enemies, the innately unclean, was being floated on national platforms.

Young nationalists took to the state's homophobic politics with abandon. Ivan Katanaev, the football hooligan who had led his Spartak-supporting comrades into battle against Chechens in the 2000s, mirrored the language of television in a 2015 interview with a football fansite. Katanaev praised Milonov and offered a deluge of aggressive, patriarchal language that targeted an amorphous blend of enemies: "I support all the initiatives against f****ts and abortions. These are questions of spirituality ... a lot of people support him. Nobody likes gay pride parades."[27] Katanaev was just giving voice to an increasingly vocal homophobic rage. Football hooligans, nationalists, and neo-Nazis were finding that their old politics were suddenly no longer just overlooked. They were celebrated. Waging war on the queers meant building the new Russia, just as beating up the Chechens had meant doing so in the 2000s.

Queer Russians in major urban centers could not escape this language. They came across stickers, graffiti, and leaflets plastered with violent slogans. "Stamp out F****ts," read stickers sprinkled across Arkhangelsk in December 2013. Teenagers found schools an increasingly hostile place to be. One sixteen-year-old reported in 2013 that "[m]y biology teacher ... spewed some nonsense about how it's 'against the laws of nature' and 'those people are sick.' And the social science teacher quoted the Bible and would not accept any other arguments."[28] School became "a living hell," forcing children to quit. This wasn't education. It was social purification. Schoolkids weren't alone.[29] Over half of LGBTQ Russians reported experiencing psychological harassment in 2012.[30]

Words turned to increasing physical violence. Networks of vigilantes used the internet to lure gay men, including minors, into meeting. Beaten, forced to strip, and urinated on, their videotaped humiliation was posted publicly.[31] Attacks at and outside LGBTQ clubs and bars, which in the 2000s had done a booming trade in urban centers, became commonplace. Reporting concerns to the police led at best to indifference. At worst, the police responded with homophobic violence of their own.[32] Prosecutions for anti-gay hate crimes were almost nil.[33]

On 9 May 2013, a gay twenty-three-year-old, Vladislav Tornovoy, was murdered in Volgograd. Police ignored the potential hate motive. One of the two killers, however, was a closet neo-Nazi with a penchant for skinhead culture and Mein Kampf.[34] That the homophobic murder occurred on Victory Day and in the former Stalingrad may have been coincidence, but it is symbolic. Russian youth in the present were being symbolically purified to defend the state from a supposedly apocalyptic European assault on the very spot that the tide of World War II was turned seven decades earlier.

The spaces in which the young had freely congregated were swamped by a language of violence that forced them to fall silent. Violent speech and action was normalized so long as it was directed against the state's latest enemy. Young Russians like Alla Chikinda and Ilya Fedotov-Fedorov would need to stuff their identities back in the closet if they weren't to be attacked in the media, in the street, or on the internet. They could never describe themselves as both "Russian" and "queer."[35]

Driven from the collective. Stripped of language. Tormented psychologically. Attacked physically. Russia's young queer community, a psychologist who surreptitiously works with LGBTQ patients today, tells me, "didn't know how to talk" about what was happening. The state had fragmented its new enemy of choice, driving it to silence in an orgy of social bloodletting.

Some responded by absorbing and performing the anti-LGBTQ language of the state. Nikolay Alekseev, a young gay lawyer, had founded the Moscow Pride march that so vexed the city's Mayor Luzhkov in 2005, fought the government in a series of public court battles over gay rights, and worked with representatives from civil rights organizations from across the globe. Whatever the battle, Alekseev was involved.

Yet come the summer of 2013, when the federal propaganda ban was passed, Alekseev was a man publicly transformed. In a series of social media posts, Alekseev laid into foreign-aligned LGBTQ entities like *Out* magazine (One of Alekseev's social media shares reads:

"A Jewish slut magazine that supports Jews and their filthy f****otry propaganda"). Before long, he was writing an op-ed for the regime's Russia Today outlet arguing that "gay propaganda laws only help." The critical Western media just didn't understand Russia's unique situation. And anyway, claimed Alekseev, only two small fines in Ryazan had actually been issued, so the law didn't matter.[36]

Alekseev had in public become, to borrow a term coined by one of the victims of his bile, "the Kremlin's pocket gay":[37] a queer self-transformed to be suspicious of the West and its deleterious influences. He promptly exited stage left for a quiet life in Switzerland. Whatever his real beliefs—and the Kremlin may well have used its enormous power to force his hand—Alekseev offered a model of self-purification for the homosexual community.

Queer youth could transform themselves into better Russians by adopting the state's language of hatred and exclusion. But doing so meant engaging in a battle with the inner self. The battle would engulf Ilya Fedotov-Fedorov.

* * *

By the 2010s, Ilya was starting to make waves on Moscow's modern-art scene. His striking works—which mixed paint, medical equipment, traditional sculpture, and drawings—explored bodily transformation and sexuality in humans and animals—insects, horses, butterflies. These fantasies on Ilya's own childhood and sexuality were snapped up by eager collectors and even displayed in state venues like Moscow's renowned Tretyakov Gallery. Ilya's stock was soaring.

But when—Ilya quietly utters the words—"they, the authorities, started using [homophobia] as a tool, using it to suppress culture," Ilya's burgeoning confidence was shattered.

"I [experienced] a kind of self-censorship. I knew that museums and institutions would not be very welcoming to this kind of thing [LGBTQ]. After I had been practicing for two or three years, they created the law. I started ..." Ilya trails off, searching for the words that can give voice to this suppressed selfhood. The clarity of his memories of the 2000s, when he grew in confidence in a safer and wealthier Moscow, gives way to stuttering hesitation.

After a lengthy pause, Ilya takes a deep breath. He continues: "That was the point when I started fighting with this." He retreated back inside the imaginary world of creation and fantasy he had created as a lonely child in hospital in the 1990s. But now, this fragile world had been penetrated by the state. An aspect of Ilya's self had been linked with Western pedophiles, satanists, and "disease." Ilya, like many others, was saddled with a perpetual feeling of inner uncertainty. His own sense of identity was collapsing. Inside, at least, Ilya was left speechless. He was paralyzed.

Ilya's growing reputation would soon lead him to residencies in Switzerland, Spain, and the Netherlands. Leaving the psychological war zone of Russia was an enlightening experience. In Europe, everything was different: "I didn't have to hide it ... I didn't want to go back to Russia. I realized I have my own homophobia inside. I realized completely that it was artificial. It's not mine. It came from this environment. I was scared."

"In Russia, you're always hiding. You're always doing this kind of manipulation for your friends, your family, your colleagues, trying to say 'I have a girlfriend' and not 'I have a boyfriend.'" Ilya's choice of word, *manipulation*, is telling. Ilya blames himself, not the state, for the lies he was forced to tell—and for his own, internalized "homophobia."

Few young Russians would have the chance to look at the state from the outside like Ilya. Young, queer Russians wrestled with the idea that they were "terrible creatures"—dirty, diseased, and undesirable.[38] Alla Chikinda had been confidently out in the mid-2000s in the Urals. She had ignored politics, finding solace in apathy. But now politics forced its way into her life:

> I was flying somewhere, and I read a newspaper on the plane. There was an article about [the anti-propaganda law] and there was an interview with Eddie Izzard. I read the article and I was like, "That's crazy! What a crazy idea!" I guess it was some kind of protection mechanism, but [before that] I didn't know anything!

Alla took action. She sought support from the sparse network of activists who covertly supported young Russians. By the mid-2010s, she was a community leader, working at the LGBT Resource Center—most in the Russian queer community refer to themselves as "LGBT" rather than "LGBTQ"—in Yekaterinburg. But Alla, whose plucky decision to speak out on LGBTQ rights has seen her embroiled in court cases in the last few years, is the exception.

Young Russians and their parents, teachers, and mentors were learning that their options had narrowed. They would need to reinvent themselves as good homophobes; to play out their internal battles in acquiescent silence; or, through self-harm or suicide, they could "cleanse" society of their existence. Drowning in the homophobic noise of the extreme right, a quarter of queer Russian youth attempted suicide in the early 2010s.[39]

The end of politics

The government struck at young, liberal Russians with blow after blow. In 2013, Aleksey Navalny announced he would run to replace Sergey Sobyanin in the Moscow mayoral election due to take place that September. Legal and administrative obstacles popped up at Navalny's every turn, and government proxies continued to harass the candidate's campaign both in person and online.

When Navalny was sentenced to five years in jail on trumped-up charges of embezzlement in July 2013, he was legally barred from standing in the mayoral election. The situation rapidly turned on its head. "The prosecution lawyers," explains Anna Veduta, "the very same guys who asked to have him arrested—made an appeal for him to be released! It was insane … It was weird to everybody. We didn't understand it. It was such a mixed message."

Navalny was allowed to stand. His team ran hustings and campaign events all over Moscow, but they were hindered constantly by hooligans who vandalized their portable campaign banners with graffiti, physically assaulted organizers, and even threw feces at Navalny's supporters.

Anna and her team found themselves under constant attack online too. "They'd ask questions to provoke you, film you, then edit it in a way to make you look bad," she says. Uploaded to real and astroturfed nationalist groups on VK and YouTube channels, pro-Kremlin videos would rapidly go viral, squeezing out space for discussion of the real Navalny and his actual agenda. Instead, the message that the opposition were a liberal, Western-funded group of anti-Russian hypocrites constantly echoed in the background of users' online experiences.

The Navalny campaign could still target the young with a savvy social media campaign. Using the internet to campaign, Anna remembers, made it feel "almost as if we were in a normal world, a normal political society." But the state's hold over the judicial, electoral, and media systems created a sense of perpetual doubt. Would Navalny be able to stand? Would he end up in jail? Were the rumors about his funding true? Was he a Western plant? Just as with the anti-LGBTQ language promoted by the state, individuals who were thinking of supporting Navalny found themselves beset by internal doubts and fissures. Only Putin and the state offered certainty.

There was little hope of disrupting the certainty the state offered. There never had been. Young men like Ivan Kondakov were already long gone, in thrall to the myth of Putinist rejuvenation. Back in September 2011, months before Anna joined her first protest and long before the Moscow mayoral election, Ivan had been returning from his latest jaunt abroad. A late summer trip to London—his favorite European city, full of great music and culture—was drawing to a close.

Ivan hopped on his plane. He began to settle in for the four-hour flight back to Moscow when a familiar face hovered into view a few rows ahead. Memories of videos his friends had shared online clicked together. Aleksey Navalny was on the same plane. He didn't approach Navalny, but that was the last straw. He'd given the opposition, he claims, a fair hearing, but "there's no such thing as a coincidence. He was in London. What was he doing there? He just happened to be in London and then two months later all the protesting started?"

Thus Kondakov's mind was made up almost two years before the Moscow mayoral vote. Navalny was just another of the "Western-funded elite." Ivan mixes in a drop of antisemitic conspiracy to boot: "George Soros was funding it all, with ideology and training: what to say, PR, that sort of thing." Putin was building things. Putin had constructed a fairy-tale empire. But the invasion of Western corruption, Western money, and Western mores threatened it all. No matter how smart Navalny's campaign, there would be no chance of reaching the conspiracy-minded young supporters of Putin. Ivan and his peers were in too deep. They would have to keep fighting off the invasion.

The anti-Navalny campaign worked. Sobyanin ran out the easy winner, receiving 51 percent of the vote to Navalny's 27 percent. A healthy dose of electoral fraud, of course, ensured there could be no errors—2013 was the last time that alternative political futures were showcased on a public stage this large.

Despite the aggressive activity to deprive Russia's young of the power and language to oppose the state, Putin's poll ratings continued to nosedive. By late 2013, barely 60 percent of Russians had a positive opinion of their president; his rating among the young was even worse. The state's most successful myth had been built on military action. What better way to invigorate the nation than to launch a war against an external enemy that—supposedly—threatened the very existence of the Russian nation? And, in so doing, to promise the revelation of a lost mythical past in the present?

Six months after the mayoral election, in the winter of 2014, Putin turned his attention to Ukraine. Russia's young—at home and abroad—were to be saved in a new, spiritual conflict.

Making Russia whole again

In late 2013, Ukrainians had taken to Kyiv's Maidan Square to protest against President Viktor Yanukovych. Corrupt, venal, and in thrall to the Kremlin, Yanukovych broke promise after promise until his people had had enough. On the Maidan, the lights of barrel fires twinkled through the long winter nights as thousands of protestors wrapped in national flags demanded a new start.

Russia's state media marched out to bat for its "brother nation": newspaper headlines roared; state propagandists fulminated on political discussion shows; the coup was sponsored by the CIA; the plotters were neo-Nazis; traitors wanted to embrace Europe and attack "ethnic Russians," as the Kremlin preferred to call Russian speakers in Ukraine; real Ukrainians loved Russia and hated the democrats.

Ukraine's government dealt with its opposition even more brutally than Russia's had. In February 2014, over 100 protestors were killed. The demonstrators were undeterred. The protests gathered momentum. The government in Kyiv collapsed. The Kremlin's historical control over the peripheries of its tsarist and Soviet empire was on the brink of collapsing with it. The forces of degeneration—America, the West, the liberals—were running rampant in Moscow's backyard. The worse things got, the more golden the opportunity for an increasingly fascistic regime to wage a war of renewal.

On 20 February 2014, Russian forces moved into Ukraine's Crimean Peninsula. Crimea's "loss" to Ukraine in the post-Soviet break-up was an unhealed wound. Crimea, like Chechnya, belonged with Russia.[40] In went the troops and, after a hastily organized sham "referendum," Crimea was annexed. Crimea was home. Russia was whole again.

The Kremlin and the Church staged a new series of media spectacles to sell the annexation as a spiritual crusade. Putin told his parliament that the West, just as during World War II, had forced Russia's hand. Moscow had to defend "Russians"—Crimean Ukrainians were, of course, nothing of the sort—from an invasion: "Russia found itself in a position it could not retreat from."[41] The Russian Orthodox Church rushed to support its brother in arms, the state.[42] Patriarch Kirill took to the pulpit at the Cathedral of Christ the Savior—the same nationalist temple that had been rebuilt as part of the great reconstruction of Moscow as imperial capital—to claim that the annexation was a spiritual quest to save "the Russian world, the great Russian civilization that came from the Kievan baptismal font."[43] And Crimea, the "most sacred shrine of the Russian civilization," had to be seized for the faithful.[44]

Nonetheless, Crimea wasn't enough. The Kremlin's forces—unmarked "polite people," as Putinists called them—trickled into Eastern Ukraine. Soon, the conflict, like the war in Chechnya, stagnated. But that didn't get in the way of a good story. Russia's media scripted an absurd melodrama that increasingly focused on the supposed plight of "ethnic Russian" children in the war zone. Driven, apparently, by a relentless lust for Russian blood, Ukrainian forces were purportedly torturing and murdering the "Russian" young. The most shocking of the obscene stories claimed that Ukrainian forces in Sloviansk had publicly crucified a three-year-old child.

Ukrainians—bloodthirsty, blasphemous, satanic murderers—were everything the saintly Russian Orthodox crusaders were not.

Little matter that the crucifixion story, cooked up by neo-fascist thinker Aleksandr Dugin, was false.[45] It spread like wildfire.[46] Soon, the same quasi-religious, racial animus was being publicly applied not just to Ukraine's soldiers but to *every* Ukrainian: they were Nazis, "animals," and, in particular, "diseased." The language of hatred that had been so effectively applied to Chechens, homosexuals, and liberals was now being directed at Russia's Slavic neighbors. In counterpoint to grotesque distortions of Ukrainianness, videos of jubilant "ethnic Russian" children celebrating their Russian "saviors" spread online through pro-Kremlin media groups.

Avowed young Putinists bought it hook, line, and sinker. Fed up with "bloggers" and liberals who were on the take and sought to undermine Russia at any opportunity, Ivan Kondakov found himself drawn into the world of politics: "Like many others I got interested [in politics] after Crimea, which was a huge moment of anti-Russian sentiment. In Ukraine, there were Nazis, and Nazis shouting 'We're going to slaughter Russians.' I opposed this totalitarian turn in Ukrainian politics." Before long, Ivan's VK feed was packed with pro-war memes comparing Ukrainians to Nazis. He and his online contacts, who liked, shared, and commented, were occupying a mythical world spiraling quickly away from empirical reality.

The war was saving Russia's young. It could save Russia—the mythic Russia whose borders extended well beyond the country's actual territory—and Russians from disease, from satanism, and from "fascism." It could save the future. The state poured money into Crimea. By constructing a $3.5bn bridge that linked the peninsula to the Russian mainland, the nation was symbolically made whole again. On the Kerch Bridge's opening in 2018, Putin explained the symbolic significance of the moment: "In different historical epochs, even under the tsar priests, people dreamed of building this bridge. Then they returned to this [idea] in the 1930s, the '40s, the '50s. And finally, thanks to your work and your talent, the miracle has happened."[47] Crimea was the new Chechnya: the amputated limb returned to its rightful place; the site of mythical dreams made real; a "miracle" won through the state's brilliant leadership.

When Russia was becoming whole again, when the future held the promise of yet more dreams to come true, who cared that the neo-Nazis fighting at the front—groups of hooligans and radical nationalists from Russia's street gangs—were actually sent there by the Kremlin?[48]

And what could the opposition say in response? After all, the liberals, the democrats, the queers were all corrupt. They were all traitors. They weren't real Russians. They didn't want Crimea. A flurry of protests, including a "March for Peace" in Moscow attended by tens of thousands of mostly young Russians, rapidly faded away. Putin's ratings soared among every demographic group.

The disillusioned generation

Reality soon began to bite. The Russian economy stumbled due to Western-led sanctions and the cost of funding an expensive war and a newly acceded Crimea.[49] Incomes shrank with the contracting economy.

Studying abroad and taking foreign holidays—the perks of the previous decade for the increasingly wealthy middle classes— became far harder as the ruble collapsed in value. Whole cohorts of Russian students dropped out of universities in Britain and North America as their savings proved insufficient to cover the cost of tuition. Tourist trips fell by one third, from 15 million to 10 million, in the year after Crimea.[50] Worse yet for the regime, many young people felt attacked as a period of personal liberties gave way to an increasingly militaristic and totalitarian culture that permitted no public flexibility in ideological or personal beliefs.[51] The middle-class dream was taking another kicking.

This time, though, the opposition had little to say and few options. The state was attacking them with performances of power on the streets and online. Opposition politicians had limited access to the ballot box, and elections were fraudulent even when smatterings of liberals were allowed to stand.

In schools, in churches, and on television, ordinary young Russians who didn't want to toe the line were told they were as diseased and evil as the Ukrainian "Nazis" the nation was battling in Luhansk and Donetsk. Caught up in internal psychological battles, they had a simple choice: seek an exit, fall silent, or reinvent themselves as Putinists.

"2014 was only a year's difference" after the hope of Navalny's run at Moscow's mayoralty, says Anna Veduta, "but it was a different world." Like many others, she was left hopeless in the face of what she remembers as the "overwhelming support" for the state's actions in Crimea. Navalny would soon be targeted with further legal repercussions and violent attacks, culminating in his near-deadly poisoning with the nerve agent Novichok in 2020. There was no sense staying. Anna left Russia for good in August 2014 to enroll in a funded master's program at Columbia University.

This was the environment Egor Polyakov found himself in when he graduated from the Higher School of Economics with plans for a career in academia or politics. Four years earlier, he had whiled away the time in dusty lecture halls imagining himself as a thrusting young Decembrist. He would reform the state. He would right all the wrongs of post-Soviet Russia.

Egor graduated into a jobs desert. Even for this affable, intelligent, and educated young man, there was no work in Western-style think tanks or policy institutes. Even the dubious "political technology" schemes that had been popular in Russian electoral politics in the previous decade had dried up. "In a normal country," he laments, "a politics grad would find such work, but that political culture just didn't exist in our country." Had he been born a few years earlier, things might have been different: "We had normal elections for governors, and graduates were in demand. But when I graduated"—he almost spits the words out—"that was all over. For good." Egor had missed the boat. The fairy tale of limitless choice was over.

By chance, Egor landed a job as a financial copywriter. It was not long until he, like many other overeducated and underemployed creatives of his generation, was sucked into the government's propaganda mill. Gazeta.ru, a state news site that has today become a purveyor of some of the more obscene propaganda floating around the Russian infosphere, offered him a staff writer position. Working at Gazeta meant good money, responsibility, and a career ladder.

But selling out to work for the state also meant sacrificing principles: "I fell into a system where censorship and restrictions were the norm." He chooses his words carefully. He did not choose his job as a financial copywriter; it was all he could find. He did not choose to work as a propagandist; he "fell" into somebody else's system. In his eyes, Egor was driven to working for the state—another echo of Russia's nineteenth century, when listless young noblemen, bored and underused, found themselves under-utilized in mandatory state service.[52] Egor could have elected not to collaborate on the state's propaganda projects. However, it's easy to understand why—even though the country was regressing into the politics of radical nationalism, myth, and censorship—a boy from the wrong side of the tracks grasped the opportunities the state provided.

With the help of Egor and his peers—the hundreds of young graduates who staffed the nation's propaganda mills—the state embarked on the construction of a new identity for young Russians. It seized on anything that could promote Orthodoxy, militarism, and nationalism. Young Russians would learn that their country "was the world's greatest, strongest nation, and that God was on their side." The USSR was a great and good father to its people, the tsarist era was a lost world of national strength and culture, Soviet life was a nostalgic dream or the object of retro cool. It was perfectly okay to enjoy Hollywood movies and the latest American music, just so long as you believed in the nation's messianic fate.

Reason went out the window in this morass of contradictions and logical mismatches. Propagandists were creating, Egor tells me, "a Frankenstein of Soviet and Russian ideologies." Russia was becoming "a fake country." With little memory of life before Putin and without any other means of understanding reality, millions of young Russians began to inhabit the alternate reality of the fascist fairy tale.

4

REMAKING THE YOUNG

It has taken me weeks to pin down Vladislav, a Muscovite in his late twenties, for an interview. When we finally do connect via Telegram, Vlad breathlessly waves hello from a hipster cafe in downtown Moscow. "Wait," he immediately interjects, "I have another call coming through …"

Vlad's boss—he works as a videographer for a state media producer—is on the line, chivvying him about some or other deadline. He'll call back no fewer than four times, Vlad's buzzing phone splintering our conversation into segments, in the next hour.

As he slaves away at work and on a dissertation for his university course in TV and radio management ("It's due next week but I haven't even started!"), Vlad's running on coffee, self-discipline, and ambition. Work–life balance doesn't seem to be much of a thing for a young media employee like Vlad. But it's worth it. He hopes that if he nails his course, he'll land a big job on the Moscow media circuit.

A gentle giant with a penchant for motorbikes, macho aesthetics, and consuming exceptional quantities of alcohol, Vlad is the life and soul of the party. He is also everything a Russian liberal ought to be. He has always eagerly sought out foreigners online to swap stories of life in Russia and life in the West. He grew up well-off in the 2000s, traveled extensively through Europe, and even, thanks to his Jewish roots, studied in Israel for a few months. Always curious about life and culture in the West, he even taught himself to speak decent English as a teen.

Somebody from Vlad's background should have been drawn to Navalny and the Bolotnaya Square protests. He ought to have been at least somewhat tolerant of queer culture, and he ought to have been appalled by the invasion of Ukraine. But for Vlad, a switch flipped in the spring of 2014.

In the week that Russian forces invaded Crimea, Vlad's VK page was transformed overnight. The young Vlad, then barely twenty, suddenly started posting a slew of nationalist imagery: a cartoon of a hulk-like, muscled Russian bear bursting free of his clothes; an image of Putin holding a gun to Barack Obama's head; and a cartoon of a Russian bear defending a helpless "Ukrainian" bear cub against a monstrous American hyena brandishing a "democracy" sign. Vlad's posts gathered dozens of likes from friends and family, and plaudits in the comments: "Awesome! Let's take a vacation in Crimea!"

Vlad wasn't outraged by the Crimea invasion. He loved it—and he joined dozens of nationalist groups on VK that fed his addiction to news of the latest flag-waving triumph, the latest pro-Russia rally, and the latest hot meme that celebrated Russia and denigrated Ukraine. So did the millions of other Russians who spread visually striking, sometimes even witty, memes and viral songs that reduced the complexities of geopolitics into palatable chunks of nationality; Orthodoxy; Putin; World War II; and, of course, anti-Ukrainian racism. Something had changed: an outpouring of nationalist euphoria spread across Russia in the wake of Crimea.[1]

"Crimea is ours!," a slogan seeded by the state, for example, rapidly wormed its way into pop culture. It appeared on everything from mugs to badges, sweets, and T-shirts. It was rendered next to images ranging from scantily clad Japanese anime-inspired drawings of female Russian troops to photos of Vladimir Putin. High schoolers marked their graduations by printing up shirts with the slogan, posing for photographs and filming videos of drinking and dancing, then uploading their content to social media en masse.

An anonymous Russian YouTuber, Enjoykin, incorporated the slogan into a nonsensical viral tune, "Floopy Flowers, Crimea's Ours," which serenaded Natalya Poklonskaya, a thirty-four-year-old ideologue appointed as Crimea's new prosecutor. Mashing up excerpts from Poklonskaya's speeches—including the absurd phrase "floopy flowers"—nobody quite knew whether it was serious or not. The song quickly went viral, racking up almost 50 million views on YouTube alone.[2]

Swimming in nonsense the words may have been, but everybody learned snippets of Poklonskaya's warmongering speeches: "blood and power"; "Crimea's ours." The language of the state's war was seeping into mass culture on a wave of virality. Every young Russian could speak the language of Putin, even if they believed they were only doing it ironically. And—reiterated at raucous parties, in catchy earworms, and in salacious cartoons—the language of Putin's Crimea invasion seemed fun.

Vladislav was along for the ride. His posts became more homophobic, more violent, and more racist. Yet he continued to post images of his "regular" life—holidays, music festivals, parties, and stills of Soviet and post-Soviet films—too. Vlad's nascent fascism was absorbed into his everyday and online life. Being a hip, party-loving consumer was not incompatible with being religious, militaristic, macho, and nationalist.

Today, Vlad speaks entirely in propaganda slogans, snippets of language he has drawn from the state media and pro-state social media groups he consumes non-stop. He despises Ukraine. He has abandoned his Jewish roots for Russian Orthodoxy. He has cut Ukrainian family members and friends out of his life: "It's the right thing to do," he brusquely declares.

Vlad has obliterated every trace of his non-Russian personhood. It is almost as if he used the invasion of Crimea and Eastern Ukraine as an opportunity to sacrifice the undesirable elements of his own personality and to cut himself off from a deleterious—a Ukrainian—community. Vlad didn't have to travel to a Chechnya, a Georgia, or even to the present conflict in person. He was participating in the war vicariously by purifying himself and launching an online crusade, displaying his transformation for his friends and family to see, and creating Moscow's fake reality of Ukrainophobia by amplifying it online.

Where did the flood of Kremlinspeak—some Russians refer to it as *novoyaz*, "newspeak," in deference to Orwell's *1984*—that sold the Ukraine war originate? And how did it draw somebody with Vlad's cosmopolitan, Jewish, and liberal background into the cult of nouveau war so quickly in 2014?

A new, Russian identity

September 2013. Putin—clad in his usual, unremarkable black suit—ambles up to the podium at the annual Valdai Club meeting. Members of the "club," a policy mill that upcycles Kremlin suggestions into glossy, think-tank-style presentations, gave polite applause. Putin dawdled his way into a monotone, twenty-four-minute oration that soon had the attendees nodding off to sleep even as the bright, sky-blue backdrop—"Russia's Diversity for the Modern World," declared the screen—flooded the auditorium with light.[3] But Putin's content was remarkable. He was outlining a vision to remake Russia's young.

In the speech, Putin developed his 2012 election-winning material. He reeled off a list of evils linked to "political correctness": pedophilia, homosexuality, feminism, militarism, and even satanism. Each evil came from abroad, and each evil was a "direct path to degradation and primitivism." The West, said Putin, was undermining "the Christian values that constitute the basis of Western civilization." Russia's young were under attack, and only a spiritual revolution—a new "national identity"—could save them.

It was time, said Putin, to focus on the inner life of the Russian citizen: "The main thing that will determine [national] success is the quality of citizens, the quality of society: their intellectual, spiritual, and moral strength." National success, national existence itself, depended on whether subjects "identify with their own history, values, and traditions, and whether they are united by common goals."

History, value, and tradition meant "Russian language, Russian culture, the Russian Orthodox Church, and the country's other traditional religions." The education system, which Putin suggested did not have to be limited to the school classroom, should continually emphasize "the role of great Russian culture and literature." That Russian culture should then "serve as the foundation for people's personal identity." The "soft cultural therapy" that Putin had outlined the previous year was being stepped up a notch. Only a project of totally remaking the young around "Russian" cultural and religious ideals could fend off Western degeneracy.

Putin signed off his Valdai speech with a coda that restated his myth of the 1990s: "We lived through and overcame that turbulent, dramatic period ... we must, and we will, move forward!" If Russia was to survive, young Russians like Vladislav were to be plunged into a war with their inner selves. They would have to emerge from battle remade and ready to move into the future: a Russian future.

This wasn't Putin's first hint at such an extreme policy, but it was the most unequivocal. The country's apparatchiks scuttled off to their policy institutes and media studios to turn the president's words into reality.

The Valdai Club itself sponsored a group of five young scholars to produce their own recommendations.[4] Contemporaries of Egor Polyakov at the Higher School of Economics—upwardly mobile, all LinkedIn profiles and visiting scholarships at leading universities in China and Europe—declared themselves "fundamentally optimistic" about Russia's future. But only, they noted, if a "non-patriotic generation" of young liberals with insufficient attachment to national history, ideology, and religion could rediscover "Christian and universal religious morality."

Russia's young, they argued, had nothing to learn from other ethnicities. After all, non-Russian minorities functioned only as "bright ethnic additions that serve to enrich the main culture. The most obvious example of this is the coexistence of sauerkraut, salted herring, shish kebab and pilaf on our holiday tables." Russian women ("faithful, devoted, and loving"), meanwhile, were to be mothers to "sacred" families.[5] The authors' heroes—to be hailed as role models in digital and educational spheres—were almost exclusively white, male, and ethnically Russian. Most of them, of course, were great military leaders. Stretching back centuries, the greatest Russians were its military saints: those who had beaten off the Mongols, attacked the Poles, and subjugated the Islamic peoples on the empire's periphery.

Soon, a new cult of nationalism and war was rampaging on and offline through popular culture, military parades, schools and universities, and new youth groups that targeted the very youngest Russian citizens en masse. Slipping and slithering its way through young people's worlds, the culture was inescapable. Just as the "undesirables"—the queers and the liberals—were being smashed apart, young Russians would be provided all the spaces and language they needed to remake themselves. The fissures and voids the government had created as it attacked the opposition were being filled.

New models and sites for fascist youth

The brash party in the world of sports and entertainment didn't let up for a second, but it became increasingly nationalistic. The Sochi

Olympics, held just before the invasion of Crimea in the winter of 2014, was the biggest show of all. At the opening ceremony, the state orchestrated a spectacle of brilliant, nationalist youth. The stadium fell dark but for a pall of purple light. The cameras cut to a video. A child's bedroom on a snowy night. A sleeping girl, clad in white, rolls over, knocking open an alphabet book. The wind riffles through the pages, revealing fairy-tale illustrations of Russia's feats and heroes: A for Alphabet, B for Baikal, C for Catherine the Great, D for Dostoevsky. E for Empire. The heroine wanders through fantasy vignettes that bring Russia's greatness to life.

U for "Us." The journey ends with the beaming protagonist mirrored in five different national outfits emblazoned with letters spelling out dominance: *Ya* for *Rossiya*. *Ya*: the last letter of the alphabet, and the Russian word for "I." The perfect Russian child becomes the reflection of empire. Sweeping out to the Olympic Stadium, the cameras gazed down as fireworks carpeted the sky in explosions of red, white, and blue. A new model of Russian childhood—imperial, fairy-tale, martial, unabashed—was being formed on the biggest of stages. Weeks later, the troops set off for Crimea.

Tune into Eurovision the next year—as millions of Russians did—and the previous decade's trite fairy-tale fantasies of impossible dreams were gone. Instead, Russia trolled its competition. The year after it had invaded neighboring Ukraine, the Kremlin sent one of its most sycophantic singers, the popstrel Polina Gagarina, to belt out a ballad praying for world peace. The cloying accompanying video was a paint-by-numbers affair of smiling children bathed in glorious sunlight. The audience booed, but Russians knew the "truth" from the state's memes and speeches: they were only waging war to create peace, to save the dream vision of their national youth and national culture.

But the patriotic drum-beating wasn't reserved for these showcase events. In the 2010s, switching on the TV, tuning into the radio, spending the evening at the movies, or even loading up social media meant an inevitable brush with the new national identity. Through choice or by force, Russia's young would be exposed to a more patriotic, more *Russian* culture—and that meant an apocalyptic culture of war, religion, and martyrdom.

Settling in for a lazy day on the couch might mean channel hopping from increasingly angry political discussion shows to the new

Tsargrad TV station, a vehicle for neo-fascist Orthodox nationalism edited by the increasingly prominent Aleksandr Dugin. Priests, hacks, and pundits railed at Western moral depravity for hours on end on this Fox News-cum-apocalyptic media cult. And this wasn't just a channel for the old: like its extremist American models, it counted large numbers of young viewers among the millions switching on.

Flicking over to the flagship Channel One, even trashy entertainment shows provided no respite. Viewers might have stumbled across *The Male/The Female*, a glossy talk show that bolted the studio rage of *Jerry Springer* onto the all-out aggression of the Soviet show trial. Since 2014, guests have entered the studio's cauldron to meet the glamorous hosts, the journalist Aleksandr Gordon and footballer's wife Yuliya Baranovskaya. A panel of pundits and a baying studio audience offer damning accompaniment to tales of collapsing apartments, alcoholic parents, and predatory pedophiles. Bouts of spittle-flecked rage delivered by the presenters are followed by tears, laughter, and pleas for mercy.

All the wrongs of the degenerate society are righted under the dazzling glare of the studio lights. Homosexuals, cheaters, alcoholics, liberals, the West, satanists, practitioners of "black magic," "parasites," atheists, and men who skip military service are destroyed. And always, the sense that the West is somehow to blame for all of this. In one early episode, a baby-faced nineteen-year-old, Anton, insinuates that his American adoptive parents were pedophiles. The watching panel thank God that "organic," Orthodox Russia has embraced him on his return home. Just as in Putin's "Direct Line" phone-ins, the show always ends with the promise that a lawyer, psychologist, or local official will "look into it" and everything will be fine. Happy end after happy, Russian end.

This is young life as pure spectacle; these are young people remade on camera. Their remaking is consumed then discussed in endless YouTube and VK comments. Users who'd followed Anton's transformation from American dream to Russian rebirth scream their approval: "Everything's possible in Russia!"; "You can be a Russian in Russia, but you can't be American in America"; "Anton's genes overcame the Americans' attacks!" Bathed in the warmth of the glamorous studio, bounded by the simple, assured of the inevitable happy end—turning into a good Russian through conflict seemed miraculous.

At the center of becoming a better young Russian stood none other than the sexagenarian Vladimir Putin. Even as his physique obviously diminished, Putin seemed to become ever more youthful, more perfect. His daily routine purportedly consisted of filmed gym sessions, hours of swimming, and abstemious evenings of hard work.[6] He made whipping boys of hockey pros in staged annual matches—even though he'd only hit a puck in anger for the first time, apparently, in 2012. Even as Putin aged, he seemed to be getting younger.

PR men and pop moguls fed the president's youthful image into pop culture. The state carefully cultivated links with popular young musicians: "We cannot afford not to pay attention to" them, as one presidential aide explained.[7] On the dictator's birthday in 2015, Timati, the country's biggest rap star and a long-time Putin fan, dropped a new track, "My Best Friend Is President Putin." In the accompanying video, Timati and his collaborator, Sasha Chest, stride out across Red Square in impossibly cool black outfits to serenade the president. Groups of young women are agog as a figure wearing a Putin mask enters a hip nightclub. Hip young skaters and gymnasts fill parks and Red Square with color and movement. The lyrics assert Putin's brilliance, growing ever more absurd as they use twenty-first-century street language to claim that the leader knew it all and had everything under control. The song and its video briefly illuminated the Runet before drifting off into the great swarm of identikit nationalism surrounding everyone from twenty-somethings like Vladislav to children like Alina.

Putin was, to borrow Chest and Timati's words, "on a level with us"—but always a little more sporting, a little stronger, and a little younger. Everybody loved him and everybody could be better by learning from him, whether he was on stage at the Valdai Club or refracted in viral memes and hip hop hits. Indeed, Chest even wrote a university dissertation about the president: "I decided that Vladimir Vladimirovich Putin would be an ideal example [of leadership], so I dedicated my work to him. It was cool to defend the work; it was super interesting to prepare for it."[8] Russia's young rap fans agreed: the piece racked up over 16 million views and 160,000 likes on YouTube alone.

But the state wasn't just puffing up its historical feathers at grand performances or churning out sharable internet hits and memes to praise the president. It was preaching the cult of war to the young like never before.

Militarizing youth culture

As the shock of the Crimean invasion receded from view, Vladislav wrapped himself up in nationalist culture. And, when it was embedded in familiar Western entertainment forms, he didn't feel for a second that he was an old-school nationalist. After all, he wasn't violent. He wasn't an extremist football hooligan. He wasn't beating up Chechens, Georgians, or even the abominable Ukrainians. He was one of the good guys.

So Vlad cued up the cutting-edge Russian hip hop pumped out by Timati's Black Star label. He watched esoteric, apocalyptic religious rants from Tsargrad, liking and sharing them on social media. He joined dozens of pro-Kremlin social media groups in which members exchanged vitriolic material, urging each other on to greater commitments to the nationalist cause.

But, most of all, Vlad engaged with a cult of war that was ballooning to absurd proportions. And in the rants and memes he has left behind online, we can see the detritus of a rhetorical war being fueled as he expunged Western cultural influences—perverse, satanic, threatening—from his self. Into their place marched the language of civilizational conflict.

In the 2000s, the opportunities to fight a war, to make the ultimate sacrifice for the motherland, were limited to far-off Chechnya and a lightning-quick conflict in Georgia. Now the war was always on, online, in popular culture, in song, on screens, and on television. And now, as war bubbled away in Eastern Ukraine, young Russians could imagine that their rituals and performances of war and sacrifice—their online attacks and transformations—really were part of a meaningful conflict. Cloaked in internet memes and trends, the war cult was reaching behind every closed door and into every device in Russia.

Fifteen years after Putin's first Victory Day parade, the sun again radiated down on Moscow as an unheralded swathe of troops and hardware were assembled on 9 May. As viewers gathered around televisions and devices to watch, the cameramen trained their lenses on serried ranks of Russian flags and red Soviet-era victory flags. Cameras soared over an immaculate Red Square, painting sublime, geometric shapes with vast corpuses of troops. They snatched at glimpses of dazzled children clad in uniform in the crowd before pausing on elderly veterans, heads reverently bowed. In swept Defense Minister Sergey Shoygu, weighed down by a treasure trove of medals and ribbons, on a glittering limousine. This was a "holy war," intoned the commentator explaining every element of the symbolism to the crowds.

Twenty minutes into the parade, like clockwork, Putin returned to the podium. He railed against his Western adversaries: "In the last decades, the basic principles of international cooperation have come to be increasingly ignored. We see attempts to establish a unipolar world. We see the strong-arm bloc thinking gaining momentum." Among the ritual—the same parade, but bigger, shinier, and staged with the TV panache of a great sporting event—warnings of another showdown with the West were becoming less a mythical specter than a promise.

Putin left the Red Square podium to join some of the 12 million Russians participating in the Immortal Regiment parade. A grassroots initiative seized by the state as the latest invented ritual, the Immortal Regiment sees Russians take to the streets in columns, bearing pictures of their ancestors and of wartime leaders including Joseph Stalin, wearing the black-and-orange George Cross ribbon, and often dressed in period costume.[9]

Wielding their grandparents' photographs as if they were Orthodox icons, Russians at the Immortal Regiment of 2015 marched alongside their president, took part in sing-alongs, and smiled for selfies. As President Putin, holding a picture of his father, told a state TV interviewer that the ritual helped Russians have confidence in "a happy future for our children," he was not flanked by aging veterans. Instead, a small boy stood to his left, and hundreds of adolescents and twenty-somethings milled behind him. The parade wasn't remembering the past. It was creating the future—a future awash with the myth of lost national utopia.

Millions of photographs instantly appeared on social media profiles along with stories of wartime sacrifices and gaudy memes that mashed up Soviet aesthetics with pictures supporting war against Ukraine. Everybody could take part in this parade—in person, online—and everybody could consume and re-consume the moment of the parade over and again as algorithms fed the mass spectacle into feeds.

And who should have taken part in the Immortal Regiment in 2015 but, of course, the new convert to the faith, Vladislav? Snapping smiling selfies and holding a tattered sepia photograph of his family, Vlad delighted in bonding with the shared memory of the past. "We owe them a debt," he wrote, "and we must never forget them." *We*. The language of community, not individualism. The language of a shared religious ritual. The martyred Soviet generation, not Christ, is the inimitable idol of this state religion. Victory Day is its national holiday, and Putin's Victory Day performance its papal Christmas message. And, as the moment of renewal was endlessly re-shared online, it left behind Red Square, the Immortal Regiment, and 9 May itself. The spirit of sacrifice and victory was transcendent. It reached away from reality and into the world of myth.

Indeed, messianic visions of national sacrifice during World War II were hammered home year-round and across popular culture. The state threw money at everything from musicians to film directors in pursuit of ever more ambitious statements of militarism. For example, popular director Fedor Bondarchuk received a record haul of $30m—most of it from the state's Cinema Fund and the state-owned VTB Bank—to produce a messianic war epic, *Stalingrad*, that would reel in a mass audience of young adult viewers.

The film retells the story of the World War II battle. In the central storyline, a group of soldiers defend an apartment block alone. They heroically withstand the German onslaught before deliberately sacrificing themselves to save a group of civilians and their comrades, thus winning the battle and resurrecting Stalingrad and the world. The story is at heart religious: a tale of martyrdom and resurrection.[10] Only sacrifice could save the world from the threat from the West in 1942.

Bondarchuk's team lay the message on even thicker with a framing device set in the present. In this subplot, the 2011 tsunami and earthquake in Japan has left a group of Germans trapped under the rubble of a collapsed building. Russian emergency workers are called in to assist. One emergency worker, Sergey, explains the story of how he came to have "five fathers": the troops who sacrificed themselves in 1942. In this framing plot, the movie depicts Russians as global saviors both in the past and present, suggests that Germans are "forgetting" the war, and reminds Russians that there is no greater good than to sacrifice oneself—today, tomorrow, whenever the state needs it—to stave off catastrophe.

Stalingrad was a phenomenon. Excitement grew as the release date approached. State ministers talked up the film's brilliance. Bondarchuk expected an Oscar nomination.[11] Trailers attracted huge attention on social media ("I cried watching it!" commented one Russian teen). *Stalingrad* smashed a domestic box-office record to take $16m in its opening weekend, and it was the runaway victor in a poll to find the public's film of the year.[12] "I love you, Stalingrad!" burst out one hysterical online commenter. Millions of teen and adolescent viewers had got the message.

If gritty blockbusters like *Stalingrad* should prove too gruesome, much younger children could enjoy the spate of TV serials and films soon released about children's sacrifices during World War II.[13] Everybody, even the youngest children, was being primed to understand that the great battle might break out again at any moment.

Educational institutions were obliging their staff and children to get in on the act too. One middle-school teacher, Olga, originally from St Petersburg but now living abroad, told me that "I didn't have to go to the Immortal Regiment but it was expected I would attend." Olga remembers that at the time "most of the older teachers just went anyway, and some of the younger ones went too. But I felt I didn't have the choice."

Class time in the days leading up to Victory Day, Olga tells me, was occupied by parades, assemblies, singing contests, and poetry recitals about the war. And during the rest of the year, kids took field trips to war museums, met aging veterans, and might even have been lucky enough to visit one of the new "military-historical" theme parks the state was constructing around the country.

Thousands of students were put through a new course on Orthodox Christian culture that linked Christianity and Russia's military past. But this wasn't really about the past. It was about—as the Archdeacon Andrey Kuraev, who authored the course textbook, put it—launching a "pre-emptive strike, though education, against extremism." The course might have been unappealing—one of my interviewees remembers that his younger brother "was bored solid" during the lessons, "but he learned the important parts of Russia's religious history." To be religious meant to be ready to fight.

If attempts at introducing military and religious patriotic education had been more style over substance in the previous decade, now they were woven through the entire educational experience.[14] And the purpose of all this? To learn—through pantomime, play-acting, and performance—to fight the wars of the present.

Graduating grade school did not see the end of this warlike performance. University students could now hear their rectors hymning the creation of "celebration platoons," institutional uniforms, and courses that would prepare better soldiers for the state.[15] But as ever in Putin's Russia, the lines between serious military preparation and outrageous pop-culture performance were muddied.

At Moscow Art Industrial Institute (MAII)—a private graphic, fashion, and art school—a group of enthusiastic young undergraduates founded a military cadet group that "trains" students as members of a "military brotherhood," the so-called "Junkers."[16] Clad in an ominous black parade jacket, modeled after a late tsarist uniform, and a peaked red cap, the MAII "Junkers" stage memorial events, tsarist "fairy tales" on holidays, and recreation period balls, and help in the community by tidying up military cemeteries. They are sometimes joined by local politicians, who cheer on the group's dynamism and zeal. The school's induction events are a miniature, uniformed reflection of the militaristic parades of Nashi, Victory Day, and political rallies: flags flutter, slogans are uttered, and Orthodox priests bless the incoming class.

The charade never ends. "Junkers" members, many of them fashion students, delight in refining the uniform every year or two, finding imaginative ways to emblazon the group's logo—a white skull—over uniforms, banners, and event flyers. Posting striking photos of themselves—tattooed and bearded young hipster men, women in heavy make-up and daringly short miniskirts—to social media, the group's members live their identity online and offline.

MAII didn't stop at the Junkers group. The school's official "patriotic hard rock" group, "The MAII Army," produced a series of music videos in the mid-2010s.[17] In the accompanying video to "The Army and I," from 2016, the group's musicians ride a tank through a military base near Moscow. Their singer—all denim, tattoos, and long hair—strides across the screen as he spits out an aggressive hard rock serenade to "remembering victory" and the contemporary army: "There's a strong force that's defending me! / It's all about me! / The army and I!" For Victory Day that year, the group put out another track, "I Want a Tank Guy!":

> On the snow-white sand
> Between the hipsters and the beach boys
> I met a tank guy
> From the special forces
> I don't need those little kids
> In their shorts and facial cream
> I just want a tank guy
> With a military machine!

Even punk-rock fashion students weren't rebelling. They were showing their peers that there could be nothing better than acting, playing, and singing your love for the state's military men.

Just as Vladislav's old identity was becoming indistinguishable from a militarized persona, so pupils and students all over Russia were finding themselves caught up in this whirlwind spectacle. Indeed, one former MAII student told me that it was hard to know how serious the Junkers group was for the school's students. Some members just enjoyed dressing up, creating, performing, and bonding. Perhaps the Junkers' skull logo was just a silly joke—"like the Jolly Roger!"—something to be laughed at and ironically reclaimed.[18]

But some, my source tells me, really did believe all of it. As one third-year student explained in 2013, "These sorts of organizations are really close to home for me. I was a cadet in school. We designed the uniform ... and now it's kind of like our school's brand!"

A pipeline from school to university and into the state's youth and military training groups was laid. A path with only one destination. A path on which decisions never had to be made. The cult of war promised wholeness, community, and joy—even if it meant playing out militarism at every opportunity.

Influencers meet military youth groups

The state's messages sank deeper into every part of the Runet. Instagram-influencer culture took off in Russia in the mid-2010s. Lifestyle gurus promised perfect lives through diets, exercise regimes, and mindfulness, accumulating millions of followers. Gamers streamed their interactions online, getting rich from subscribers and advertising income. The Kremlin spotted a good thing and offered money to those willing to spread its message to young audiences, who could barely tell the difference between a real and a paid-for post.[19]

But, Kremlin money aside, young Russians leapt onto the influencer bandwagon by creating lifestyle brands with a distinctive, nationalist twist. In 2014, after she had given birth to her first child, Alla, who was in her early twenties, was bored at home. Her husband worked all hours to make ends meet. Most of her friends were at work or at home with their own children. And, living in Russia's southwest, there were no bougie Moscow coffee shops to frequent in the local town. So she created a world for herself as an apocalyptic Orthodox momfluencer.

Alla's racked up thousands of perfectly curated images of a dream Orthodox family life. She posts selfies in fashionable dresses, topped off with a traditional headscarf, and tells her thousands of followers how "dreams come true" as she attends church and makes pilgrimages to monasteries (tagging in churches' and monasteries' own social media accounts, some of which have hundreds of thousands of followers in their own right).

For Alla, religion is inseparable from war. She praises the military heroes of the past—the mythologized Aleksandr Nevsky, who fought the Mongol invaders in thirteenth-century Russia—and welcomes war as a way to save the nation today. Posting an image of her beaming children, she tells her 14,000 followers that "[war] is God's strongest remedy; it is more healing for our fatherland and the Church than all societies, speeches, and slogans ... if you added an undoubted faith in the Providence of God to this remedy ... then your pain would not be in vain." Alla's perfectly photogenic kids frame a familiar message: war and destruction save the young, save the nation, create miracles.

Alla's followers, like any group of young moms, were eagerly swapping tips on parenting in the comments to her posts. But the tips they swapped were all about extreme nationalist upbringing, war, and sacrifice: where to get the right education, where to go to church, and what the nation's enemies were up to.

Orthodox influencers like Alla have popped up all over Russian social media spaces. Adopting the language and style of Western lifestyle influencers, they appeal to young Russians. But they tell their audiences that war is a healing, divine force necessary to save the nation. It might be washed over in the comforting warmth of Instagram filters, but "clean living" Russian style involves a lot of dying.

But the government wasn't leaving the field clear for outlandish student groups and small-time influencers. It was about to dig up the skeletal framework of the Walking Together and Nashi projects, plug them into an internet cult of war headed by its own influencers, and set to training a generation of real child soldiers.

* * *

Olga Zanko may be barely thirty-two years old, but she's already a familiar sight in Moscow's political circles and on Russian patriots' social media feeds alike. Yet Zanko's aloof student-council-president manner, gimlet-eyed stare, and youth belie her political brilliance.

In a stellar rise to political fame, Zanko has already become a Duma deputy. In July 2022, she was voted the tenth most popular member of Russia's parliament, and the opposition already singles her out as a leading Putinist.[20] But Zanko doesn't have much in common with the anonymous gray faces of the previous generation. She is a leader of Russia's military cult for the 2020s. Her image and influence have been marching relentlessly through the Runet ever since she washed up in St Petersburg from the tiny town of Borisoglebsk as a teenager in the late 2000s.

Full of ambition and driven by nativist conservatism, Zanko—with the support of an eager state—founded Victory Volunteers as part of the seventieth anniversary Victory Day celebrations.[21] The group invites young Russians to participate in campaigns to look after war memorials, care for veterans, attend Victory Day parades, and share family and personal memories of war online and in person in non-stop campaigns.

The group's VK, Instagram, and Telegram feeds are jam-packed with dreamy, soft-focus images of deliriously happy young Russians—all white, as are the veterans they help—wearing matching blue-and-white T-shirts and hats as they go about their "volunteering." The visual content is accompanied by a familiar blend of Putin quotes, Soviet-era slogans, vague inspirational quotes about remembering history, allusions to messianism and saintliness, and images of wars past and present. The Volunteers aren't just stuck in the past. They're apparently building the future for the next generation: "We're proud of the past, we value the present, and we look to the future!"

Since its founding in 2015, Victory Volunteers has swept across Russia: 135,000 users follow its VK page, 300,000 "volunteers" have registered to participate in events, and the organization has over 1,000 offices across the nation. And while the organization has benefited from the Kremlin's support—Putin has personally blessed its work—the key to its success is Zanko's role as influencer-in-chief.[22]

On her VK feed, Zanko projects a spotless image of traditional Orthodox family values and Putinist patriotism. Days and evenings out with her husband, family meals, selfies, and visits to church mingle with sycophantic praise of Putin, updates on Zanko's work as a Duma deputy, and photo sessions at Victory Volunteers events. Now and again, vitriolic anti-Ukrainian content interrupts this idealized dreamscape.

But Zanko makes the dream wholly accessible. She interacts with her fans, answering their comments, providing them with polls ("Should organizations that are 'traitors' receive state funding?"), and modeling patriotic behavior. After the 2018 presidential election, when she assisted Putin's campaign, Zanko posted a message of support for volunteers:[23] "Thank you post [heart emoji] ... We honestly did follow all the great work you each did and couldn't not thank the best volunteers from V.V. Putin's headquarters." Followers luxuriated in the acclaim: "Olga, thank you for your warm words, for your support, for your belief!!" Zanko's young fans inundate her page with sycophantic birthday greetings, applaud her every move, and express their desire to be just like her. With every post, the whole community watches other followers build themselves up into feverish excitement. This is a place they can really belong, and it's a competition to show that you're the one who *best* belongs.

And with just a couple of clicks, those same fans can meander into participating in the work of Victory Volunteers from anywhere and at any time. In one event, "Access Code: Stalingrad," users were urged to participate in an online campaign to learn about Stalingrad. A series of simplistic but eye-catching Instagram-style graphics introduces key lessons about the battle while offering prizes to those who participate in a live event. The language of the presentation borrows from the gamified rhetoric familiar to any social media user: participants are promised "inner secrets" and a "new look!!"; hashtags serve as gathering points; the posts are liberally sprinkled with peppy emojis. The first advert for the event was shared by 150 users and seen by at least 27,000 people on VK.[24]

Victory Volunteers, with its prizes, youth-culture vibe, and snappy graphics makes participating in a project to learn to be a better kind of Russian *fun*. And, what's more, young Russians don't need to fill out any application forms or commit to ongoing meetings to join in. In the world of social media, the fascist rally knows no bounds, and the meetings of the fascist youth group can continue 24/7.

Indeed, when I spoke to Irina, an eighteen-year-old from a small, remote town in Arkhangelsk province, she tells me that she doesn't go to Victory Volunteers events in person—they are few and far between in towns as small as hers—but she follows the organization's VK feed, likes its posts, and takes part in some of the campaigns. She enjoys the idea of winning prizes and making friends online; she regularly exchanges messages with fellow followers online; and she admires Zanko, who's "a good idol, somebody who cares about young people." Isolated in remote towns like Irina's, teens all over Russia can breathe in a little of Zanko's political stardust by reaching out to and marching alongside their role model online.

Irina, like many young Russians, says she's not interested in high politics, and she's ambivalent towards Putin. Yet the material she engages with online has started to influence her VK profile: she has just decided to list her religion publicly as "Orthodox Christian," and she has shared clickbait fake-news stories about Western atrocities in Africa.

And when I ask about Ukraine today? She may not be an outright warmonger, but Irina messages me back with an almost verbatim rendition of the state's slogans, "I know that bad things are happening in Ukraine. Russia has to look after its own." Irina has found community and role models in Victory Volunteers. But she's also reforming her worldview and inner beliefs in a serious way as a result.

The state has found a means in Victory Volunteers to spread its message even to those who might never have joined an organization officially. In the virtual sphere, the "soft cultural therapy" that Putin advocated in his 2012 election article operates insidiously, almost imperceptibly. You might not even notice, like Irina, that it's shaping you or that you're sharing it. You might consequently still consider yourself to be politically apathetic. Now headed to university in Moscow, Irina plans to get more involved in Victory Volunteers events.

In the state's other great youth project of the late 2010s, however, "soft cultural therapy" took a back seat.

* * *

Pester power is just as effective for Russian kids as for their Western peers. Whether it's the latest iPhone, a subscription to an online game, or borrowing a few rubles for a day out, young Russians usually find a way to extract what they want from their harried parents. Nikita's parents never had much money to spare—his mother is a kindergarten teacher and his father a furniture maker— but back in 2017, when he was twelve, Nikita wasn't after money. He wanted their permission to be like his friends.

Nikita's peers weren't spending their evenings and weekends playing ball in the courtyards of the crumbling, Soviet-era apartment blocks they inhabited in Saratov, in the southwest of Russia. They were donning khaki boots and pants and a distinctive red T-shirt and beret, then heading off to the local hall to practice marching and chanting. They were learning to be young soldiers. And like thousands of their peers across the country, they were learning the battle cry "I'm ready to fight and die for Russia!"[25]

Soviet and Russian children have long received forms of military training in schools and extracurricular clubs, but enthusiasm for active preparation had flagged through the 1990s and 2000s. The Youth Army, masterminded by long-serving Defense Minister Sergey Shoygu, aimed to correct that situation on its lavishly funded launch in 2016.

The group has four core goals: "social development," a program of civics education about the relationship between "young boys and girls" and their community and country; "physical development," a focus on healthy living and strength through competition; "intellectual development," aimed at forming a "positive attitude towards constitutional duties and preparing the young for service in the Armed Forces"; and "moral and spiritual development," which explores "honesty, faith, dignity, and love for the motherland."[26] Through the Youth Army, the state explicitly seeks to mold the young into soldiers of Russian nationality, history, and Orthodoxy.

Youth Army members spend vast swathes of their time parading. They parade on national holidays. They parade after school. They parade in gyms. They parade in the community. And when they're not marching, they're taking classes, they're meeting serving troops, or they're helping veterans in the community. But, most of all, they're preparing for battle.

Relentless physical training, capped with annual sports competitions, is meant to keep the members in tip-top shape. At summer camps and after-school events, even the youngest members—those aged seven—learn to take apart and reassemble grenades and AK-74 rifles, while older teens practice throwing grenades and firing weapons.[27] They learn about how to defend themselves and their communities in the event of nuclear and chemical attacks by dressing up in protection suits and gas masks.

Morally and physically drilled, attendees graduate from the program ready to enter society with a nationalist mindset that promotes Orthodoxy, fear of the West, and a positive relationship with the state and the army.

But the group dresses up this serious military preparation in a wave of youth-culture fun. In 2018, former cosmonaut Roman

Romanenko, who was then head of the Youth Army, sold the organization as a route to non-stop patriotic education, socializing, games, and competition: "We run a whole host of events to do with studying history and geography, and events that have a bit of competition, like our 'Victory' military sports competition, hikes, expeditions, and 'memory guards.' And we tell kids about their ancestors' great military feats so they won't ever forget them."[28] Just like everything else in the new Russian national culture, extreme militarism was all just fun and games.

A glossy Youth Army magazine distributed to members and newspaper readers in 2017 is a bizarre advert for the group's mix of militarism and family-friendly fun.[29] On the cover, Defense Minister Shoygu appears in the fake military regalia he was now wearing at Victory Day parades. Inside, frothy stories—"Grandfather Frost Has Joined the Youth Army!"—complement New Year's greetings from lightweight Europop singer Valeriya: "My little heroes! I wish you a happy new year … you are the pride of our nation!"

But young readers leafing through the glossy supplement could also read all about Russia's latest military hardware, army recruitment efforts, and the history of World War II. Smiling teen Youth Army members are pictured playing laser tag, which is "a new way to train for battle in any weather conditions!" They're just having a good time, aren't they? Yet dressed in camouflage and wielding imitation firearms, they look for all the world like real soldiers.

On the back cover of the magazine, the smiling face of a blonde-haired, blue-eyed Youth Army recruit in Crimea beams past a headline: "The Crimean Youth Army regiment is being reinforced on a mass scale. More than a thousand people have joined the movement. The bright years ahead will see them train in both theoretical and practical aspects of military preparation." The Youth Army was never about games. It is about mass indoctrination to funnel children seeking belonging into the fight for Russification in Ukraine—to funnel children into a war that could create "the bright years ahead."

Russians rushed to sign up. By 2019, 380,000 children between the ages of seven and eighteen were already members. Most came from the poorer southern and western regions of Russia that border Ukraine and Belarus.[30] Schools, community groups, and private businesses were all encouraged to form their own branches.[31] Most enlistees are average kids looking to fit in, and their parents are generally supportive. After all, militarism has long been supported by most Russian parents.[32]

Back in Saratov, Nikita got his wish. His parents signed him up, and he spent four years dressed up in uniform; parading on national holidays; attending historical education classes; and—his favorite part, since he's "always been interested in things like special ops"—learning to use firearms. He was such a keen "young soldier"—as the group's members are known—that he helped organize additional events in his school, aiming to educate his peers and, perhaps, attract some to join the movement too.

Today, Nikita is a real internet addict. He spends evenings locked away in his bedroom consuming Japanese anime and bizarre, ironic Russian memes. But he also wages war on perceived slights against his country online, attacking "lies" from abroad; defending Putin, who he says is in a "difficult position"; and claiming that Russia needs a strong military to keep itself safe. He says that he loved his time in the Youth Army so much that he plans to postpone going to university to sign up for the Russian army as a contract soldier.[33] The unfolding disasters of Russia's military efforts in Ukraine hold no fear for Nikita. He has had a taste of the fun and games of military life—and he knows that he's ready to fight.

If Nikita is anything to go by, the Youth Army has been a roaring success. Thousands of young Russians like him might enjoy Western culture, but they are also entering adulthood equipped with hands-on skills, pumped up with aggressive support for their country, and confident that the state is a foster parent to rival their biological family.

The state's search for bodies to prepare for war, though, didn't stop at gentle pressure. Some parents reported finding themselves feeling pressured to enlist their children, as employers and school principals touted the benefits of the organization. Worse, the Youth Army has sought out recruits in orphanages. It claims that joining up is a solution to the alcoholism and criminality that sucks orphans in.[34] The state is, in its own words, "liberating children from the burdensome search for the self" through membership in the Youth Army.[35] Join up, allow us to instill morality in you, and there is no chance that you will end up diseased, degenerate, and disordered like the victims of Western perversion.

But, as with any totalitarian regime, the search for bodies to feed the war machine begins by preying on the poor, the isolated, and the vulnerable. As it was psychologically breaking apart non-Russian "outsiders," so it was offering routes back into the fold through its youth programs. Perhaps a remake of 2010's *Christmas Trees* might see Varya, the orphan heroine, finding her fairy-tale ending not with an enchanting message of hope from the president but with an invitation to join the local paramilitary youth group. She wouldn't send a message for the president; she would speak the words she is told: "I'm ready to fight and die for Russia."

Volunteering for the online war

Snowballing beyond the government's own media channels, the state's insipid symbols, songs, myths, and memes took on a life of their own as they spread online. Anybody could tune in at any time, night or day, to catch a moment of the fascist rally, the harmonious community, and a vision of a better self. Anybody could contribute to the non-stop glamour of the flag-waving, neo-fascist rally.

Ivan Kondakov, already suspicious of Western "traitors" like Navalny and proud of the gains he had made under Putin's leadership, didn't need any financial incentives to join this cacophonous world. And when he did so in the late 2010s, he went all in.

Ivan had long been an amateur musician, playing piano in school and singing in an Iron Maiden covers band at university (even if he would have preferred to be playing Deep Purple, his favorite group, or something by Russian rock groups Aria or Korol i shut ("The King and the Jester")).

In March 2020, when Moscow was under COVID lockdown, Ivan found himself at a loose end. Inspired by the bawdy social media personalities who dominated pro-Putin corners of the Runet, Ivan observed that there was no conservative, patriotic voice among Russia's modern comic singers, "so I decided to do something about it. I'd been a decent guitarist and wrote songs back in college, so I decided to write something funny, sarcastic, and satirical."

With the help of a neighbor who owned a home studio, Ivan quickly cobbled together a few tracks. The lyrical content came easily. Ivan played a range of different characters who mock liberals,

Westerners, pacifists, and homosexuals: "Grandpa, am I gay? / No, grandson, you're a dick!" goes the refrain of one his early tunes. Ivan imagines a dialogue between a homosexual grandson—"The girls don't want me ... I guess I must have a different orientation / I'm different because of my rear entrance"—and his good, Russian grandpa: "There's no rainbow in your arsehole." The piece gained thousands of plays across YouTube, VK, and Telegram. Young Russians found the crudity hysterical.

After scoring a couple such viral hits, Ivan was approached by producers at the Tsargrad TV channel to host a weekly show. Kondakov used his platform to launch racist attacks against Ukraine, the Black community, the United States, and what he terms the hypocritical, clownish liberal "fighters for justice" that make up the political opposition. Ivan's TV show was canceled when Tsargrad switched to a web streaming format, but the budding singer had made contacts galore. He's been widely interviewed since, featured on several state-run TV channels, and wined and dined by politicians.

Ivan runs YouTube, TikTok, and Telegram channels with thousands of subscribers and millions of views. When shared by Telegram influencers like the journalist Yury Podolyak, individual videos can rack up more than 1.5m views. He's particularly proud, he tells me, that some of his poems have even been cited on *60 Minutes*, the nightly rage-fest that masquerades as political discussion on the Rossiya-1 channel. Indeed, Ivan's so busy that he spends one day a week in Moscow just doing media work while juggling his aerospace work and childcare responsibilities. He seems rather surprised by all his success, struggling—like many viral stars—to describe quite how fast it's all happened for him.

For the boy from poverty-stricken 1990s Arkhangelsk, this is a deeply personal project. Performing online defends the world that has offered Ivan untold opportunities. And for Ivan's many fans, the singer provides yet more language and themes to share, quote, and quip when "traitors" raise their heads above the parapet on social media.

Here, then, is a very ordinary kind of fascist: Ivan is still young, he's a digital native, and he borrows liberally from the state's language of conspiracy, hate, religion, and war to expound his theories of the world to a willing audience. He doesn't care about money or fame, and nobody is forcing him to produce this material. But he also doesn't care about the violence wrought on the excluded and the othered as a result of his work. The Runet is today packed with men like Ivan, feeding the social media ecosphere with extreme content that's promoted by the state and finds its way into young Russians' social media feeds. Thus off they go, like Nikita, to fight for the motherland—on the internet and off it.

The most extreme of voices had wandered into the center of Russia's political discourse. And that meant celebrating even the most extreme individuals as valuable contributors. After Crimea, Ivan Katanaev, the Spartak Moscow supporter and self-professed fascist who had taken part in racist and homophobic actions in the late 2000s, began to pop up in the media again.

Katanaev had, he claims, undergone a spiritual rebirth and embraced an extreme nationalist form of Orthodoxy. He had joined a new "civil religious" organization, Sorok Sorokov, which was founded in 2013. The organization claimed its mission was to construct churches in Russia and provide humanitarian aid to Donbas. In reality, it was a front for a racist, anti-Islamic, and anti-Ukrainian violence: "Russia cannot exist without Orthodoxy," explained the founder, Andrey Kormukhin, while commenting on the threat of Islam; "We are fighting for *our* motherland."[36] Katanaev had replaced the chaos of the football stadium's extreme racism with a state and Church-approved equivalent.

In a 2015 interview with Spartakworld, a Spartak Moscow fan site, Katanaev—still just thirty-one years old—declared that:

> We need a revolution. People in *Novorossiya* ["New Russia," comprising Eastern Ukraine] are fighting and dying for their faith and for their country. … When they get back to Siberia, the Far East, Samara, Bashkiria, Moscow, will they want to live in the kind of society [liberals and gays] are creating? No. … The only way to stop them is the Russian Orthodox Church.

This was a rallying cry to join movements like Sorok Sorokov, to battle Ukrainians online and in person, and to drive liberals and homosexuals out of Russian society. Indeed, in a subsequent interview for one of the biggest sports sites in Russia, Katanaev ratcheted up the xenophobia to an even greater degree: "Ukrainians are just Russians who've become like cattle."[37]

As the Ukraine conflict unfolded, Katanaev used a LiveJournal blog to make his worldview even clearer. He declared himself a proud Russian nationalist, announced that it was only "under Russia's wing" that other nationalities could flourish, and suggested that a vibrant Russia would edge out "the old lady of Europe" in a moral and spiritual conflict sparked by events in Ukraine. Turning out to an anti-war counter-protest, Katanaev labelled the opposition "f****ts," "freaks," and "traitors"—the "unclean" were to be swept away by war.[38]

Katanaev was no longer some isolated figure, whipping up uncontrollable hate from the touchlines of society. He and the football hooligans he now encouraged to join the "revolution" found common cause with a state building a cult of war. And the state welcomed young men like Katanaev with open arms, giving platforms and clout to their "humanitarian" work in Donbas, and inviting them onto television stations and to media interviews.

Hailed as role models—young, Orthodox, white, and openly fascistic—Katanaev and his peers found themselves center stage in Russian culture.

The split generation

Back in Nizhny Tagil, Alina turned ten the year that Putin returned to the presidency. She doesn't remember the rippling pluralism of the 2000s. The language she uses to describe the world is drawn from a much narrower group of state-approved sources.

In school, she learned all about Russia's heroic military past and its historical responsibility to save the world from the threats that seemed always to be arrowing their way toward the country. She and her parents would settle in for evenings on the couch flicking from *Game of Thrones* and Russia's *The Voice* over to *The Male/The Female*. News and politics shows buzzed away in the background of family dinners.

Like many of her peers, she got her first smartphone when she was barely into puberty (albeit Alina, thanks to her father's healthy income, laid her hands on the latest iPhone and not a flimsy Chinese Android device). She joined Instagram and VK. She followed the hot influencers and celebrities. She had music by everyone from Drake to Timati on repeat. She saw her classmates joining the Youth Army. Her family didn't participate, but she heard all about the Immortal Regiment on Victory Day. Clicking, commenting, sharing, her idols and her peers brought the world of nationalism, glimmering and flashing past at a thousand posts an hour, into Alina's mind.

The world of Kremlin politics seemed miles away. But everywhere, reified and repeated over and again, the culture of extremism was being embedded into Russia's youth culture in an identical way. And Russia's extremism might have been violent, warlike, but its vision of battle promised wholeness and harmony—even if that meant smashing apart the non-Russian elements in society.

For those who wished to immerse themselves in this welcoming language, the spectacle of the fascist rally was accessible at any time and from any place. From Arkhangelsk province, Irina could log onto Victory Volunteers events. In Saratov, Nikita could bond with friends at a Youth Army parade or summer camp. In Moscow, Vladislav could watch war movies and share his Victory Day photos online, and Ivan Kondakov could gather a legion of online followers with songs of hatred and violence.

Indistinguishable in form from the flood of Western shows, reality TV, and Hollywood movies that filled the schedules, the state's "Frankenstein" nationality offered up waves of opportunity to be included, to be whole, to be on the side of the good and the righteous.

Young Russians—from idols like Katanaev to peers like Vladislav and Nikita—could use the state's raw materials to transform themselves into "ideal" Russians. Those on the outside found that no language, no dress, and no culture could possibly allow them to be homosexual and Russian, to be an ethnic minority and Russian, or to be a pacifist and Russian. The categories were as irreconcilable as Putin had made them in his 2012 election victory speech: this was a country of *us* and *them*, separated by a whirling and contradictory mass of images and symbols constantly on display on television, in film, and online.

In reality, the endemically corrupt and deeply incompetent Russian state didn't have the knowledge, capacity, or will to live up to its own ambition to reshape the inner lives of the nation's youth.[39] The sell was only made harder as Russia failed to emerge from its post-Crimea economic funk. A dwindling and disenchanted middle class—and plenty of young, patriotic Russians like Egor Polyakov—were fed up.[40]

The state's cultural producers were often wrong-footed. YouTubers and online reviewers tore into the more absurd government cinematic productions with blistering and sardonic comments. One disenchanted Moscow resident who described himself to me as a genuine patriot grew tired of the state's productions. The state's newest war movies? "A load of shit. Not worth the watch. All those *Tanks* [a 2018 state-funded movie about the World War II-era T-34 tank], and that Zoya film where they fight for the Icon. Good God, it's all *nonsense*."[41]

Sometimes the state's efforts were too much even for a dyed-in-the-wool Putinist like Ivan Kondakov. When Timati released an absurd song to support Moscow Mayor Sergey Sobyanin's re-election (the piece hails a consumerist Moscow led by Sobyanin free of "gay parades"), the video gathered a record 1.4m dislikes on YouTube. Ivan derides the song as a piece of craven advertising: "A couple of shout outs for the mayor is one thing, but this is so blatant. No idea what the performers were thinking, and the people that paid for it must be idiots. But *state* idiots!"

Egor Polyakov blames the creaking, top-down hierarchy of the state for these failures. He was poached for a job at the state-run news agency TASS in 2017. TASS, remembers Egor, "had such an archaic method of working. The website was old fashioned and barely used; they hired me to work on it. It gained in popularity quickly." But stellar results meant nothing for the government's "PR agency," as Egor calls it, which was "so giant it couldn't comprehend anything at all."

Frustrated by this behemothic organ, Egor found himself at odds with his bosses. He spent weeks working on a story about civil rights lawyers supporting NGOs and protestors, two of the state's most abhorred *bêtes noires*. His editors canned the article and grilled him about his motives: "I was made to feel ... as if I was an opposition activist working on the inside." Egor jumped before he was pushed. TASS didn't care that Egor had done sterling work on its website. He rocked the boat, so he had to go. All the while, the political opposition throughout the late 2010s ran rings around the state with savvy online campaigns.[42] As Anna Veduta puts it, the state's media managers "have no idea how the internet works, or what makes things popular."

The state couldn't be lightning quick and incisive like the opposition. But when it came to reaching young people, it had two weapons they did not: the sheer firepower to fund production after production and to hire influencer after influencer; and, worse, the brutal iron rods of the Russian legal and legislative systems. The "censorship of noise" and the censorship of the courts were powerful arms indeed.[43]

Opposition leaders came under attack. Navalny was charged with further trumped-up crimes and assaulted, first with acid then almost fatally with Novichok. Boris Nemtsov was murdered in 2015. Activists like Anna Veduta and Alla Chikinda found themselves and their allies facing increased violence. The state was not just turning a blind eye to homophobic, racist violence carried out by militia-like mobs and vigilantes.[44] Its police and its hired heavies were carrying it out more than ever before.

The state went on the offensive online too. It seized control of VK in 2014. Then, when it failed to ban Telegram in 2018—a project too technically complex for the flailing administration—the state simply co-opted the platform by establishing its own channels and flooding opposition channels with bots and trolls. In 2017, LiveJournal blogs with more than 3,000 daily readers were classified as "media outlets" and could no longer be written anonymously, forcing LGBTQ activists afraid of attacks or being charged as "propagandists" away from the platform. Media were subjected to ever more arbitrary harassment. Increasing numbers of journalists were forced into exile abroad.

And the state made it ever harder to access information from abroad—in 2017, it banned the virtual private networks (VPNs) that Russians were using to circumvent website bans.[45] Finally, in 2019, a "sovereign internet" law was introduced. Russians would be "protected" from foreign content. The state would surveil and control every part of the internet, restricting access to thousands of sites it deemed "extremist"—which, in practice, could mean anything.[46]

The state was winning. Military draft dodging declined by 66 percent between 2012 and 2019. Young men attracted by above-average salaries and fired up by raging, nationalist language signed up to work as contract soldiers. Schools, television screens, and internet portals were full of the language of patriotism, war, and religion. Neo-Nazis, Christian fundamentalists, communists, and Soviet nostalgists were linked in overlapping bubbles of reality. They might have had their differences, but each bubble was charged with violent hatred for enemies real and imagined at home and abroad, and adults in each bubble were actively shaping their young around a new vision of national militarism and religion.

In Nizhny Tagil, Alina soaked it all in. By 2022, this nineteen-year-old could draw on a whole Frankenstein toolkit of conspiracies, symbols, memes, and objects of hate. She knew how bad the 1990s had been. She knew how much her peers enjoyed the Youth Army. She knew how valuable the Immortal Regiment was. She knew the West was to be treated with suspicion.

She knew that the invasion of Ukraine could mean a new and better, a *Russian*, world. A world worth sacrificing everything for.

5

FASCISM UNLEASHED

As daylight recedes on 30 September 2022, Red Square comes alive. Thousands of people have packed the cobbled square, stretching from the Kremlin's wall, snaking around Lenin's mausoleum, and reaching out to the stores and shopping malls beyond. Hundreds of identical flags wave in unison. A vast stage and television screens cut off the twisting onion domes of Saint Basil's Cathedral from view.

The state is marketing its latest additions to Russia: the four illegally occupied territories of Donetsk, Kherson, Luhansk, and Zaporizhzhia. The stars are wheeled out one by one. Girls from Donbas mime the words to a trashy backing track: "Glory to my motherland!" A teenage girl from Luhansk appears, draped in a camouflage jacket, to read a poem. A round "Z" sticker sits above the national flag on her chest. The waving flags are stilled in reverence as the actor Ivan Okhlobystin, once the star of Russia's version of the sitcom *Scrubs* and a former Orthodox priest, strides out from the wings: "This is not just a patriotic war. This is holy! This is a holy war!" he cries.

Colors. Symbols. Flags. Songs. Fun. Religion. Youth. War. The watchwords of the Putinist spectacle. The man himself has to follow. Out he comes. Putin addresses the crowd. "Take a giant breath and shout on my command": he leads the masses in three cheers for the troops' sacrifices, for Russia, and for the future. Young faces in the crowd beam with delight.

But behind the scenes, reality is collapsing in on Russia's military pride. February's plans to seize Kyiv rapidly crumbled. Midsummer's quagmire has turned to early fall's storm. The Ukrainian army is

117

advancing on all fronts. The invaders are humiliated. Videos of Russian troops with ramshackle equipment and rusty rifles surrendering to Kyiv's troops trickle into internet feeds. Thousands of the empire's troops lie dead on the battlefield. The president and his media acolytes rattle the nuclear saber, promising to wipe out Ukraine and Europe.

A disastrous attempt at mass recruitment—the absurdly titled "partial mobilization"—has seen chaos break out once more as hundreds of thousands of young Russian men have headed for the exit. Dragging hastily packed holdalls, they've made their way to traffic jams that snarl dozens of miles away from Russia's southern borders. Explosive demonstrations against the forced recruitment rocked regions hundreds and thousands of miles from Moscow before fading out again.

On the home front, the country is faring no better. Consumer goods, microchips, car parts, and aerospace components are in short supply. The dream of a booming new world order trading with China, India, and Central Asia withers as Putin's political peers shrug at the war and rub their hands at the economic barrel they have the Russian president bent over.[1] Once his juniors, now his masters, they're dictating the terms.

The state has hastily assured its citizens that everything is fine. Opinion polling suggests that only a small majority of the young were ever in favor of the conflict.[2] Support has gently ebbed away every time the latest disaster unfolds, even if a clear majority in every demographic still state their support for the war. Surely all but the most fanatically convicted young are fed up of this catastrophic military spectacle?

The deluded and the damned

Two days after Putin's Red Square rally, I log onto Vladislav's VK feed. He has just updated his profile photograph. Clad all in black, a bulletproof vest around his chest, his hair is wrapped up tight under a skull-and-crossbones bandana. On his chest, another skull: the military insignia of his unit. He poses next to an Orthodox cross in a ruined church's yard. Vlad is at the front.

Ever since the invasion began in February 2022, Vladislav's VK page has been flooded with conspiracies, lies, and calls to violence.

Scrolling backward, waves of videos and photos overwhelm the senses. Bodies, guns, armor, suffering, tears, the past and the present are wrapped up in the Russian national colors. Lashings of orange and black, the colors of Russia's memorial World War II ribbon, wash over the page.

A single theme surges repeatedly to the surface: children. Suffering children. Lost "Russian" children. Joyful "rescued" evacuees from Ukraine. Vladislav addresses the dead children of the World War II past. "Don't worry," he writes next to a photograph of doleful Soviet children captured in black-and-white as they awaited arrest by the German invader, "we're fixing it now!" World War II, the war to save the future, continues unabated. Russia has to save its young; the world's young.

I get in touch. After much debate—Vlad is busier than ever as he juggles work, study, and his social life—we set up a call. We exchange pleasantries, but I hold my breath.

I summon up the courage to broach the touchiest of topics: "Can you tell me about your support for the war?" Vlad's demeanor instantly changes. The smile melts away. His pixelated face fixes the video screen with a steely glare. Free-wheeling chatter gives way to a sermon.

"There is no war," Vlad declares. "The Russian people have been asked to support a special operation, and support it they do. Nobody will ever tell you they support the war. So you have to get that right." Nailing the terminology is as important as getting the facts right. Indeed, it turns out that the only way Vlad would—the only way he can—describe the ongoing war is through phrases and slogans that come directly from Kremlin propaganda.

But why, I wonder aloud, is the "special operation" so important? Vlad can barely conceal his disdain for those who don't support the war:

> Those who support the special operation are the people who can really, truly empathize with the suffering of people in the Donbass. You follow me? You have to understand they don't support any war; and they'd rather not even have a special operation. [The opposition] hope that everything can be controlled with diplomatic and economic measures, even though they know that *Russian* people are living in the Donbass, in Ukraine. It's a terrible thing.

So Russia is simply rushing to the defense of the vulnerable residents of its historical peripheries. As in 1941, Moscow has no choice but to defend "Russians" against a Nazi aggressor in a brutal conflict.[3] The religion of holy war has utterly captivated Vladislav.

Fixing the camera with a wide-eyed stare, his voice modulates upward as if imploring me to understand, to have faith too. "*Yen*"— even English-speaking Russians can never quite nail the sound of my name—"this is a genocide. We know what it's like to lose something. Twenty-five million people in the Great Patriotic War." *We* know, but *you* do not. As an outsider, Vlad believes that I can't possibly understand Russia's unique history or its lonely wartime present.

Vlad's voice drops into a measured whisper as he turns to the topic of NATO. NATO's soldiers, he confidently proclaims, are carrying out a "creeping occupation" of Russia by "grabbing a couple of centimeters here and a couple of centimeters there." NATO and Ukraine are entirely to blame—he continues his lengthy sermon— for the present conflict. The Ukrainians signed the Minsk peace agreements after 2014, he tells me, but "they didn't fulfill a single demand of the agreement. Not a single point! They just kept kicking Russia! For eight years there's been a war going on, and the Ukrainian armed forces have been continually on the attack. There was no way we could continue negotiating."[4]

Innocent Russia is just trying to protect "Russians" and keep the peace in Ukraine. Expansionist NATO and genocidal Ukraine ride roughshod over every agreement they make. Vlad tells me all of this without pausing for breath, winding himself up more and more as his tirade goes on.

Now he switches into a world of pure fantasy, fluently spinning out some of the more unhinged conspiracies the Kremlin has floated in recent months: Volodymyr Zelenskyy has been trying to obtain nuclear weapons; "The US and Ukrainians have biolaboratories there where they're doing all sorts of stuff."

He's picked all this up from the nationalist Telegram and VK channels that have exploded in popularity in recent months. Vladimir Solovyov's channel has grown exponentially, rocketing from 288,000 followers on the eve of war to 1.1m followers barely six weeks later. Leading frontline war correspondents have become stars overnight.[5] Dozens of new channels—many obviously amateur efforts—have been spawned.[6] Each channel constantly reposts other channels' content; a perfect circle to amplify propagandists' wild conspiracies.

Vladislav interrupts his lecture to quiz me: "What about the US–Ukraine agreement to deliver weapons to Ukraine? When was that signed?" He gives me a second to answer, then repeats the question, a teacher chiding a delinquent pupil: "*When was that signed?*" I'm not allowed to answer: "Google it! In the middle of January! That means they wanted war! And why did Ukraine call up 40,000 reservists on 23 February? Because they wanted war!"

Vlad cannot imagine that these stories, drawn from the state-aligned social media groups he frequents, might be misrepresented. It's impossible that Ukraine might have been calling up troops to counter the threat of the Russian forces massing on its borders. Inconceivable that Russia might be anything but the innocent victim in all of this.

Vlad is impervious to logic. "What about Bucha?" I ask. "A provocation!" Vlad launches into another series of comments on other supposedly staged events from Kosovo—a favorite *bête noire* of the Russian media—to Syria and Ukraine. We go around in circles as I, with increasing exasperation, try to gently challenge Vlad's misinterpretation of reality. But nothing I see is real. None of my evidence matters. Indeed, Vlad believes it's the Ukrainians—and me—who have had the wool pulled over our eyes by Kyiv's "very serious psychological operations against their own people."

On his VK page, Vlad continues this crusade against reality. He launches volleys of rhetorical fire against the "liberals" and "queers"—the young opposition who go to protest and "don't believe in Russia." When his Ukrainian distant family members and friends posted critical comments back in March, Vlad blew them off. Then he blocked them. There's no room for nuance in this world.

Vlad doesn't care about the weeds of international agreements, timelines, data, and rigorous analysis. His world is a fairy tale made of black-and-white opposites: happy and sad, attack and defense, safety and danger. But there is no happy ending in this fairy tale. In Vlad's world, history is always careening ever faster towards Russia's destruction.

That means the present and the future have to be defended in perpetual warfare. Such is Russia's lot. Russia has to act to save itself:

"We have a right to a buffer zone!"; "We have to save our—*Russian*—children." But above all, salvation lies in destruction. He tells me that there's only one way to end the war and to keep Russians safe: "Ukraine will be divided up into governorships—Malorossiya, Novorossiya, and so on" to be ruled from Moscow (Vlad uses nationalist terms that translate as "Little Russia" and "New Russia"). Ukraine is simply too dangerous to be allowed to exist. Instead, a new, greater Russia will reign over its historical territory.

And then, Vlad imagines, Russia will be powerful enough to counterbalance the nefarious United States. Russia's culture will flourish. Russia's children will be safe forever. This is a heady concoction for believers.

Vlad was determined to act. He decided to travel to the warzone as a military journalist. He would assist the state in its "information war." Always respected in Russian cultural history, today's journalists are every bit as much "veterans" as regular servicemen.[7] Vlad would become, he tells me, an Orthodox "information soldier" protecting the world from the threat of NATO and a nuclear-armed madman ruling over Kyiv.

In late summer, he put his beloved motorcycle up for sale on Avito, a popular auto-trading site. The state won't fund the travel of minor media functionaries to Donbas, so Vlad had taken it upon himself to get to the front. A few days later, he updated his profile photo to a selfie showing himself in military fatigues. Now, wielding his video camera, he is capturing the action from the front. No amount of setbacks will persuade him that Russia should back down.

There is no retreat when the existence of the Russian idea, the existence of Russia itself, is on the line. For young men like Vladislav, this is a cause worth dying for.

The great sacrifice

A cavernous studio is lit with bright, multicolored lights. Enormous TV screens filled with captivating bursts of color surround a stage. Hunching over into a microphone, Vladimir Solovyov almost whispers as he addresses a gathering of young Russians:

> We're the greatest country! Not because we're wealthier than everybody else. No! Not because our life expectancy is the highest.

No! We're the greatest country because we have the greatest destiny! We're standing firm and protecting the children the UkroNazis are killing with our bodies! We're fighting on the side of good. Your brothers and fathers are at the frontline. The aim of human life is not to go on living happily ... to buy a car or an apartment. You can only live when you know what you're prepared to die for.[8]

Solovyov's young audience is captivated by the zealous preacher creeping across the stage. Attendees at this "educational conference" organized by Znanie ("Knowledge")—just one of the dozens of state-sponsored NGOs and groups that have popped up to "educate" Russia's young in patriotism in the last few years—are learning to play their role in war.

Billboards have popped up around the country displaying the faces of the "heroes of victory" who are fighting and dying for the motherland in Ukraine. The all-pervasive "Z"; the orange and black of the George Cross; and splashes of red, white, and blue swathe the faces of young men in a patriotic miasma. The low-rent Photoshop work and shoddy print quality of these symbols, consigned to dusty roadsides in rotting provincial towns, may be banal simulacrums of exquisitely crafted Orthodox icons, but their function is identical. They remind the viewer that there can be no greater act than to imitate the martyred saviors of the state's political religion.

The state is telling its people, and above all its young, that Russia's mission in Ukraine is messianic. Only through a supreme act of destruction can the world be saved, no matter how much sacrifice it entails. A new world order, a better future, is to arise from Russia's collapsing economy, from the ashes of obliterated Ukraine, and from the graves of Russian troops at the front. This is "constructive destruction" in action.

The spiritual message of death and rebirth the state is preaching has become indistinguishable from the language of religion. While Solovyov preaches on the stages of educational conferences and TV shows, Putin plays the role of secular priest in this state evangelism. The "high commander," as he has been styled recently, preaches sermons on myth and war to the nation's young. Speaking to graduating students at a military high school in June 2022, Putin declared that "Russia has always gone through trials ... Russia is now going through another time of trials." Gone is any hint of the language of Western retail politicians. Instead, the archaic and the biblical. Back in 2005, Putin claimed that the country had to suffer the pain of the 1990s to enjoy the "blossoming" of the 2000s. Now it suffers again in constant self-sacrifice.

In Russia's churches, believers gather to hear the same message of martyrdom from their priests. On 24 February, the first day of the war, Patriarch Kirill declared that "[v]alor and courage, courage and determination, ardent love for the fatherland and readiness for self-sacrifice—these qualities have distinguished our people for centuries, who have passed through the crucible of many trials and tempered their character and strength of spirit in them."[9] Russian servicemen in Ukraine, Kirill declared four months later, "are showing amazing examples of courage and self-sacrifice, and it all comes from their inner moral sense."[10] The Russian Orthodox soldier, full to the brim of state-religious morality, is ready for heroic self-sacrifice.

The day after the Kremlin announced its partial mobilization, Kirill once again took to the pulpit. His words echoed through the hall of Moscow's Cathedral of the Armed Forces, a new, state-funded behemoth decorated with scenes from Russia's glorious military past: "Christ was resurrected, and all shall be resurrected alongside him! Go bravely and fulfill your military duty! Know that if you die for your country, you shall be with God in His kingdom."[11] Endure sacrifice to save the nation; die in Putin's war to save your soul. The audience bowed their heads in reverential awe.

Russia in 2022 is awash with this language of destruction. Nightly talk shows feature politicians, journalists, and pundits out-competing each other to make the most outrageous statements: Zelenskyy is a Nazi; Russian can nuke Europe in 200 seconds; the United States is on the brink of collapse; Joe Biden has months to live, thanks to cancer; Russian troops will win the war any day now; Ukrainians are murdering Russian women and children.

State politicians and agencies openly plan and execute the destruction of any hint of the Ukrainian in captured territory. Signs of Ukrainian history and culture are being purged from schools, from billboards, from historical memorials, from festivals and holidays, from television, and from politics.[12] And, in Russia's next-door "brother nation," thousands of Ukrainians are being killed, their graves unearthed in discovery after gruesome discovery as Russia retreats.

Yet in destruction, young Russians like Vladislav see dynamism. In Ukrainian death, they see the rebirth of Russian life. And they applaud as, at home, the purifying destruction is wrought like never before. Putin addresses the nation, demanding that degenerate and queer Western culture is to be ruthlessly "spat out ... like an insect."[13] Putin has declared war on the "fifth column, the national traitors—those who make money here"—not just the wealthy but any opposition, since all opposition in the Kremlin's world must be funded by the West—"but live over there, and 'live' not in the geographical sense of the word but in their minds, in their servile mentality."

Comparing those who live in the West "in their minds" to anti-semites and Nazis, Putin reaches for the language of the Stalinist Purges to advocate for a "self-cleansing" of society of these opponents, these "scum and traitors." If the effort to remake Russian minds in 2012 was a battle, now it is a war.

And that war has been waged with a fearsome combination of erasure and violence. Traitors are being unearthed just about everywhere. The police and security forces are being purged of those accusing of holding *verboten* views. Teachers are being fired for making "errors" in their descriptions of the war. Beloved celebrities—everyone from young upstarts to national treasures like the singer Alla Pugacheva—are tarred as "foreign agents" to be destroyed, from the pulpit and the politician's desk alike. Teen lifestyle Instagrammers are charged under draconian laws that forbid "discrediting" the army; held up as examples of minds gone astray, they are pilloried as "scum" by angry social media users. One pundit proposed concentration camps for Russian opponents of the war.[14] The public search for Ukrainian saboteurs and spies in classrooms, on the streets, and in the mind reminds everybody, constantly: the enemy is within.

And the most threatening internal enemies are those who seek to create alternatives to the state's world of constant battle: writers, journalists, and opposition politicians. Journalists are arrested for reporting on civilian deaths in Ukraine, even if they don't blame

Russia.[15] Online personalities like the YouTuber Yury Dud, an idol for many young Russians, are accused of spreading "homosexual propaganda." Petr Ivanov, a member of the opposition Yabloko Party and an independent journalist, is severely beaten.[16] Navalny is thrown into solitary confinement for weeks on end. The state attacks with the courts and the police. Its vigilantes throw themselves into the fray. Naturally, attackers do not face justice. They are doing the purifying work the state demands.

Anton Barbashin, the young editor of the news site Riddle Russia and a man once accused of spying for the British government by Solovyov on television, tells me that things are more intense than they ever have been. Anybody minded to criticize the regime in even the slightest way has got the message: "Better pack your bags and go," says Barbashin. And for those that remain? "You never know—you might be the next one." The state is cleaning out the sty with the most extreme violence.

At the far end of the spectrum, the real fanatics believe they are waging a final, spiritual battle against the non-Russian. Tsargrad hosts Orthodox priests who compare the present to biblical prophecy: "If you resist and rebel, you will be devoured by the sword." Fringe figures with vast cult followings like Aleksandr Dugin take to social media to declare to their followers that the war is "a battle between Russia and the Antichrist."[17]

Plenty of the young are joining in with this apocalyptic circus. The Eurasian Youth Union, a group Dugin founded in the mid-2000s, has seen a surge in membership. It has staged pro-war rock concerts, historical conferences, and "homophobic picnics," covered to great acclaim in local media. The group, long moribund, seems bursting with life at the idea of the final war.

It received an even bigger boost when Dugin's daughter Darya, the photogenic hope of the country's most radical fascist block, was killed in a car bombing in August 2022. Dugina was rapidly turned into a saintly martyr by her young adherents. Dugina died, they claimed, in "a war in which we all, whether we like it or not, are taking part. There is no front and no rear … We are certain that Darya's martyrdom will not be in vain." At last, they claim, Russians will understand that "We are all in another Great Patriotic War!"[18]

The apocalyptic rhetoric is inflated to absurd levels. The state brandishes threats of nuclear war at the West, of nuclear attacks against Ukraine. Propagandists like Solovyov and Russia Today editor Margarita Simonyan matter-of-factly declare that nuclear war "is what it is. We will go to heaven, while they will kick the bucket!"[19] Eager tabloids christen the commander at the front "General Armageddon."[20] At the bottom of the pile, the believers are enraptured. The young millennial parents who follow Orthodox lifestyle influencers know what to believe: "The apocalypse is here, it will happen in 2024!"[21]

And the apocalypse—the greatest sacrifice of all—will purify Russia. Destroy Ukraine. Save Russia. Save every ethnic Russian child. Whether meeting ministers, the media, or groups of young children, Putin never misses an opportunity to remind his listener: the troops are sacrificing themselves to create a world in which smiling, happy children will have the right to call themselves Russian, to speak Russian, and to joyfully live in a world of exciting circuses, verdant forests, and glittering cities.[22] The state is sending its boys to die, but only to save their younger brothers and sisters. The "Nazis" in Kyiv and their puppet masters in the West won't have it any other way, so Russia risks everything to fight.

Creating the war of the young

Luzhniki Stadium, 18 March 2022. The eighth anniversary of Crimea's annexation. The precise spot where, ten years earlier, acolytes had rallied around banners proclaiming "We will defend our country" as they prepared to vote Putin into the Kremlin for a third term.

The stadium was packed with a heaving crowd. Thousands of supporters—some enthusiastic patriots, others "encouraged" to attend by employers or universities—had been bussed in. Opposition journalists were kept clear, and a heavy police presence ensured no trouble broke out.[23]

Out onto the stage stepped a group of young, white athletes clad in immaculate Team Russia tracksuits emblazoned with the letter "Z." The audience cheered as they recognized Olympic gymnast twin sisters Dina and Arina Averina and figure skaters Nikita Katsalapov, Viktoria Sinitsina, Evgenia Tarasova, and Vladimir Morozov. Glittering medals hanging around their necks, the athletes waved and smiled to the crowd. Behind them, a gigantic screen displaying the slogans "For a world without Nazism" and "For Russia." The perfect picture of patriotic youth.

Athletes were accompanied by musicians. Polina Gagarina, who had trolled Eurovision with her brash song of peace after the Crimea invasion, sashayed onto stage with a George Cross ribbon pinned to her chest. Her rendition of "Cuckoo," a piece by the Soviet rock rebel Viktor Tsoy rewritten as a nationalist anthem to soundtrack the 2015 World War II movie *The Battle for Sevastopol*, attracted the loudest cheer of the day. Gagarina's tune, all pent-up rage and threats of violence, was a defiant call of individual and national militarism—even if the rebel Tsoy had meant the song otherwise.

Then Oleg Gazmanov, an uncool but surprisingly spritely seventy-year-old crooner, bounded onto the stage to pump out fifteen minutes of patriotic *popsa* anthems: Gazmanov's hits "Forward, Russia!" and "Made in the USSR" summed up the nationalist mood. Accompanied by young troops in dress uniform, wearing their George Cross ribbons twisted into "Z" shapes, Gazmanov had the crowd enthusiastically singing along with his military-patriotic hits. Glittering, entrancing, and lively, Gagarina's and Gazmanov's performances wrapped the war up in a comforting blanket of familiar entertainment. Russia might have been invading its "brother nation" and making a great sacrifice, but it was all good fun.

When Russia Today's Margarita Simonyan appeared on stage, the audience were primed for a serious message. Simonyan sold them on the idea of national renewal—a "Russian summer":

> Eight years ago, Crimea returned to Russia. I have never experienced a feeling of such joyous pride as during that, the Russian spring. ... But spring cannot last forever. The Russian summer is coming. Mother Russia is going to the Donbas, which is right on its doorstep. Crimea has come home. For good. No ifs, no buts. And that's a marvelous thing.

Then, as always, the headliner: Vladimir Putin. The leader explained how "over these years, Russia has done a great deal to help Crimea and Sevastopol grow," then spoke on the importance of defending Donbas, where "a genocide" is being conducted against "ethnic Russians." Putin, forced to pause as technical difficulties interrupted, built to a climax: "At this point, I recall the words from the Holy Scripture: 'Greater love hath no man than this, that a man lay down his life for his friends.' And we are seeing how heroically our military are fighting during this operation." Military sacrifice was a spiritual, utopian mission.

The whole charade of youthful glitz, fun, and glamour of the Luzhniki performance had just been a prelude to these lines. To die for ethnic Russians was to renew the earthly world—to bring about the "Russian summer"—and to attain heavenly goals. The "fairy tale" Putin promised on his accession to the presidency at the turn of the millennium was now embedded in the language of fascistic, messianic war.

The Luzhniki concert broke the Runet. Pro-war social media channels—some run by the state, others by keen patriots—hummed with excitement. Excited group moderators shared dozens of live updates that attracted thousands of views and garnered hundreds of supportive comments. Users were over the moon about the large turnout, inflating the figure apparently of their own accord so that over 120,000 had supposedly attended.[24] In reality, Luzhniki's capacity is 81,000, and the record attendance for any event was just over 100,000, at a Soviet-era football game. But the unreality of the story didn't bother Russians eager to bathe in the splendor of what they perceived as a great communal enterprise: "It's like something out of a fairy tale!"

The Luzhniki concert was a Nashi march on a phenomenal scale, broadcast around the country, and tailor made to be cut up and shared widely on social media—a chaotic but eye-catching Nuremberg Rally for an online world. Clips, pictures, and videos snaked their way through Russians' feeds. Not least of all, the young pictures of athletic perfection that had appeared on stage shared behind-the-scenes clips on their feeds: the Averina twins alone have over 600,000 followers on Instagram, where they share photos of themselves, their family life, and their sporting endeavors.

If Ukraine was a war about youth, then it was also a war *by* youth, a youth ready to make sacrifices to create heavenly, utopian Russia from the ruins of war. The "fairy tale" marched onward. And, fueled by social media communities, plenty marched to meet it.

* * *

Ever since the Luzhniki concert, the state has been trying to conduct its cacophonous orchestra of tropes, memes, motifs, and cadences to sell the story of the war in Ukraine as a war for Russia's youthful future.

The nation saw plenty more big performances in the summer of 2022. A run of concerts around the country tried to capture the magic of Luzhniki, but the Z-list stars on parade in remote Barnaul and Krasnoyarsk had nothing like the appeal of Gagarina, Gazmanov, Simonyan, and Putin.[25] The punters stayed at home, preferring to watch TV and browse social media than hear forgotten bands whose last hits had come in the 1990s and 2000s.

Victory Day 2022 was, in terms of the Red Square parade at least, a subdued affair. But the government used the day to gee up the population with more performances of national strength, faith, and messianism, projecting the essence of World War II onto today's war. In his Red Square speech, Putin delivered another religious sermon: "The defense of the motherland has always been holy," he insisted, and claimed that remembering the dead would keep them "forever young." He reserved special praise for Russians' dedication to their "faith." It could have been faith in victory, in nationalism, in Russian messianism, or in Orthodoxy. Whatever it was, the Orthodox priests watching from behind Putin's tribune applauded and nodded sagely. After all, any level of destruction could be justified if it kept Russia and its sacrifices "forever young."

The Russian media landscape is punctuated by lavish spectacles like Victory Day and Luzhniki, but not a day on state-sponsored social media or TV goes by without a new story about the young. Ukrainians are shelling or shooting children. Young faces fill eyes and ears with tears and screams. Soldiers clad in balaclavas and face masks pose for publicity snaps next to smiling, blonde Ukrainian children. The children have been "rescued" from the "Nazi bastards" who use women, children, and newborns as human shields.[26] Correspondents lay flowers at the "Alley of Angels," a memorial to Donetsk's dead children constructed in 2015. A cycle of destruction, rescue, and resurrection is constantly re-staged; little matter that it's the Russians who provoked all this suffering and could end it by leaving Ukraine.

State TV viewers were confronted with the constantly teary face of Yuliya Baranovskaya, the presenter of *The Male / The Female*, in a

series of specials aired in April 2022. In one episode, Baranovskaya
visits children "voluntarily" evacuated from Donetsk to a seaside
resort in Russia. "See for yourself the emotions on the children's
faces," implores Baranovskaya. See the emotion. Wallow in it.
Know that it's more real than asking difficult questions about facts
or causality.

Her voice cracking, Baranovskaya introduces interviews with the
child "refugees." Thirteen-year-old Ivan comments, "Ukrainian soldiers ... aren't, well, the nicest people. They don't like children."
Fifteen-year-old Sofia tells the story of how her school was bombed,
putatively by Ukrainian forces, on 25 February: "There were bodies
lying in the offices." Twelve-year-old Inessa describes her father,
who is fighting in Donetsk, as "a hero." The children cry too. As
they speak, the screen spews out images of destroyed buildings and
bloodied corpses.

"Every day the children try to call their parents. As they dial the
number, their hearts freeze. They don't know whether anyone will
pick up." Baranovskaya struggles to speak as saccharine music soars
over the footage. The joyful children, in matching uniforms and
chanting Soviet-era Pioneer tunes, laugh and smile. Thank God for
Russia, the savior of children.

Russian audiences are gripped by these viral stories.[27] Each atrocity is accompanied by melodramatic outpourings of public, social
media grief that rapidly spin into calls for extreme retribution: "God
protect you now, my children!"; "What a tragedy. [Prayer emoji]
God save you!"; "We don't need to beat an enemy like this. We have
to KILL them! Guys, don't spare the prisoners." Calls to save children descend into a rhetoric of extreme violence and aggression that
justifies—at least in the posters' minds—a war with no limits.

Just like the rhetoric around "homosexual propaganda" and liberal values in 2012, and the myths of 1990s suffering and 2000s
regeneration, today's propaganda obsesses over the fate of children.
No image of the future is more powerful than that of the child:
messages about the plight of "Russian" children in Donbas have
proven far more resonant with ordinary Russians than those about
abstract goals like "denazification."[28] Creating a new world where
Russia's children are safe justifies everything. It breaks down all
moral limits. It demands the total purification of society from every

possible enemy. It demands the purification of the self. And it demands the destruction of the Other, the anti-Russian: Ukraine.

None of it makes sense. The bloviated propaganda of performance and ritual has been elevated to the realms of the absurd.[29] But to the faithful, it all makes perfect sense. As they sink deeper into the fast-paced world of fairy-tale war, many are struggling to tell what's real and what's not—and many don't seem to mind. They are the supporters who, like Vladislav, have leapt to Russia's "defense" by joining up or by fighting online.

The world of war enthusiasm

The invasion was the moment that Ivan Kondakov had long been waiting for. The time when, finally, the state would stop pandering to the people attacking it from outside and deal with the "traitors" within its own borders. In the first week of the war, he plastered a large red "Z" over his VK profile photograph. Peering through the partially transparent letter at his face and beyond, onto his page's feed, it's hard to find much of Ivan left.

But he's eager to chat. It's a chance to spread the gospel of war. When I ask him about the nature of the war, Ivan repeats everything Vladislav and the state have already told us a hundred times over. Ukrainians hate everything Russian, but Ivan doesn't blame them. They are, he tells me, "cult members" who've been brainwashed by "American psychologists ... who've done them over 100 percent professionally." And, of course, he is sure that the war will bring about a new world: Russia "is fighting not just against Ukraine but against the whole of the West for a new world order. We're working so that Russia can—*will*—be one of the centers of world civilization again!"

He might not be volunteering for the front, but Ivan's doing what he can for the war effort by going into a virtual battle with Ukrainians, liberals, and homosexuals. He's releasing new music, self-penned poetry recitals, and TikTok-style vox pop sermons. "I'm no soldier," he tells me, "but at least I can do this." And plenty agree that his work is an important part of the war. The extreme nationalist vlogger Mikhail Onufrienko recently described Kondakov as "an instrument of information war."[30] Even if he's not risking life and limb to stymie a Ukrainian advance, Ivan is a soldier defending the world of unreality he and his peers have constructed.

He's been extraordinarily productive in recent months. His wartime works attack the gamut of Russia's enemies. Kondakov's number one target is Ukrainians. Russia, he tells his audience, loves the infantile Ukrainians. Europe will abandon them at the first whiff of trouble.[31] But Ivan speaks of Ukrainians with hatred, not love. Much of his opprobrium is leveled at Zelenskyy, whom he attacks in antisemitic doggerel as "y*d-like." In one poem uploaded to his social feeds, Ivan lays into Ukrainian refugees. "Summer, croissants, and Schengen are all they want!" he spits into the wobbling smartphone frame; Ukrainians are just money-grabbing conmen whose dreams will come to naught when the West grows tired of helping them.

But Ivan isn't satisfied with attacking Ukrainians. He's taking part in the state's mission to purify Russian society. In his world, internal enemies are everywhere. Whether they're queer—"sodomites" are Nazis who commit "crimes against humanity"—or liberal, they're all undermining the war effort.

It didn't take Ivan even a fortnight after the invasion to cook up "Pacifistution," a three-minute pop song that attacks liberal Russians who oppose the war as stupid, selfie-loving, and shallow traitors who get everything from Russia but still dream of going to live in depraved London. Kondakov thrashes out a guitar backing, crooning into the camera from the same leather office chair he occupies when we talk: "Paci-paci-pacifistution, we think we're against the war but we're really against the country!"

His 10,000 YouTube subscribers rushed to applaud Kondakov's efforts: "This is going straight in the dictionary!"; "Brilliant! The truth and nothing but the truth!"; "These pacifists are everywhere, even in the civil service." Shared and liked thousands of times, off Kondakov's melodies march to the information front.

Kondakov isn't just performing for a niche audience of Telegram users and YouTube viewers. He has a weekly slot on a Moscow radio station and pops up on state TV channels. A local Orthodox radio station has funded full video clips for his works. His social content is shared by right-wing channels with large followings.[32] He premiered a new piece about the coming Russocentric age, "The Time of Z,"[33] for the hacking-cum-troll group Cyber Front Z, a

Kremlin-sponsored factory launched in 2022 to coordinate attacks against anybody perceived to have slighted the war effort. Ivan was even invited to speak about his "information work" with young people at an educational conference in Volgograd.

One of his poems was even read out by Aleksey Zhuravlev—a hawkish former communist who in February appeared at a PR event in military uniform to declare that "all of Ukraine will be Russian" and attracted global attention when he claimed that Russia's nukes could wipe out Europe in 200 seconds in April 2022—on *60 Minutes*, the state's flagship nightly ragefest-cum-news-discussion show. Ivan is delighted: "Really serious people are listening to me. I get recognized on the street, in elevators, and all over the place!"

It's almost sad to have heard Ivan describe his own journey from childhood poverty to youthful success in cosmopolitan Moscow and, now, onto the most extreme form of Russian nationalism. He's a witty speaker, a talented songwriter, and has real charisma. Yet his language and worldview is so morally objectionable that it is hard to find any common ground at all.

There are plenty more young Russians hoping to follow in Ivan's footsteps.[34] A wave of young artists, singers, and poets are enjoying moments of stardom as they launch their works into the constellation of nationalist groups on the Runet, hoping that something from their personal social media page will go viral. And, when state media operatives amplify these young creatives' work, the war effort is flooded with youthful energy.

Yura is a fourteen-year-old from the Russian provinces. For the last couple of years, he's run an Instagram account for his amateur art. He uploads his surprisingly competent drawings and paintings: characters from HBO dramas; the logo of his favorite football team, CSKA Moscow; scenes from the popular online game *World of Tanks*. First line drawings, then slightly wobbly watercolors.

Yura's growth as an artist is all there. Over time, the colors are hardened, the shades are refined, and the images are clarified. Increasing numbers of patriotic scenes—Soviet soldiers, Russian troops—have crept into Yura's stream. Today, his feed is packed with "Z" art: Russian troops saving kittens at the front, wielding guns and Russian flags, and meeting Soviet troops in Ukraine; battlefield scenes from the war in Ukraine; and portraits of battle-scarred, masculine troops. Each invocation of the troops recalls, in Yura's gauche way, Soviet-era Socialist Realist art, which depicted heroized soldiers at war with the state's enemies, and Russian Orthodox icons, which provide believers with models for spiritual reflection and daily imitation.[35]

The copypasta language Yura slaps into the art's captions only reinforces the sense that this young man's artistry is based on imitation, not originality: "Strength in unity!"; "Unlike the UkroNazis with their fantasy 'Ghost of Kiev' we've got real heroes.[36] Our cause is just. We will win!" His artistic world channels the language of the state.

Just like any teen artist, YouTuber, or TikTok amateur, Yura simply wants to fit in. Imitating the twenty-something and thirty-something role models who are making a career out of nationalistic creativity—men like Ivan Kondakov—is a great way to do so. But Yura's adolescent yearning to belong is founded in apocalyptic fantasies of destruction and Russian triumph. He's been bowled over by high praise from nationalist accounts, and even reached the final of a patriotic art competition run by a pro-Russian news channel's Telegram account. Yura has found warmth, praise, and respect in Russia's pro-war community.

"Vindemiatrix"—the artist won't reveal her real name—is just eighteen but has become one of the most widely shared war artists on nationalist Telegram channels. Hers is a more refined artistic talent and palette than Yura's: she allows color to drift around her frames, leading the eye through dreamy fantasy landscapes. Red blood spatters across screaming skulls. Surgeons, surrounded by streaking black marker lines, tend to a child's foot. Russian troops, paint and line fraying at the edges, complete lonely marches across vast swathes of white space. Silken "Z" letters wrap their way around unarmed soldiers clasping children to their chest.

Photographed in elegant, Instagramesque, minimalist settings, next to cutesy jars of flowers and white cups of coffee, Vindemiatrix's work is made playful, appealing, and clean. Yet it is every bit as warlike as the state's most extreme propaganda. In mid-June, for instance, Vindemiatrix published an elegant line drawing of a young boy dressed in a beret and camouflage uniform. Delicate red and white watercolor accents set off the drawing with the national colors. Alongside the photographed drawing, the artist has deli-cately arranged a Russian flag arm patch, some wildflowers, a beret, a dog tag, a military backpack, and a George Cross ribbon. In the accompanying description, she includes a brief poem that suggests children might join the Spetsnaz, the Russian army's special forces:[37]

> I know the Spetsnaz will enlist them,
> Those, the young, better than us,
> And with no fear of change or darkness,
> Pass our names to our grandchildren.

The image seems familiar, harmless. But it transforms the child into a patriotic soldier of the present and the future. Only through military service will "our names"—a Soviet-era poetic synonym for memory of the sacrifice of World War II—be preserved in Russia's messianic history. Sending the next generation into battle to die for the cause is essential. Young Russians like Yura and Vindemiatrix are cutting up and reimagining the government's stock language and visual forms. The war in 2022 is being absorbed into youth culture; its extremism laundered through social media culture. And the people driving this phenomenon are young volunteers, not the state's hardened propagandists.

Occasionally, the state's media workers pluck talented young-sters from the online crowd, thrusting them into the spotlight as the faces of war. Akim Apachev, born in Mariupol, gained prominence as a frontline "war correspondent," sharing his impressions of the fighting—simple reiterations of state propaganda claims—to his social media accounts. In June 2022, Apachev released a duet with an unknown singer, the twenty-three-year-old Darya Frei, puta-tively another Ukrainian.

Sung entirely in Ukrainian, Apachev and Frei's song hymns the war as a religious conflict that is creating a new world. "In Azovstal"—the steel-production plant where heavy Ukrainian resis-tance was only ended after several weeks' intense bombardment and a nightmarish siege—"they're burying demons / The Mother of God is birthing a child," sings Frei. In the video, Frei wanders the apocalyptic destruction left behind in Azovstal. Wearing a virginal white shift and wrapped in the national flag, the ethereal young singer seems to embody the spirit of a young Mother Russia. In place of destroyed Azov stands an embodiment of fragile mother-hood. In place of Ukrainian stories of reality stand Russian fantasies of rebirth. A myth of fascist erasure. Indeed, Apachev didn't disguise his intentions: "Ukrainian is our trophy. We're taking this language for ourselves."[38]

Yet social media fascism picks up and drops its stars just as quickly as viral stars come and go anywhere else. A second song, "Us," though promoted through state channels, didn't have the same public appeal. Apachev and Frei receded from public view as fast as they had arrived. However, their work is available in perpetuity. Shared by media personalities and on everything from traditional Orthodox Christian VK groups to absurdist internet culture communities and nationalist Telegram channels with no oversight from the state, images and songs by amateur artists are thrown into the public sphere.[39]

The real action selling the war to the young isn't taking place on state media. It's online. Across Russian social media and in Russian cities, Russians have been playing out their own performances of war support. They share photos that combine the heroes of the present and past wars, hand-drawn memes that depict the "ghosts" of World War II fighting in today's Ukraine, videos of troops singing tsarist-era religious songs set to juxtaposed images of the past and present, and dressing up in period costume to imagine themselves as the participants in a war that took place eighty years ago.[40] They share songs by men like Kondakov. They like sumptuous, appealing artworks by Vindemiatrix. They admire Yura's youthful efforts. And they applaud their brave sons, like Vladislav, who speak of World War II so positively and even volunteer for the front.

With each like, with each comment, with each share, the fascist idea is restated and renewed: war is inexorable and essential. Each time a clip or a meme flies through a social media feed, the war's supporters find strength, community, wholeness. Fed by destruction, their world is being endlessly constructed and it is becoming ever more indistinct from the reality: Russia's military is failing in Ukraine.

The momentum is irresistible. Drip by drip, the fantasy grows even as it crashes into reality. Young Russians don't need to be as far gone as Vladislav, Alina, or Kondakov to understand why the sacrifices of today's war matter.

God is with us

When we connect, twenty-three-year-old computer specialist Kostya has been hanging out at the family *dacha*, a beloved site of languorous childhood summers, on the outskirts of Moscow. An intense, whip-smart young professional, Kostya has raced up the career ladder since graduating a couple of years ago. He's already a project manager for a team of DevOps engineers working on a big Android app. Kostya lives to work: "The devil makes work for idle hands," he smiles.

Kostya is a real believer in Russia: "I love my country. I was brought up to love my motherland. The state acts to defend you, on your behalf, and in the interests of the people. They do things for the greater good." Like Vladislav, he views the Ukraine war in simple binaries: "Russia, home" is the place he wants to be, and everywhere else is something to be feared. Indeed, he's only ever traveled outside of Russia once, as a teenager on a trip to Germany.

Kostya says he's not fit for military service, but he's considering going to work for the state despite the low salary compared with the private sector. And if he gets a real call-up? "They won't take me because of my health. But I'll offer to do what I can." Like Kondakov, he believes that war work doesn't just have to mean firing a gun at the front.

And as for why the war is happening? "I'm still not entirely sure, but I'm confident that it's the right thing and that things will become much clearer in the future." Kostya has total faith in the leadership: "The idea that [the war] is without grounds or is mad is impossible. I read a group of military experts and economists whom I trust and cut through the rumors. They provide their own hypotheses." He buys into the state media machine not because he can understand its dubious reasoning but because it provides calm and direction when everyday life in wartime seems to be rudderless.

He's not worried about the war's impact on his industry. "Big companies, especially those that provide services to European companies, have had to lay off staff. But, do you understand,"—among my interviewees, "do you understand" almost always segues into a piece of conspiratorial government propaganda—"Russia's IT industry is big and strong! You've got Google, we've got Yandex. You've got Facebook, we've got VK. Google Cloud has problems?

There's somewhere else to go. There's a solution to all the issues!" Kostya reiterates some of the bolder claims made in the media by politicians and pundits. It's no big deal that things look bleak today. The motherland has an alternative for everything. Give it time and a homegrown industry will spring up to replace everything that's being lost.

"Soon," Kostya assures me,

> we won't be following examples from America anymore as we have done in the past. We used to try and follow the same path as Europe and compare ourselves to Europe. People followed American trends and wanted to move to America. They dreamed of it. But that phenomenon is going to become noticeably weaker.

Kostya barely has to think about what he's saying. He talks, like Vladislav, at increasing speed, rattling off a checklist of Putin's nationalist talking points about national self-sufficiency:

> People will soon start looking to different countries and cultures. The state will push Russian culture to the fore. People will learn more about their own history. Right now there's a phenomenon where the young generation know bits and pieces about the history of France, England, and America better than about the history of Russia. That's cool right now, but it's not good.

Kostya tells me that soon, Russia will produce steel, computers, microchips—everything it needs, just as it did "during the Soviet times—"and if not, we can buy from China. It's good that we have that option. But China has its own interests." He finishes his speech: "We can become more and more independent. We can use what we have at our disposal: culture, technology, industry."

Kostya's hardly naive: "Will this be hard? Will it require a drop in living standards for now? Yes. But we'll come out the other side. We can't do it all in a day." Kostya is ready to accept huge changes in his day-to-day life in order to return to the Soviet style of "self-sufficiency" and to build a new world that is less American and more Russian. The Ukraine war is an act of destruction necessary to realize the long-promised, mythical national fantasy.

"We're Russians, so God is with us." The constant refrain heard everywhere online. Russia *has* to win, because it always does. Divine providence makes it so. Egor Polyakov, who was working for the popular news site Lenta—which, like almost every news source in Russia, is effectively under state control—when the war broke out, elaborates. He and his fellow journalists observed that Russians "believe the propaganda narratives about [Russian] greatness and the return of a mythical past. [They think] the whole world envies us, 'We have so much land, so many resources!'."

Flocking toward patriotic, Orthodox, and militarized online communities, many in today's Russia are not just passively absorbing the government's propaganda. They are actively seeking it out and, through creative efforts that span the amateur to the professional, imitating the state's great performance of military strength and national vitality at every opportunity. And despite the reality on the ground in Ukraine and on the home front, there's no sign they're any less sure of Russia's messianic destiny. They're just waiting for Ukraine to crack. For Russia to launch the real war. For the moment when Russian destiny leads them to victory.

"I look at the TV propaganda and it's just absurd. It's mad. It starts crazy and then veers off into the world of the absurd. But it works. [My young colleagues] believe it all." Nikolay, a civil servant from the provinces, tells me that today's new civil servants—the Egor Polyakovs of 2022, highly educated and looking for a place to exercise their talents—aren't budding Decembrist revolutionaries. They're yes-men who want to emulate idols like Olga Zanko. His young colleagues, laments Nikolay, "don't know how to do anything but shout 'hurrah!' the loudest."

Nikolay is no liberal. He's long been involved in organizing World War II remembrance events. But even he is seeing a change: "Adult, intelligent people believe it. People like that live in a world of formulaic propaganda. They believe the whole circus, and they're terrified of coming across alternate facts, because that would mean the destruction of their little world." In their world of propaganda creations—of barriers erected, a world where empirical reality can be rejected in favor of waves of lies—there is nothing but the government's language, symbolism, and ideals.

* * *

Fifteen years ago, the Russian wing of the British neo-Nazi group Combat 18 published a rallying cry to its followers, its latest tantrum about the perceived threat of ethnic minorities living in Russia:

> Our Native Land, Russia, is living through the most troubled period in its modern history. Every day pain, death, and chaos are wrought on Russian homes and families. Every day the enemy, which has rooted itself in OUR State, is pulling the noose around the Russian People's neck tighter. The enemy has gone mad from hatred for everything Russian.[41]

The "Russian nation," claimed the authors, are forgetting "the history of Great Russia"—its "victories and triumphs." Hope, they supposed, lived on in "our Russian youth," over whom "nobody will EVER emerge victorious." Theirs is the Russia of "freedom and justice," of "Ilya Muromets, Dmitry Donskoy, Evpaty Kolovrat, Suvorov, Kutuzov"—a list of mythical-historical national heroes, all later listed in the Valdai Club's 2014 report on rebuilding Russian national identity. In their racist screed, Combat 18 create an image of a Russia under attack from all sides, at home and abroad. Only a generation of historically literate and warlike young patriots could save it.

A few football hooligans and neo-Nazis may have believed in it, and the state may have hyped up those groups to intimidate the opposition, but this was fringe stuff in 2007. Nobody in the Kremlin spoke this way, and young Russians weren't being pumped full of such extreme language.

But in 2022, Combat 18's declaration is inseparable from the language of the state. Aryan families proclaim their love for the motherland. Manliness is indistinguishable from martial imagery and, in turn, from patriotism. Images from the tsarist and Soviet imperial pasts are dovetailed with fantasy visions of messianic, apocalyptic futures. The enemies of the state are distorted, diseased, vermin, *nelyudi*—unhumans. But hope lies in the young generation. The smiling children of the motherland welcome war and destruction as conflict ushers in a Russian utopia.

This is the language of plenty of young Russians, from hipster patriots like Vladislav to online personalities like Ivan Kondakov and artists like Yura. And today, Russia's talking heads aren't backing away from this rhetoric. They are calling for more, better, "ideological propaganda" to prop up their motherland's genocidal urgings.[42]

The neo-Nazis of the 2000s and 2010s are along for the ride. Since his trips to Donbas in 2015, Ivan Katanaev has reinvented himself as a tech-friendly sports-marketing guru. Katanaev, not yet forty, posts pictures of himself speaking at a government-sponsored conference at the Luzhniki Stadium and doles out advice on how to make it in the industry. Alongside selfies dressed in snappy suits, hip glasses, and relaxed sports clothes, he boasts of an idyllic life of luxury travel and self-realization.

But alongside this idealized version of hip entrepreneurship are frightening justifications of war tinged with the language of biblical apocalypse and Russian exceptionalism. Russia, he says on his social media channels, "should fight to the last Ukrainian." The country's "time has not yet come … after the collapse of the USSR, we wasted two decades just to remain a sovereign nation." He compares the events of 2022 to Moses leading the Jews through the desert: "Forty years weren't just spent looking for the path forward but on the regeneration of the people." When Putin tells children that Russia is enduring a "time of trials," he is speaking the language of the Orthodox neo-fascist ultra.

Katanaev tells his followers that "there's going to be a new generation. With a new consciousness. I absolutely believe it." War, Katanaev believes, will cast out "American war movies," McDonald's, and "all this liberal garbage—BLM, LGB"—the adoption of which has been "a great example of how to fuck everything up all by yourself."

There are many more model, macho young Russians. Like Katanaev, they have tempered the rage of youth into militant, nationalist Orthodoxy. They mix hip, Silicon Valley cool, native-soil entrepreneurship, and a public disdain for anything not Russian. Simultaneously, many advocate destruction, genocide, and apocalyptic war as a means to purify the nation and create the future.

And Katanaev is not alone. Indeed, who is fighting Putin's war in Ukraine? Not the urban millennial middle classes, who turn away from committing real destruction and try to avoid being conscripted. The Russian army is riddled with young neo-Nazis.[43] Mercenary groups open their arms to fascist regalia and the behavior of the death cult. They promote hatred on the internet, spreading gleeful tales of destruction in Telegram and VK groups. And, as they receive the approval of at least some of the online masses, it is these young men the state is turning into saintly martyrs.

This is the Russia of 2022: a place where fascistic destruction and regeneration are ordinary, a place where fascist language and symbolism run rampant, and a place where it can be cool to be a fascist—even if the locals call themselves "anti-fascists." And the "anti-fascists" are willing on the war at home too. They cheer as the state seeks out the enemies in their homes, their schools, and their online communities. They howl with delight as the state chokes the opposition of air and words.

Purify harder, wage more war, don't give in, scream the military preachers: God is guiding us to fight "absolute evil," and "God needs Russia."[44]

6

THE UNMEANING OF PROTEST

On 24 February, Lera, a twenty-two-year-old music teacher from Moscow, awoke as dawn's light was beginning to creep between the neighboring Soviet-era apartment blocks and through her bedroom window. Like most millennials, a bleary-eyed Lera always reaches for her phone before getting out of bed. What she found on 24 February left her stupefied. Trying to thumb through her social media feeds, Lera was frozen: "It felt like they would issue a correction to the news. They would announce that the opposite was true. It had to be." Lera was stunned. She knew exactly what the invasion would mean for Russia.

Lera slipped out of the sardine-can apartment she shares with two other young teachers, but the clogged air of Moscow's busy streets didn't help. "For the whole of the first week, the first month, I had a constant headache. I couldn't think. It was terrible. Tragic."

A native of Vladivostok who had moved to Moscow four years earlier for college, Lera was torn by indecision: "I didn't know what to do. Resign and get a ticket to go abroad? Leave all my Telegram channels, wipe my phone? Stock up on iodine in case of a nuclear war? Fly home to my parents? What would be worse: emigration or staying here?" The pro-war crowd, full of ideas, goals, and missions, were invigorated. Lera wasn't so certain what to do.

On the first night, Lera headed straight from work to downtown Moscow to protest. The "vegetarian times" were over, but she was ready to risk a beating from the police to make her voice heard. But what she found wasn't anything like the tales of the rambunctious, exuberant protest movement of the early 2010s that inspired her anti-Putin stance (she's a big fan of Navalny). The group she stumbled into was rudderless:

There weren't many protestors. There were no organizers like I guess there had been with Navalny's protests. I didn't know exactly where or when the protest would be, and there was a lot of conflicting information. I just followed the crowd out of the right metro exits. But people were all spread out.

"The police were very aggressive," Lera tells me. She shows me video recorded on her phone of a group of police officers throwing a young woman to the ground so violently that her head smashes into the pavement. The police wander off, sated. Lera casts her eyes downward, blinking back a tear. Fragmented, leaderless, and facing arrest and extreme violence, the protests died out quickly. Lera didn't dare return for a second night on the streets. Paralyzed, she has been standing still ever since.

When I ask men like Vladislav or Ivan Kondakov to describe the war, they launch into untrammeled rants driven by wild conspiracies. They have all the slogans they need to explain exactly what's happening and why it matters. Whenever unexpected news breaks, they can just return to their comforting world of harmony and national power, sharing the latest conspiracy meme to get some quick likes and communal affirmation.

Lera can talk eloquently about her profession, her side hustle as a photographer—teachers in Russia are atrociously paid, so many seek extra work to make ends meet—her hobby of stand-up comedy, and even her ethnic background. The latter's a particularly difficult topic given that she is part of Russia's long-oppressed Korean minority. But Lera can barely speak of the war at all.

When I ask her about protests today, Lera's eyes dart around the room as if checking nobody is watching. She pauses. Her eyes drift downward. Her answer trails off into nothingness: "People … people … well … they're staring down the barrel of jail time." She almost fails to utter the sentence, even though it reiterates a talking point that has been voiced on government propaganda platforms countless times in the months since the new laws were introduced.

Moments of silence carve through Lera's life, casting dark shadows between her and the warmth of the collective. The situation in her school has become difficult. "Every school I know of"— she has spoken to her teacher peers in other institutions—"has received a questionnaire from the state asking about staff members who were born in Ukraine. I don't know what it's for, but they've gathered the data. They haven't done anything with it yet. But for now ... for now ... direct pressure ..." Thinking through the ramifications of the survey, Lera loses her words. Finally, she confides her worry: that she, as a Korean, may too have to be logged as a form of "non-Russian."

Lera has learned to shut up. Not to participate. Not to draw attention to herself. Not to speak to her friends about her anti-government beliefs. She doesn't post anything questionable online. She and a handful of anti-war colleagues adopt the same approach at school:

> We try to keep quiet, not say anything, and not pay attention to anything that doesn't directly affect musical education. So we don't volunteer to participate in any children's military concerts and all that sort of stuff. It would be more dangerous to do that sort of thing for the school and its staff ... if we want the staff and school to keep working. There might be inspections. None of us wants any attention from official bodies.

It wasn't always this way. Lera discovered the opposition when she moved from Vladivostok to Moscow in 2018: "It was like an awakening. Everything's going on in Moscow. It was just like ... *wow!*" For the first time after a childhood spent learning to suppress her ethnic origins through rote learning of Russianness in school history and civics classes, she felt connected to the possibility that there might be alternative ways of being.

"I started hanging out with some new friends who were students," she remembers. "Some of them were very firm opponents of Russia's politics. When I was surrounded by those sorts of people, I learned the names of people like Ilya Yashin and Ekaterina Schulmann, and I signed up for a whole lot of Telegram channels."

Lera only joined this community by chance. A world of nods and winks drew her—when she was already willing—into a world of alternative discourse. And she was willing not because she was determined to become a rebel, but because she had grown up in diverse social spaces—the Korean, the Russian, Vladivostok, Moscow, and so on—that exposed her to different voices, identities, and political narratives. The government's world of memes, soundbites, and slogans are, to Lera, completely impenetrable and illogical. She shares none of them, mocks them when she sees them, and blocks those who upload or use them. It would be easy to mistake Lera's new silence for a learned apathy. But she is not apathetic. She simply lacks the community and the language to express her frustration.

Many of Lera's peers are brimming over with anger at a government they see as increasingly distant, stagnant, and bereft of ideas. Anton was just twenty-one years old and still living with his parents in Novgorod when the 2014 invasion of Crimea and Eastern Ukraine brought his plans for a big career as an engineer crashing down.

Anton's father, an engineering professor and ravenous reader of global literature, was an old-school Russian intellectual. As a boy, Anton would listen with eager ears to his father's friends discussing politics and culture over tea and vodka. He wanted nothing more than to be like his dad. He enrolled in an engineering program, scored top grades, and was all ready for a career in construction.

But Anton's hopes of a high-flying career in engineering collapsed along with the economy. When he graduated in the summer of 2014, just as the post-Crimea economic consequences were beginning to be felt in Russia, Anton found that there weren't that many good opportunities to use his engineering skills in a recessive economy. The best he could do was spend the next two years running errands for his mother's business.

Did a young man like Anton support the invasion of Crimea? "Of course," he says, "I was—I am—a patriot." He gives me the state's soundbite without a second's hesitation: "I thought it was the right thing to do, that they needed protection. People in Crimea wanted to join Russia." Anton might claim to be uninterested in the state's ideals, but he still learned to speak its language fluently. Crimea was the right thing to do. Anton would just have to be more like his mother, a self-starter who'd made it on her own in the early 2000s.

He worked exhausting shifts, studied online to gain extra qualifications, and constantly hustled to make ends meet. Anton, despite his intellectual credentials, believed that Crimea was a mission worth sacrificing his personal success for.

By February 2022, Anton had just settled into a job as a car salesman. His role was simple: to trawl classified sites looking to cut deals with private car sellers then shift the vehicles at a heavy mark-up for an auto dealership, taking a commission for himself. Then, the war came.

Anton's spitting with rage. Inflation and supply shortages caused by the war—Russia's car sales have slumped by over 80 percent year-on-year—have destroyed his new career: "Everything's got three or four times more expensive. We have huge problems. We might be able to get new cars. Maybe. But we'd have to bring them through Kazakhstan or Vladivostok. There are no spare parts. What cost 2,000 rubles last month is 12,000 today. It's impossible." Unlike Lera, he has no problem expressing his anger. He throws up devil horns with his hands, rocks his head, and roars some lines inspired by nu-metal group Lumen: "I love my country so much, but I hate the state!"

Now he's looking back at everything that's happened in the last eight years: "I didn't think too hard about things back then. I didn't think 2014 was a breaking point. But what's happening now is only because they said that Ukraine would attack us or NATO would establish bases on our borders. And that seems pretty strange." But Anton hasn't expressed his concerns to anyone bar his fiancée and, anonymously, to me. And he certainly won't dare to take to the streets: "Nobody wants to protest, because nobody wants a truncheon to the head."

The internal "fight" that Ilya Fedotov-Fedorov described as the state waged war on queer Russians in the mid-2010s has spread to every young Russian who questions or opposes the war. They find themselves trapped in a perpetual war not just with the state's heavies but with the imagined specter of a state that might be present everywhere, ready to seek out and annihilate non-conformism.

The opposition is stagnating. They have no language in common with the Putinists. And when they do say something, their words are blown apart by the nationalists' barrage of irony, performance, and spectacle.

So they choose: abandon politics and stay silent; flee the country, an un-Russian "traitor"; or engage in an absurd game of protest with a regime that pulls all the strings.[1] The war might not be overwhelmingly popular, but finding a place to nurture alternatives to the state's harmonious military vision has become near impossible. What looks like political disengagement is a fragmentation of meaning carefully cultivated by the state.[2]

Fleeing the regime, finding the voice

For many, the exit door is more tempting than ever. Some estimated that 300,000 Russians, most of them young, had left the country by the end of summer.[3] When Putin announced the "partial mobilization" of military-aged men at the end of September, hundreds of thousands more young men made for the exit. The well-off residents of Moscow and St Petersburg who had passports, money, and family connections weren't going to sacrifice themselves for a holy war—even if the state easily found the number of bodies it needed to fill gaps at the front by trawling the provinces for poorer or more conservative recruits.

The exodus has been headed by the country's coolest singers and musicians, who are using their profiles to raise money for Ukraine and refugees by touring abroad.[4] Ordinary Russians, however, head for ex-Soviet countries with lax visa regimes where there are already substantial Russian-speaking enclaves—Georgia, Armenia, and Kazakhstan—or holiday destinations with cheap living, like Turkey and Thailand. Many with Jewish heritage are seeking Israeli passports.[5] Young IT developers find they can work remotely, while others look for work in hospitality, real estate, or anything else that turns up. A handful of brave Russians have even decamped to Ukraine, where they are assisting with humanitarian aid and fighting against their homeland.[6]

But others are finding that leaving is less a luxury and more of a necessity as the state steps up its war on the non-Russian.

* * *

Alla Chikinda sighs. "In the past year and a half," she laments, "things have deteriorated. The pressure is stronger. [Lots of] activists and organizations have been included on the foreign agents list." As a result, they are forbidden from working with children. Those children, forced into a psychological confrontation with a hostile state and culture, need help like never before. Alla tells me that she's seeing more of the same comments every day: "I'm afraid to leave my home. I'm afraid to walk hand in hand with my boyfriend because I might get attacked. I'm afraid to wear a rainbow badge on my jacket because I might get beaten for it." Fear is more ingrained than ever.

The campaign to "purify" Russia of LGBTQ "perversion" is speeding up.

A new law against all "homosexual propaganda" was passed by the Duma in November 2022. Russians are bombarded with daily viral stories about Western "depravity": trans activists target children, pride parades "indoctrinate" the young. Every revelation, from discussion of war to material on schools, is accompanied by outrageously homophobic comments by state politicians and media presenters. "Pedophiles," "pederasts," and "f****ts" are everywhere, and they're coming for Russia's kids.

And it's become ever more difficult to speak out. Some LGBTQ support networks have fallen silent in the wake of the war's outbreak.[7] The state has used its legal powers to close queer-aligned organizations, offering bizarre justifications that twist logic into unrecognizable shapes. In one judgment, the charity Sphere was shuttered because it "engages in political, not charitable, activities … every part of Sphere's work is aimed at altering laws" around traditional marriage "supported by the majority of the citizens of the Russian Federation."[8] Organizations that might be tainted as "foreign agents" or closed down as "political" shutter themselves away or hide in the shadows, afraid to speak out or even tacitly offer support to young, traumatized Russians.

Long forced to fight himself inside, Ilya Fedotov-Fedorov had had enough. He could no longer tolerate the legions of curators and gallery owners who stymied his work. Over and again, he heard the same: "It's too provocative for us; it's too much; we're not that modern." Message received. Even the most abstract allusions to queer issues were now unacceptable, and few would risk their own necks to show Ilya's work.

Summer 2021, and Ilya managed to land a show at the hip Anna Nova gallery in downtown St Petersburg. His delicate reflections on medicine and nature—blue cells on canvases, delicate hanging sculptures, stark medical machinery—spilled and wove their way through the gallery's white rooms. As cell turned to human, animal to machine, Ilya constructed an allegory for transgender transformations. This was an unashamedly queer space, right in the heart of Putin's beloved hometown.

But, Ilya explains, the state fought back. The gallery's owner sent out a PR release to the throngs of media that had usually been keen to cover Ilya's exhibits when he was showing in Moscow's Tretyakov and riding high abroad. What appeared in the press simply rewrote Ilya's reality: "The text ... was about me, then something about butterflies, then half of the text was about trans people and my friend. Ninety-nine percent of them excluded the part about the trans people." He sighs, "even the liberal media, the *opposition* media, did it. I think it was only Snob, which is edited by a gay activist, that didn't."

The media had simply obliterated that element of Ilya's work, stripping him of the power of self-expression. Indeed, at Ilya's gallery opening, the state put the frighteners on in person. "A woman, a state journalist, came up to me." Irate, angry, she jabbed her fingers and demanded, "'Ilya, aren't you scared to do this kind of topic? I have some questions for you.'" Ilya didn't want to speak. He tried to walk away.

The journalist marched after him, demanding answers about the West and Europe. None of this had anything to do with his exhibition. He was being drawn into saying something foolish, controversial, or perhaps, given the homosexual propaganda laws, illegal.

Ilya spotted the ruse straight off the bat: "I knew she was pushing me to say that the West supports my art and the gay/trans/queer topic, but that Russia doesn't. She pushed me. I gave a vague answer, saying 'I have different issues in Russia and the West,' but it was scary." Ilya was intimidated into silence.[9] The exchange stuck in his mind. He felt the state's eyes boring into his neck.

"It's not that I want to be political, but they make me political," he laments. Ilya's existence as a young queer man is inherently political. The aggression of the state media, self-censorship even of the independent media—while it existed—pressure from the online crowd, and internal self-censorship of the artist creates a vacuum. Instead of creativity, dynamism, multifaceted polyphony, young artists are forced into a simple choice: stay silent or collaborate with a state that that can twist whatever words and ideas they do produce.

When war broke out in 2022, Ilya knew that life had become impossible. Controversial works about transgender issues and those like his *Centaur*, a piece about Soviet troops engaged in rape and animal abuse that Ilya had planned to exhibit close to Victory Day in Moscow, would no longer fly: "I felt the horror of war. I was trapped." He had heard of prominent LGBTQ Russians sent to jail on trumped-up charges. He knew that, as a gay man, no matter what he produced it would be deemed "propaganda." He didn't want to leave his family. He didn't want to sever his fragile connections to his community. But he had to leave.

With the help of artist friends, Ilya applied for an emergency visa to travel to the United States under a special program for artists of outstanding ability. Within weeks, he had left Moscow for good. Today, Ilya is living in New York. In between crashing his bicycle, figuring out the unwritten rules of American laundromats, and furnishing an otherwise empty Manhattan apartment, he's finding his feet and re-finding his voice. Standing outside the closed world of the state's homophobic circus, he can find new ways of being.

But it's not so easy for those without connections or language abilities. Lera may be able to obtain a residence permit in Korea thanks to her family ties. Like most other ethnic Koreans in Russia, though, she has been assimilated into Russian society. She speaks no Korean. Going to her ancestral home would mean abandoning her career and, of course, her parents and elderly grandparents. However, going abroad might mean shedding a performance of Russianness she feels she has been forced to make: "If I do manage to go abroad, I'm glad I can pass as an Asian. I am an Asian." She has, against her will, been recast by the state. She has been made a traitor. A non-Russian. Only by rejecting Russia entirely and becoming Asian can she find a way to speak again.

A voice, a battle, a flight

The queer and the marginalized are silent or on the run. The street protests Lera attended in downtown Moscow have spluttered out. The skirmishes that broke out in the wake of the mobilization announcement in Russia's republics have been extinguished by brutish police and local heavies. But the Russian art of youth protest isn't quite dead yet.

When I get in touch with Armen Aramyan, he and his girlfriend are settling into sparse digs in Berlin. He loves his new home—"Moscow was so busy and cramped and nobody cares about anybody"—even if he did just spend the night in hospital testing out his German-language skills after falling from an e-scooter and breaking his arm. He laughs the incident away. He'll be fine.

It barely seems possible that Armen has just been on a helter-skelter ride to escape Russia unnoticed. Mere months earlier, he was on the brink of losing his sanity, made paranoid and depressive by the state's judicial torture machinery.

Armen's background reads like a carbon copy of Egor Polyakov's. He grew up in a single-parent family in Moscow. Bullied in school because he was an Armenian immigrant—back in the early 2010s, ethnic bullying was rife even in liberal Moscow's schools—Armen was nevertheless a top student. He spent his evenings reading and surfing the net, where he loved the forum Dvach, a Russian and even more nihilistic version of the American 4chan where everyone and everything is fair game for mockery. Armen followed in Egor Polyakov's footsteps to enter the Higher School of Economics.

However, he always felt like an imposter at the university, where he studied philosophy. Lots of those around him only wanted to be there to get the name on their CV, but Armen cared about his studies and about the student community.

One afternoon in a local cafe in 2017, he and his fellow students hit on the idea of founding a magazine to bring together students in their department. "We wanted to do something even if we didn't quite know what," they agreed. But when Armen pushed his peers to do something more radical than a lifestyle magazine—"where to drink lattes on campus!" he jokes—most of the team jumped ship. Even these liberal students didn't risk rocking the boat in the way that Armen imagined.

Doxa was the product of Armen and his team's hard work. The magazine's coverage was brave. Its writers discussed corruption and student rallies, motivations for those attending Victory Day parades, and—their undoing—events at pro-democracy rallies in 2019. First their focus was on the Higher School of Economics and Moscow, but they soon expanded to Russia as a whole. This was dangerous, challenging content.

Swaddled in the language of Western anti-patriarchy and feminism,[10] Doxa couldn't have been better designed to get the state's hackles up. First, the university administration distanced itself from the publication. Warnings poured in from the state's proxies. Then, the state's media watchdog, Roskomnadzor, demanded it remove videos about pro-Navalny demonstrators in Moscow. Armen and his co-editors grasped that "things were going wrong. We were paranoid. I wasn't really scared, but I was trying to switch off my emotions. I became very cautious."

Then the security forces came knocking. In April 2021, Armen remembers, the police burst into the magazine's offices. Smashing their way through files, computers, and furniture, they made Armen feel "completely vulnerable. There was nothing I could do. But I knew it wasn't death. It was just police violence, and at least I would live through it." Armen tried to resist: "They demanded the pin code for my phone, but I wouldn't give it to them. They threatened me, saying all kinds of stuff about jail sentences. They got really angry and pushed me. It was almost absurd."

Days later, Armen and his co-editors—Natalya Tyshkevich, Alla Gutnikova, and Vladimir Metyolkin—were arrested. They were, the state claimed, encouraging minors to behave in illegal activities. The same old story, then: the enemies of Russia are those who speak the language of the West, who offer alternative narratives of the world, who tempt the young down immoral avenues. The state knows best. The state's language is right.

Armen was placed under house arrest and banned from using the internet. Cut off from society and stripped of his ability to speak, he fell into depression. But the worst thing, he tells me, was not the detention: "It was this abstract, bureaucratic stupidity. I couldn't get out." He was trapped in a topsy turvy world in which the regime could transform meaning and logic at will. Soon he figured out that he could sneakily use the internet and, with a bit of DIY hacking, even fool his ankle tag so that he could leave home. Yet the state had planted an idea in his head: he was "constantly calculating what I could and could not do. I could go onto the street. I was free but not free. I was afraid somebody was looking." The state was made up of "stupid bureaucrats. Bureaucrats with guns." But the damage was done. His mental health nosedived.

The case suddenly came to court in April 2022. It had nothing to do with the war, but making an example of some young free-thinkers would be the perfect accompaniment to the wider crackdown on journalism and the enemy within. In Russia's judicial system, almost every accused criminal is found guilty. Armen was no exception. He and his co-defendants got off lightly. Under a two-year "corrective labor" sentence, they would be free to live in their own homes but would have to pay a portion of their income to the state as punishment.

Armen knew that in the absurd world of Russian justice, he was not safe. Worse, he thought, "they might try to use us as kind of hostages against the rest of Doxa's team. If we stayed, there would be new prosecutions and Doxa would be silenced." He and his girl-friend applied for foreign passports. Their request was denied, so they hatched a different plan. They would go to Armenia, which required only a Russian internal ID.

The journey was simple. Nobody stopped them traveling. They were not followed from Moscow. No FSB operatives halted them for interrogation at the border. Armen was a recently convicted criminal, an enemy of the state whose case had received domestic coverage, but the regime barely cared that he'd left.

The state had already staged its spectacle and acquired photo-graphs and a script showing a court stamping out the voice of a student publication. The purpose of the whole affair was to inflict silence, not punishment. Armen enraged the judge in his case by attempting to make an anti-war speech from the dock. Not a word of this was, of course, reported in the state media. Meanwhile, inside, Armen was beset by doubt and paranoia. Russia was "cleansed" of his presence.

Three months later, the German Embassy in Yerevan produced temporary travel documents for both Armen and his girlfriend. They were free. Above all, Armen is free to continue waging his war against the absurd world of the Russian state from abroad. And he's doing it where it matters. By targeting young Russians online, he and his team are creating tiny bubbles of opposition.

Doxa soldiers on online. In recent work, writers have asked why Central Asian students still come to Moscow to study despite the Ukraine war and their racist treatment; covered the state's new patriotic educational projects; and interviewed the expat artist Nika Dubrovskaya, who implies Russia is a "fascist state." The magazine publishes an anti-war newsletter and spreads real news about current affairs on its Telegram channel.

There are plenty more creative youngsters finding ways to counter the torrent of pro-war content that's flooding TV screens and social media feeds. Some have looked to their Belarusian neighbors for inspiration. Two years before Russia's Ukraine invasion, Belarus was consumed with protests after the incumbent president, Aleksandr Lukashenka, rigged the election against his challenger, Sviatlana Tsikhanouskaya. Since Belarusian security forces became increasingly violent—torturing and even killing opposition members—protestors cannily used social media, symbolism, fake adverts, and QR codes to display their messages. In Russia, social media-savvy protestors have created adverts for "IKEA Sales!" and, responding to a perceived supply shortage, "Sugar for 50 rubles!" Users who follow the attached QR codes find themselves directed to anti-war sites and opposition media outlets based outside of Russia.

On the streets, individual protestors have launched actions designed to catch the eye on social media. Female protestors dressed in virginal white—ironically mirroring the costume worn by Darya Frei in her pro-war video—cover themselves in fake blood and wield anti-war signs in prominent public places. Young Russians arrive on Red Square bearing placards inscribed with asterisks in place of the words "no to war" and even blank placards.[11] The protestors are dragged away by gangs of uniformed police officers.

Meanwhile, although the state's "foreign agents" are obliged to send regular reports to the state on their activities, its bureaucratic forms are so empty of purpose that they can be remade. The artist Darya Apakhonchich rendered her report absurd. Ignoring the state's questionnaire on her activities, she scrawled over the page with doodles and handwritten missives that attacked the war: "The inhabitants of Ukraine live in ordinary houses. They go to work. They bring up their children. Why is the Russian army bombing them?"[12] Rather than rewriting herself according to the state's slogans and models, Apakhonchich simply rejects its power over language out of hand.[13]

These young creatives are rendering the state's control over language and image absurd—making the state itself appear fragmentary, even surreal. Visions of young Russian protestors, layered in Instagram filters, counteract the state's spectacular performances on Red Square and the pro-war crowd's homegrown art and music. The protests make law enforcement look absurdly heavy-handed as they engage in a battle against blank signs and cartoonish scribblings. The state's power is momentarily diminished as social feeds are interrupted by alternatives to the mass online rally.

Yet if they are to prove effective, these protests need an audience ready to at least consider the message. For the pro-war audience, the feminist, liberal, and pro-democracy content created by protesting Russian youth is evidence that these young Russians have sold out to the perverse West. They are just purveyors of what Ivan Kondakov would call "pacifistution." Indeed, Kondakov's Telegram posts reach on average four times as many Russians as those of Doxa. This is an uphill battle.

The authorities aren't disoriented by these playful, chaotic protests. They make their arrests and carry out their violence. When reality doesn't suit the state, it simply rewrites it. Some young protestors are sent to psychological hospitals—echoing the response to anti-government protests in the Soviet era, when dissidents who protested the 1968 invasion of Czechoslovakia on Red Square landed up in psychiatric wards.[14] Others are dragged into trials where judges berate them, prosecutors read out absurd charges, and impossible claims are proven. One lawyer working on behalf of a young queer protestor described the system's absurdity to me:

> I tried to give something of a character reference by using screenshots from the defendant's Instagram feed. The judge said, "Instagram is deemed an extremist organization on the territory of the Russian Federation." I answered, "Yes, Meta ..." The judge interrupted, "Huh? You want to use evidence from an extremist organization?" I explained, "Yes, it's not forbidden to use it." The judge: "But it's extremist! What do you think you're doing?!"

Defendants are powerless as the state reinvents the meaning of language on the fly. And the watching crowd bays for more blood. The protestors are as bad as the Ukrainians. Destroy them all. Save the country's future.

Enter Egor Polyakov, fed-up with his state media bosses, to attempt to use the state's own arsenal against it. Perhaps he could still become the Decembrist revolutionary he'd long ago dreamed of being.

A grand performance of protest

Now working as an economics reporter for the major news site Lenta, for years Egor adopted the same tactic of passivity that Lera plans to follow: keep your head down, play the role everybody expects of you, don't cause trouble. Nothing in his back catalogue of reports on the financial ripples caused by Gazprom's trade wars with Ukraine and Russia's corrupt diamond trade indicated his growing disillusionment.

But inside, Egor was frustrated by the callous indifference of his bosses, increasing censorship, and the total stagnation of a state he had once believed might be capable of change. In 2021, he explains—just as for Ilya Fedotov-Fedorov—"things got a lot worse, quickly." The censorship hardened. The propaganda grew more absurd. Egor's rage against the corrupt "Frankenstein" state hardened.

The invasion of Ukraine in 2022 broke Egor. Fueled by the opposition channels he was quietly reading and the news from abroad that he easily followed thanks to his impeccable English, he explains with as much verve as the pro-war zealots: "Anyone with any common sense would say, 'If you've got so much land and so many resources, why the fuck would you need somebody else's?!' The masks were off. Everything became so singular in meaning. There was no sense looking inside myself for any more justifications." From the inside of the propaganda machine, this hopeful young man could see that the veneer of "Russia's rebirth" as justification for the war was wafer thin.[15] Egor didn't believe a jot of the fascist propaganda the regime was churning out.

But Egor didn't just plan to quit his job or quietly slink out of the country. He hatched a plan for a spectacular, propaganda-sabotaging protest. "I knew I wanted to do something at the start of March. I began to make plans and think through how to make them a reality."

Egor quietly recruited a colleague, Aleksandra Miroshnikova, to assist. They set to work cooking up an elaborate plan to sabotage their employer, Lenta, and to humiliate the state. They picked a date: Victory Day, that most holy of days.

"We exhausted ourselves in the days beforehand. We were doing our day jobs. We worked and worked, then after work, we worked on our project. On 8 May we worked late into the night. I only slept a couple of hours."

Fatigued, afraid for his safety, and nervous about the consequences, Egor was ready.

Waking up early on 9 May, Egor was crippled with nerves as the moment approached. "The whole day I was crazy stressed. My hands were shaking. I couldn't eat a thing—even though I usually eat like a horse." Egor was already on his way out of the country. He swapped SIM cards several times and kept on the move to evade law enforcement.

By mid-morning, the hour of the grand protest had arrived. He gulped. His hands shook. click. "It was so easy. I just logged in, did the job, and hit save."

One of the 20 million regular readers who happened to visit Lenta at that moment would have been astonished to discover not the usual screed of pro-war propaganda but a whole catalogue of articles exposing the government's lies, railing against Putin as a "pitiful, paranoid dictator" and attacking "the twenty-first-century's bloodiest war."[16] Headlines linked to detailed anti-government articles. Egor and his partner's sabotage wasn't just a hidden message floating through the social media flotsam and jetsam of the Runet. They had totally rewritten one of the country's biggest propaganda outlets. Egor briefly spoiled the state's great ritual celebration of militarism, mass sacrifice, and Russian messianism. He had seized the power of language away from the state.

The backlash was surprisingly slow: "Everyone was dining out on the president's speech and the [Red Square] parade. Then two of my bosses called to yell at me. I yelled back. Then the screenshots, the messages, and the calls began." They haven't stopped coming. Months after the event, Egor has barely a second to pause for thought as he has fielded calls from journalists all over the world and seen his effort discussed widely on opposition Telegram channels.

Not that it made much difference. In Russia, where the state has a monopoly on information—a monopoly on reality—the damage was simply vanished: "Most of the articles were up for forty minutes or so. Some were there for a few hours, tucked away in less obvious places." Naturally, the heist went unreported in the Russian state media. And then, the state began to erase Egor's past too. Most of his older articles from Lenta were quietly removed.

Egor wasn't surprised. He had always half-expected his enterprise to fail. He felt sure that he would be discovered, that he wouldn't have the right permissions to alter Lenta's website, or that the articles would be taken down within seconds. Speaking to Mediazona—an independent media outlet labeled a "foreign agent"—Polyakov described his actions as a "performance": "We have a gigantic audience, which I also put a lot of effort into, so Sasha [Aleksandra] and I decided that such a performance would be the only true one." The effort was symbolic. A scrawl of graffiti painted on the state's walls, then washed away and painted over as if it had never happened.

The state didn't heed Egor, but Russian nationalists, always in search of an object for hatred, noticed his handiwork. Users called for Egor's imprisonment, public shaming, and even execution. Moderators of the state-sponsored Cyber Front Z Telegram group assailed Egor and Aleksandra Miroshnikova as "clowns" who had "had a sudden attack of conscience after feeding off the state for their whole career as 'journalists.'"[17] VK users attacked Egor as an anti-Russian agent of liberalism:

> Why did they choose 9 May for this "civic act" (which is anyway like taking a shit on the Eternal Flame [in Moscow])? And why did these "heroes" go straight to the liberal media to ask for asylum? The "heroes" chose the exact moment when their shit would get noticed. And then they called out to "liberal" society, "Look at us, we shat all over the bloody-handed regime!!! Come save us!!"

Anything in Russia can be turned, as these nationalists did with Egor's protest, into a Western-funded, anti-Russian conspiracy.[18] It didn't matter that Egor and Miroshnikova had worked alone. For the nationalist faithful, they had to be lunatics, irrational and detached from reality.

His protest erased from the public consciousness, the real conflict remained within Egor. The very idea of challenging the regime had sent him into an internal tailspin. "For months on end, I had had internal arguments with myself, with my own conscience. Arguments, counterarguments, fights. Beating myself up and ironing myself out. I was incredibly afraid of the security services. I was sure they'd go totally next level crazy."

Egor knew the inside of the system. He had seen its lumbering incompetence from the inside. He knew that even Aleksandra only had the roughest knowledge of his exact plans. Yet Egor had internalized the idea that the state was surveilling everybody, everywhere, so he convinced himself that they couldn't *not* know what he was up to. Challenging the state's power first required combatting an internal sense of fear and obedience.

The day after his protest, Egor continued his amateur spy games. He headed for Azerbaijan, fearing that his door might be smashed down by security operatives at any moment. But nothing happened. Nobody came for him. He was simply written out of the public gaze and ignored. And since the state has not chosen to turn him into a player in one of its media performances—the target of ire on the nightly talk shows, the subject of criticism on its propagandists' vast Telegram channels, or the victim of vituperation from a Duma deputy—he remains, in his words, "an insignificant man." Nonetheless, the terror still hasn't quite gone. He fears that "the security services will take their revenge somehow or other," even after several months and even though Egor is in Azerbaijan.

Egor was a tiny cog in a great, grinding machine. The state is already training a new generation of graduates to play the role of public commentator. Conferences and training programs sponsored by the government are showing young minds how to "interpret events" on television, radio, and online.[19] The Marxist *politruki*—political instructors—of yesteryear are being replaced by a new breed of graduates—smart, sharp, social media savvy—who can serve as society's chorus. They will, as Egor and his peers have done at Lenta and countless other outlets for the past decade, expound on why defeat can mean victory, sacrifice can mean rebirth, and collapse can mean construction.

When Egor graduated from the Higher School of Economics a decade ago, he was lured into the state's world by the promise of a career and stability. He would have an outlet for his intellectual talents. There are ever fewer opportunities outside the state's purview. Young men like Armen Aramyan and Egor Polyakov are silenced, erased, or ritually destroyed in public show trials. Today's generation is even more likely to accept their lot and join the chorus of fairy-tale-creating "analysts."

Still, Egor has in a way beaten Putin's regime at its mind games. Long beset by doubts, fears, frustrations, and the sense that his life was being wasted on a hateful propaganda project, his protest allowed him to break free of the regime's hold over language. Settling into his temporary lodgings, Egor could finally put aside the internal fights and arguments. For the first time in years, he exhales, "I slept easy. It was incredible."

The Kremlin's real activists

Switch on the TV or log onto social media and the message is everywhere. The anti-Kremlin protestors are liberals. Leftists. Queers. Feminists. Traitors. Scum. They are dragging Russia back into the past, back into stagnation, back into trauma. Vladimir Solovyov, clad in ominous black jacket, conducts his circus of pundits. They pillory pro-Ukrainian protestors in Europe as a dying breed of self-obsessed liberals more interested in identity politics than traditional family and national values—and even, echoing Putin's words, as actual Nazis. Anybody protesting against the war wants to halt the march toward the future. They are anti-youth. Real Russian NGOs attempting to intervene on behalf of, for example, Ukrainian women refugees find that they are ignored or attacked. For them, "the entire world seems to be falling apart."[20]

But in the state's infotainment war, it's the government's supporters—whether "protesting" in Serbia, trolling Europeans with protest actions and provocations, or organizing humanitarian aid or military support—who are the real activists. Full of spontaneous enthusiasm, they channel the youthful energy of the *narod*—the people, the nation—and they are leading the march toward the new world.

The state is creating new "activist" groups of young Russians to cultivate this energetic aura. Rocketing to fame as the regime's bot and propagandist Telegram and VK accounts share their content, these groups are staking the claim to being the real "activists" in

Russia—even if their "activism" simply means parroting everything the state has told them.[21] These astroturfed groups have inherited the Nashi flame.

The Belgorod-based Katyusha "women's movement," for example, appeared from thin air in the summer of 2022. Named after a mythical Soviet World War II-era rocket launcher, the group engages in a slate of pro-military activities. The members—photogenic young women from across the country—have produced a wholesome pin-up calendar dedicated to the navy. Each month's image displays a different armed forces base in Russia (and one in Crimea) alongside an image of an idealized mother. Wedding rings and pregnancy bumps are on prominent display.[22] Some images highlight Russia's old allies abroad (Venezuela: "South America is the right America!"). Others rehash familiar aggressive slogans: "Russia's here forever!"

In another activity, the group made rough medals from frontline shrapnel. Each medal was marked with an ironic phrase: "For the rebirth of fascism." The group sent the medals as "rewards" to Western leaders. The work was obviously assisted by the state. Katyusha's videos are slick, well formatted, neatly edited productions. Its members' matching T-shirts and its provocative style imitate the approach of everything from Walking Together to the Luzhniki stadium concert in March. And the message that links it all together: war is essential and good, for war saves the young and creates the new world.

State media personalities rushed to lavish praise on what was a totally unknown group when its first Telegram post appeared. Solovyov, for example, distributed photographs and a slickly produced video clip detailing the effort made by what were described as "activists." In the first week of September, Katyusha's posts reached over 3 million Telegram accounts. Users were bombarded with the idea that "activism" could, when it was produced by good Russian mothers only looking out for Russia's troops and Russia's children, be patriotic. The certainty of meaning unspools as the state's youth campaigns are woven into smartphone realities.

* * *

Late summer, 2022. The impending trial of the Ukrainian soldiers captured after the battle for Azovstal is all over TV and social media. The detainees are threatened with death. But even such grave matters are sucked into the state's great performance. Denis Pushilin, leader of the self-declared Donetsk People's Republic, is inescapable. He's constantly on screens, ranting about "the Nazis from Azov."[23] Vladimir Solovyov trails the event as if it were a show about to arrive on a streaming service. "It should," he breathlessly announces, "happen by the end of August!"[24]

A video hits the Runet. A camera walks viewers into a dingy room. Half-finished metal skeletons twist into shot. Viewers are being led on a tour of the cells that will hold the "criminals" and "mercenaries" from Ukraine's Azov regiment. The video is shared in endless Telegram threads. Channel moderators add rhetorical flourishes to the performance: "They're preparing cages for the animals in Mariupol." Their readers engage in contests of performative hyperbole that snowball from the obscene to the downright grotesque: "They should build a gallows too!"; "They should hang them right in the square in Mariupol"; "We should make them play hangman, or Russian roulette!" Rippling through the background, the language of holy war, national renewal, and youth: "Do it for the kids"; "Eternal memory to our angels [prayer hands emoji]"; "God is with us!"[25]

Jail the enemy to save the children; kill the "scum" to purify the nation. The state howls down its opponents with its superior discursive firepower. This justice is designed as grotesque, voyeuristic clickbait for social media consumption, not for the delivery of legal process. The crude, mob-baiting infotainment show trial of *The Male/The Female* is being applied not in minor cases of social wrongdoers—queers, liberals, alcoholics, the non-Orthodox—but in cases of life and death.

The news that the Azov defenders were cheaply swapped for Putin's universally detested ally Viktor Medvedchuk causes a ripple on extremist groups that quickly dies away. The crowd watches on online, fired up by snippets of staged reality, death-penalty trailers, and the promise of wrongdoing against Russia's future punished. After all, the real spontaneity, and the real flag bearers of the future—the real "activists"—are on Moscow's side. Now, Moscow is taking action to shore up its reality by shutting off the outside like never before.

Nasha Russia: the disconnective society

Kostya, the twenty-three-year-old IT pro from Moscow, boasts to me that the West has Google, but "we" have Yandex. The West has Facebook, but "we" have VK. He goes on, listing dozens of other Silicon Valley applications and services that Russia can easily replace. For young patriots like him, it doesn't matter that banning platforms like Instagram, which underpaid Russians use to take part in the gig economy by selling goods and services, undercuts living standards. Reshaping society requires, as the confident young career man puts it, "sacrifices." He and other IT professionals might have lost a few project opportunities when access to some services evaporated, but in the long run the war is creating something new: a stronger, unique, self-sufficient Russian IT industry. Little matter for Kostya that Western analysts are pessimistic about the chances of this dream being realized.[26]

The regime's plans to create a national "firewall" have always been limited by contingency and technology. Today, though, the state—thanks to the tacit support of citizens like Kostya and its monopoly on information—is about to make it much harder for the young to find information from the outside. Its boot already on the neck of the fragile, fractured opposition, it's going to press even harder, making sure that the only reality tomorrow's Russians ever see is the one constructed by the state.

The Russian state has for years been waiting for an excuse to sever its people from independent journalism and from connections abroad.[27] In 2019, it even conducted a test to cut off the country's internet from the outside world completely. The Ukraine war, thanks to the ghoulish specters conjured up by propaganda—online threats, fifth columnists, and internal enemies—has given the regime the trigger it needed to go a step further.

The state is banning opposition outlets left, right, and center, making it harder to access their websites without using a VPN. Access to Instagram and Facebook has been restricted. Search results are skewed toward the "correct" sites. Opposition channels on Telegram are flooded with more bots and trolls than ever before. Anti-war celebrities find their social media posts drowning in abuse from angry users, often orchestrated by pro-Kremlin groups like Cyber Front Z, which provides users with copypasta invective to direct at "enemies." Labeling outside sources as "extremist," the state funds subway adverts warning travelers against using technology to attempt to access forbidden sites. Duma Deputy Maria Butina, notorious for her conviction for spying in the United States, suggested, on an episode of *Evening with Vladimir Solovyov*, jailing parents who permit their children to use VPNs.[28] Finding outside information—alternatives to the state's world—is getting harder.

In tandem, the parallel online world Kostya describes is under construction. Where Western credit-card companies no longer function online, the government replaces them with its own Mir system. Celebrities cut up their Visa and Mastercards, laying out the pieces in the shape of the letters "Z" and "V" and photographing the results to share on VK and Telegram accounts. Politicians—led by young influencers like Olga Zanko—loudly broadcast their retreat from Instagram and Facebook. The government runs competitions between its domestic internet giants, led by Yandex, to introduce new cloud storage services to replace those that had been provided by Google and Apple.

In reality, Russia's homegrown internet alternatives are usually poor imitations of superior American and European platforms, and users find simple ways around bans by using free VPNs. As the state closes one VPN, a dozen more pop up in their place. Russians swap information about the latest and best VPN via closed Telegram channels. Even the government knows it's fighting an uphill battle without deploying technology more complex than it possesses—and the president's spokesman, Dmitry Peskov, has admitted to using a VPN himself.[29] Like 30 million other Russian users, even nervy Lera is still using her Instagram account.

But the state's present struggles may not persist. Kostya welcomes news of the state's new assaults on online freedom—they'll keep the nation's youth safe from what he thinks is a "fashionable" interest in rewriting Russia's heroic history. Pro-government Russians are likely to accept censorship of the internet, which they see as a threat to national and individual security.[30] The quality of homegrown services has come on in leaps and bounds in recent years, with delivery and ride-hailing services rivaling anything Silicon Valley has to offer.

Indeed, some Russians who have returned to state-sponsored platforms are surprised by how palatable they have become in recent years. Sasha is a young web developer from St Petersburg. He's recently reactivated his VK account: "The network gets a bad rep [with his peers], and a lot of people left for Instagram, but it's light years ahead of Facebook." Despite VK's government associations, even a tech-savvy guy like Sasha is happy to use it for convenience's sake.

Russia is inching towards digital isolation. Entering a unique "disconnective society," as the scholar Gregory Asmolov puts it, Russians are being starved of information.[31] And digital Russia is already being disconnected internally. The opposition may see itself as locked in a grand power struggle with the state, but its work is carried out in the nooks and crannies of obscure digital bubbles.

The world of subcultures and communities that the Runet birthed in the mid-to-late 2000s—the time when queer Russians could find likeminded souls online and graduates like Anna Veduta could stumble across the inspiring rhetoric of youthful opposition bloggers—is long gone. Even Dvach, the rambunctious forum that gave Armen Aramyan space to breathe after another day's racist bullying in Moscow, is accused of collaborating with the security forces' strong men.[32]

The opposition seems to be carrying out the tasks an opposition is meant to. It protests. It posts. It agitates. But few are listening. In the brief moments when the opposition does make an appearance in the world of the Putinists, its script is simply rewritten by the state's infotainment performances. An objective journalist concerned for their community is turned into a "foreign agent" who must be relentlessly pursued by the mob online and in person. An enemy combatant is not just an opposition soldier. He is a mythical Nazi monster who should be gawped at, pilloried, then murdered. Anybody who questions, subverts, or interrogates the state's justifications for its war must, by definition, oppose the campaign to save Russia and Russian youth from the threat of the Other. Nobody on the inside of Russia's world of nationalism is going to be persuaded by Instagram-friendly, anti-war QR code campaigns. The opposition barely seems to scratch the consciousness of the nationalists.

Only the patriotic crowd seem able to imagine a sense of a future that moves beyond stagnation: a Russian future, a disconnected future, a future of *nasha—our—*Russia. They've got something that offers glimpses of wholeness, collectivity, and belonging. All the opposition can offer is exclusion, fragmentation, and transitory snatches of belonging.

Olga Zanko, the young influencer and Duma deputy who founded Victory Volunteers, confidently declares to her online acolytes that "I am the youth! The time to realize our potential is right now! Strive, create, try, and everything will come good!"[33] She hails the Russian rescuers of Ukrainian children: "You can't leave a child in despair alone."[34] The fascists are marching ever further into their fantasy world of constructive destruction. Theirs is a world of belonging, togetherness, future. And, as the authorities cut off the flow of information from the outside, the fascists' world is the only one the young may ever know.

* * *

Lera calls me the day after we first speak. When I pick up, words of sheer panic tumble from her mouth: "Is this going to be okay? I told my parents about our chat and they're worried. Are you sure it's totally anonymous? Can they find out about me?" *They*—the authorities—are a fixture in the minds of every Russian who questions the government's wisdom. Alone in her room, speaking on a secure line, Lera is tortured by the state's gaze. She fears being publicly turned into a "traitor." She fears for her life. She fears for her family.

The next Lera, the next young person of color washing up in Moscow with big dreams, won't join the protest movement. They won't watch Navalny videos. They won't read Doxa. They'll keep their head down. The state is always there, on the inside.

7

THE Z GENERATION

Hand on hip, confidently drawn up to full height, a teen girl holds a camera. The bright light of a flash scrapes across the mirror. Clothes, posters, make-up, and schoolbooks tumble out of the dark background. The picture is framed by a two-word caption: "#RealMeWishList #YouthArmy." A reflection stares back. Red beret perched on a neat, brunette bob. Red T-shirt. Eagle logo. Khaki pants. Military boots. More photographs slide past in an endless loop. A stamped and signed government form. An ID card.

Maria is fourteen. She has just joined the Youth Army. And the first thing she has rushed to do is put on her uniform, take a selfie, and upload it to show her friends on TikTok. She wants the world to know where she belongs: in the world of the child soldier. Maria might be playing teen dress-up, but as she gazes into the mirror, gazing back is a fully formed young soldier. Beyond the veil of performance, nothing else.

I spoke to Yury, Maria's father. He, his wife, and Maria live in a small historic town on the Volga River in Russia's southwest. War seems ever-present here. Monuments to the World War II fallen are sprinkled about the town. Volgograd, where the Red Army turned the tide against the Wehrmacht in November 1942, is just a day trip away. The residents here live in history, surrounded by monuments, memorials, and parades. Part-Soviet, part-modern, their lives are always in the shadow of conflict.

The war in Ukraine isn't far off either. The army is a popular choice for young men who leave school with little hope of a well-paying career at home. The town easily reached its mobilization target in late September. Few had to be cajoled into going to war. They willingly signed up.

Despite growing up in this militarized bubble, Maria is an unlikely child soldier. Her family is relatively well off. Yury is a professional in the chemicals industry. Maria's mom is a freelance graphic designer, while her grandfather rode his luck in the 1990s to found a successful local business. He helps the family out by funding what remains a comfortable lifestyle eight months into the Ukraine war.

Yury is no great Putinist, although he's hardly an outspoken critic of the regime. He was somewhat taken aback when the anime- and ice-cream-loving teen Maria asked to join the Youth Army. But, like the many other politically passive Russians, he didn't say no.

Filling out the application was easy enough. Candidates today can download the "Young Soldier" Android app ("The Digital Home of the Youth Army!"), fill out a few details, take a photo, and—hey presto—a digital soldier is born. Encounter any trouble and a helpful "consultant" is waiting on the Youth Army's live chat box to answer any question you might have. Purchasing Maria's uniform was just as easy. All Yury had to do was click from the Youth Army's homepage through to Wildberries, a popular online retailer. Then he loaded up his online cart with all the T-shirts, tunics, combat trousers, berets, and boots on the Youth Army's kit list. The prices, which have risen 25 percent in the past six months, were a sore point: just the basic kit runs to 16,000 rubles (around $250) today. The package turned up at home within days of the order being placed.

Now, Yury drives Maria back and forth to a typical line-up of Youth Army events: parades, classes in physical discipline and assembling AK rifles, team and community activities, and so on.

However, he has been most surprised at how she's been drawn to the online Youth Army community: "She's spending a lot of time on her phone, messaging, watching videos." Mostly that means TikTok. The Chinese platform has hoovered up the youth market since it launched in Russia in 2017. Today it has 30 million users, a number that's expected to grow rapidly in the coming years.

TikTok responded to Russia's invasion of Ukraine by blocking Russian users from seeing foreign content. And, eventually, from uploading content at all. But tech-savvy young Russians have all but ignored this ban, and the platform has done little to support it. Thanks to the Chinese social media giant's assistance, the Youth

Army's militarism can spread to a captive audience.[1] And when Maria's not on TikTok, she can use the Youth Soldier app to access an events calendar, play "educational" games, and connect with her peers in what the app promises is a "secure environment." The more she does on the app, the more points she gets—and the greater the chance of getting a prize from her regional division. Even filling out an application to join gets points in the great "Youth Army Quest."

"Secure," of course, means free from outside influences, free from opposition channels, and free from anti-war voices. Separated from the West, driven by addiction-feeding algorithms, and full of simplistic but striking video content, Russian TikTok is the perfect breeding ground for neo-fascist content (a fact that hasn't gone unnoticed by state media personalities like Margarita Simonyan, who signed up and already counts over 400,000 subscribers).

Scrolling through Maria's TikTok feed, which she updates several times a week, I can see how she is transforming herself into the sort of child soldier who'll be ready for war. In her videos, Maria exposes every aspect of her teen life and dreams. Dances and lip syncs to popular Western tunes and Soviet films mingle with laconic comments on humdrum teen dramas. Every few posts, the adolescent outpourings are punctuated by the world of the Youth Army. Maria attending a parade. Maria getting ready to march. Maria in uniform.

The two worlds melt into one another. Sitting in her bedroom, Maria cocks her head, flicking her beret toward the camera. She points to a caption on screen: #volunteer #loveyourself #youtharmy. Paramilitary youth group as upbeat internet self-help slogan. After a bust-up with her mother, she stands to attention, saluting the camera, and declares, "Mum, guess I'll just go live in the barracks!" The Youth Army is a second home, a place of belonging, a place where dreams come true, a place where Maria can become a better version of herself: #RealMeWishList.

Maria's friends comment: "Tell us about the Youth Army"; "What do you do there?" With a mix of curiosity and envy, they gaze at Maria's fairy-tale self-confidence. They'd like to belong too.

Russia's young opposition finds itself short on language, symbols, and communal spaces. But young soldiers like Maria know exactly how to behave and where they can find belonging. They wear their commitment to the state's military messianism on their sleeve online and offline. They're ready to fight the state's mythical enemies of the past in a war for peace today. They're learning to adore the state's violence.

Maria is beginning to express her inclination toward a darker kind of patriotism. In the wake of the February anti-war protests in Russia, she posted a pair of videos praising the state's riot police: "Guys, you've chosen a difficult but noble path!"; "If I had to be arrested by anybody ..." It's not hard to imagine that in a few months or years she'll follow in her older peers' footsteps into a world of extreme nationalist hate.

Maria and her Youth Army comrades are being told that they might have to die to defend the state. Growing up in Russia's disconnective society, they're embracing the cult of revanchism, sacrifice, and death. Their *real me wish list* is being formed by the state's youth program.

The state is rampaging through childhood, militarizing every aspect of youth from pop culture to schools, universities, and extracurricular activities. Beloved cartoon characters like the benevolent Soviet-era stop-motion creature Cheburashka are turned into Z-uniformed soldiers, child heroes are decorated with awards and celebrated by military groups for civil acts, and the president congratulates young war heroes and child "soldiers" for their patriotism. Anything and everything is being rewritten to fit the fascist narrative.

Building on the online and offline approaches of branding, performance, meme, and vitality it has developed over the past twenty years, the state is embarking on its biggest project yet. It's not abandoning the Youth Army to fizzle out, and it's creating yet more youth groups to buttress the Army's work. Urged on by older mentors, and increasingly isolated from alternative paths, the young are growing mistrustful of outside influences—and growing into a mindset more extreme than anything the Russian Federation has seen before.

The Youth Army: to the front

Maria isn't a one-off. Youth Army membership has exploded after a major recruitment drive. The state is aiming to have 3.25 million children—a fifth of the school-age population—by 2030. This ambitious target is a far cry from the tens of thousands of youth involved in 2000s groups like Nashi (many of whose "members" were really just attracted to one-off events by the promise of goodies and rewards). The state's putting its money where its mouth is, allotting over $200m a year to funding the Youth Army.[2] Organizations like Volunteers for Victory, new school-age Pioneers groups, and kindergarten projects are receiving lavish budget contributions too. In the southwest of Russia, where Maria has joined up, almost 20,000 new recruits have joined the Youth Army cause to form eighty-five new "platoons" in the past year.[3]

Maria's friends are watching her transform into a confident child soldier on TikTok. Audiences across Russia are seeing thousands more children do the same on state media. Journalists in far-off Sakhalin cover "flashmobs"—an old Putinist pantomime, without the spontaneous, chaotic enthusiasm of the Western conception of the flashmob—at which young "soldiers" explain their dedication to taking part in the group's civic activities:[4] "Since we're patriotic, we go to participate twice a month, every month, in events like this both in the city and beyond." The media cover "battalions" renamed in honor of today's war heroes as they learn to use bayonets like the heroes of nineteenth-century battles and spend days at World War II memorial sites.[5]

Chechen despot Ramzan Kadyrov uses his vast social media following to boost stories about local Youth Army events, sharing clips of leaders declaring, "We're for Russia! We're for the president! We're for peace! We're for a world without fascism! Together we are as one!"[6] The Youth Army leader's invective ends with a declaration of military fealty to Kadyrov: *"Akhmat sila!"*[7]

In the Hall of Military and Labor Glory, an ornate imperial cave of gold and white marble tucked away in the Stalingrad Panorama Museum in Volgograd, Medvedev is filmed declaring that if Ukraine's "bloody clowns" attack occupied Crimea, "Judgment Day, quick and brutal, will be upon them all instantly." He is flanked by a nonagenarian veteran and an immaculately uniformed teen Youth Army girl. She listens intently as Dmitry Medvedev's words resound around this temple of war.

The Youth Army is pictured again and again, ready to fight the wars of the past—of the Napoleonic Wars, of World War II, of the

Chechen wars—and the wars of the present. Their individuality ironed into hard, uniformed lines, today's young soldiers are the inheritors of Russia's heroic military flame.

The young soldiers' experience in 2022 is dominated by the "special military operation" in Ukraine. Young soldiers bearing "Z" flags take part in bicycle rides in dual celebration of the "special operation" and Russia's "Day of Physical Culture," a Soviet-era festival dating back to the 1920s. Their peers see the heroes of today's war transformed into mythical heroes in murals on local buildings.[8] In school gymnasiums, they learn to pack and unpack parachutes under the watchful eyes of "veterans" from today's war. In the group's classrooms, children write letters to troops at the front. In the community, they gather food, blankets, and other essentials to send to "ethnic Russians" forced to flee from the conflict zone.

Children as young as six take part in art and poetry contests to celebrate the events of the present, drawing sketches of Russian troops rescuing children in Donbas. Some of the poetry read by the entrants is drawn direct from the world of online extremists like Ivan Kondakov. One boy, Platon, appeared bedecked in Youth Army medals and a "Z"-shaped George Cross ribbon to read a poem written by a local schoolteacher as part of an entry for a national festival of patriotism:[9]

In the center of Europe, Bandera's descendants—
Fascists and toadies—have been growing
for months and years like a tumor.
How did we Slavs allow this?
The first blood was spilled on the Maidan!
Only the Russian soldier
Can finish off Nazism in its own lair.

"We hope you win!" commented his detachment's VK group as they virtually waved him off to take part in the national festival: "Be glorious, our country! We're proud of you!" Online, offline, in Moscow, in the provinces, in school, in church. Any child can take part, and anybody can witness this grand spectacle of generational creation.

Indeed, the Youth Army is also being used as an indoctrination tool in occupied territories. In Crimea, 29,000 children are now members, approaching the government's target of enrolling 10 percent of the eligible Crimean population by the end of 2024.[10] Boys and girls who might have grown up looking to the outside world as part of a Europeanizing Ukraine are sucked into the Russian state's neo-fascist, nationalist program of violence at the youngest possible age. They learn to behave like good Russians, to be ready to defend the motherland, and to worship the military martyrs of World War II and the tsarist past. As one critic put it, "the children are inculcated with hatred for Ukraine … and morally readied to die for Russia and for Putin."[11]

Youth Army brigades are already being founded in the newly occupied territories. Young recruits file into halls, the light catching on shards of glass in bombed out windows, to listen to military concerts. Sunlit videos depict new members saluting murals and monuments to the invaders—their "rescuers"—and the former Youth Army members who have been sacrificed at the front. Ceremony, parade, media attention, and monuments throw the invaders' victims into the world of psychological remaking. It's all there to be photographed, captured on camera, and shared on social media. The Russianizing of Ukraine is processed and reprocessed. It is a militarizing, social media cultural genocide—the "proof" in the nationalists' world that the "special military operation" really is rejuvenating the nation, saving the children from the perversities of the West and its Nazi hordes.

But this is no transient viral phenomenon. The Youth Army is a serious military group. The European Union added the organization to its sanctions package in the summer of 2022, labeling it a "paramilitary" group. Ukraine's ombudsman for human rights, Lyudmyla Denisova, released an online statement expressing fears that Russia intends to use Youth Army members on the battlefield in response to its enormous troop losses.[12] Denisova's fears are not unfounded. Some adult recruits tempted from the streets of provincial cities into the army by big pay packets receive as little as two weeks' training; the recently conscripted may receive even less. Senior Youth Army members are likely to be physically; militarily; and, most importantly, ideologically ready to wage a destructive racial war in Ukraine. Given the right equipment and under the right command, they may prove far more resilient on the battlefield than their unwilling or mercenary elders.

The Russian media is whipping up expectations around the young soldiers' capabilities. In response to the EU sanctions, state media channels posted pictures of children training with firearms accompanied by headlines as flippant as they were confrontational: "The only reason the Youth Army is on the EU's sanctions list is the West's fear of Russian children!"[13]

Russia's children aren't just being "saved" in Ukraine. Out of the destruction, the Russian media claims that the Youth Army's members are being made into supreme warriors that can wage war against the nefarious West. Today's youth aren't swing dancing their way through glamorous Moscow or nodding along to hip hop odes to Vladimir Putin. All over the country, they are TikTok dancing their way toward Russia's messianic military destiny.

Just how did the group shift itself from being merely one of many Putinist projects in 2016 to the heart of nationalist hopes for Russia's future? How has it become the sort of fresh, tech-savvy organization that can reel in young teens like Maria?

Young faces of leadership

In 2018, Roman Romanenko was appointed head of the Youth Army. A forty-nine-year-old United Russia Duma deputy and former cosmonaut, Romanenko was a bland functionary whose minor space heroics—he spent time on the International Space Station between 2009 and 2013—could have been lifted from a Soviet-era textbook. His monotonous tone of voice was as uninspiring as his pallid appearance. Romanenko was no hero for a generation of Instagram-loving child soldiers. He stepped down in 2020.

Into Romanenko's shoes hopped Nikita Nagornyy, a twenty-three-year-old, chisel-jawed, Olympic gold-winning gymnast. Blessed with the rippling physique of the professional athlete, the clean-cut face of a teen boy, and the social media savvy of the very best, Nagornyy has the chops to lead a paramilitary group for the digital generation.

On paper, Nagornyy leads a team that includes senior politicians, administrators, and army chiefs. In reality, he plays a symbolic role as the ultimate idol—fit, healthy, patriotic, white, and militaristic—for a generation of Youth Army members. And Nagornyy, who's almost never pictured without a broad grin slapped across his face, delights in playing that role.

Nagornyy has built a vast social media audience, with 1.3m followers on TikTok, 781,000 followers on Instagram, 365,000 on YouTube, and a further 12,000 on VK.[14] In some ways, his feed is indistinguishable from that of any other young fitness influencer. He posts inspirational videos, snippets of his intense gym sessions, behind-the-scenes lifestyle shots, exchanges and selfies with other athletes, and training and workout advice.

Nagornyy's public persona, however, is a perfectly curated model of the Russian patriotic ideal. His workout videos are awash with national colors. Non-white, non-ethnic Russians rarely appear. He appears in traditionally Russian settings like the *banya*, the steam bathhouse, praising the sauna as a place for physical and moral development. Nagornyy pops up alongside everyone from the Averina twins, who appeared on stage at Putin's Luzhniki "Z" concert in March 2022, to the national hockey hero and avowed Putin supporter Aleksandr Ovechkin.

Brightly lit, perfectly filtered photographs spill across Nagornyy's social media feeds. Each is accompanied with bubbly statements expressing Nagornyy's boyish excitement at his latest adventure: "Sharing a dream come true. Hockey legend Aleksandr Ovechkin signed a hockey stick for me [shock-horror emoji] Limitless delight, guys." What young Russian boy or girl wouldn't want to spend a day living Nagornyy's perfect influencer life?

But Nagornyy's patriotism doesn't end at the superficial. He's spreading a serious message about the importance of war. On 8 May, he uploaded a somber lecture to his VK page explaining the importance of participating in Victory Day to his young followers: "I'm proud that every parade I was at is imprinted in my childhood memories. And I only ever missed a parade when I was training hard with my team for competitions."

The following day, Nagornyy paraded with his Youth Army group on Red Square. Later, he logged onto VK to upload a shot of himself in uniform, same broad smile as ever, to explain how important the day's ritual is: "The military march strikes up and ordered rows of tunics march across Red Square. This is the parade in memory of Victory in the Great Patriotic War!" Nagornyy's young fans fell over themselves with excitement, leaving 1,200 comments filled with heart, biceps, and Russian-flag emojis: "Bravo, Nikita!"; "Happy Victory Day, Nikita!"; "You're a real hero!"[15]

The discussion rapidly turned from past wars to today's conflict. One commenter who suggested that Nagornyy shouldn't be celebrating war due to events in Ukraine was howled down by the mob of young fans: "Maybe before you post you should think for a second about whose country you're in, you fuck-up?"; "Go to Ukraine! We don't need fascists here! Bon voyage!"

Nagornyy (or his social media team) did nothing to intervene in the vitriolic arguments. The Youth Army chief himself has, after all, lavished praise on the "special military operation" and, in particular, on efforts to "educate" Ukrainian children into Russian culture and behavior.[16] Carrying out virtual attacks on those who don't toe the line is just one way for young Russian children to learn to belong and to purify the country of the degenerates.

From the comfort of their adolescent bedrooms, children can play at being the fascists, hooligans, and thugs the Putin regime has always courted. And what's more, Russian children don't have to be a member of the Youth Army or even to follow Nagornyy to stumble across this content. They see their friends doing it online. In snatches of performed violence scrolled past on feeds, shared by friends, carried out by peers, a whole generation can learn to harden themselves, remake their identity, and attack those who don't follow the mob.

There are dozens of young, often female, athletes coming to public prominence who play the same role as Nagornyy. Twenty-one-year-old Veronika Stepanova, for example, won cross-country ski-relay gold at the Beijing Winter Olympics in 2022. A graduate of the Youth Army, Stepanova is another model of physical and performative perfection for Putin's fascist state—one who seems to sum up the ideal path for a young soldier from the ranks of the paramilitary group and into the role of state hero.

Like Nagornyy, Stepanova is a creature of social media. She shares her every moment online for thousands of followers. Like Nagornyy, her feed mostly comprises athletics training and banal posts that appeal to her youthful following. Hers is the voice of a positive, optimistic, and modern young woman: she slaps emojis all over her posts and photographs, enthusiastically raves about her latest adventures, and gushes about her friends and social life.

But Stepanova's whole identity is tied up with the Youth Army. Looking back through her feed, it's easy to find images of a teenaged Stepanova at Youth Army summer camps. Veronika in camouflage. Veronika bursting with laugher and clutching an iPhone. Veronika at a military tactical exercise. Veronika—to use her words—as "the little soldier with a big heart." Joining the Youth Army is fun. It's something any teen might do. Hang out with friends, have a laugh, enjoy the summer. Learn to fire guns and participate in military-patriotic life. Become a hero.

Today, the "little soldier" trains rhetorical fire on the West. In interviews, Stepanova speaks in a confrontational, slogan-heavy style. She aggressively attacks her foreign competitors and lauds Russia in interviews and on her popular social media feeds.[17] She hopes Russia keeps fighting in Ukraine, and she hopes Russia wins.

And Stepanova lends her youthful image to the staid events of the state. In April 2022, she met Putin in one of the Kremlin's state rooms to receive the vaunted Order of Friendship award. Delivering her acceptance speech, Stepanova gazed across from the podium at a watching Putin. With a smile, she declared, "I'm extremely proud to be receiving such a prestigious award from the president of our country. Thank you that you've raised the country's banner so high. We won't let it down. I promise." Video of the speech tore through the Runet, shared by everybody from Youth Army recruits to media personalities like Vladimir Solovyov. Stepanova doubled down in a follow-up interview: "Russia is back, strong, proud, and successful … we're on the right track, and we will definitely win, just as we won the Olympics."[18]

Role models like Stepanova sprinkle rejuvenating stardust on the aging leadership, its Ukraine war, and projects like the Youth Army. And, thanks to social media, the stardust glitters non-stop. Stepanova and her athlete peers keep on posting long after the cameras stop rolling at PR events in the Kremlin. They're living a real Putinist life.

Children see that they can belong to a world that is fun, online, and modern, participating in the old machine, imbuing it with the aura of youth, even as it falls apart before their very eyes. And, if they want to be like their heroes, if they want to fit in, they can imitate the language and actions of "little soldiers with big hearts" like Veronika Stepanova. The fun, however, is built on a myth of violence and endless war.

The Nikita Nagornyys and Viktoria Stepanovas are still few and far between. Most of the Youth Army's work in Russia's provincial cities is being carried out by a much older generation, by the middle-aged and senior Russians who look back on the USSR with fondness. Thanks to social media, though, they have a means to connect with their kids—without the help of the techy millennials who aren't much interested in Russia's battles and just want to be left alone.

Social media Stakhanovites

A rotund head of gray hair hovering over a camo-bedecked paunch harumphs into the camera. Leaning back toward the Soviet-era wall-paper behind him, Maksim clears his throat.

"They're OUR KIDS," he bellows. Everything Maksim says is expelled at maximum volume, a parade ground habit the sixty-something can't shake even years after leaving the army. "They're the future! We have to educate them!" Maksim despises the Western and American influences that he believes are eating away at the younger generation. A world of video games, social media influencers, and Hollywood movies isn't what he fought for in Afghanistan as a young man.

When the USSR collapsed, Maksim felt the prestige of belonging to a superpower's military ebb away overnight. Like so many of his generation, Maksim adores Putin. He believes the president has given Russia some self-respect back. He's thankful to the president for leading the defense against hordes of "Nazis" threatening a repeat of World War II in Ukraine today. He believes that Ukraine is still part of the "motherland" and that today's conflict is really a war between Russia and the United States to decide the fate of the Slavic peoples.

Maksim was ready to die for his country in the Soviet era and, now there's something worth fighting for, he's ready to do it again. His VK page is awash with the symbolism of the war in Ukraine. His profile photo has been overlaid with a Russian flag and a slogan, "For Russia!" He's joined dozens of pro-war groups that span the Orthodox Christian to the radical nationalist. He shares post after post of state-produced fantasies about Russia's purification and its military "just cause."[19] Two weeks into the war, Maksim even declared on his VK feed (already plastered with flags, patriotic videos, and "Z" memes) that he was ready to take up arms and show the West "how the SOVIET marines were taught to defend the motherland!" It's all something of a charade. Maksim's in his mid-sixties and not in the shape that he once was.

But if Maksim—despite the news of forced military call-ups for older Russian men that regularly sweep social media groups frequented by cosmopolitan professionals—won't be joining the columns headed for Donbas or Kyiv, he still has a role to play in building Russia's future. Indeed, his role might matter more than most, for Maksim holds a ranking position in the Youth Army.

Maksim rushed to sign up as a Youth Army leader back when the group was formed in 2016. Since then, he's been beating the parade square with his young, uniformed charges. His platoon is as well versed in the mythical martyrs of Russia's and the USSR's heroic military past as they are drilled in firearms and physical exercises.

And Maksim is trying to use social media to drum up interest in the group's work. His posts over the last two years comprise hundreds of videos and photographs showing his young recruits, immaculately dressed in distinctive khaki pants and red tops and berets, attending training. They stand guard at war memorials. They fire guns. They proudly bear standards at Victory Day parades. There is nothing of Maksim's own family or personal life—his life is subsumed in the work of the Youth Army.

More recently, Maksim has been eagerly sharing the war work his young charges are undertaking: photos of letters scrawled in clumsy children's writing to the "defenders of the fatherland" at the front, folded into the triangular shape familiar from World War II-era field post; videos of military displays at children's fetes; clips from the latest two-week "shift" at the Youth Army's militarized summer camps.

Maksim's page isn't all one-way traffic. He's followed by the parents of his "young soldiers," as they are called. Millennial moms and dads shower every post with formulaic praise and strings of emojis, squealing with virtual delight at their offspring's latest display of fealty to the state.

It's not just the older generation watching. Maksim's kids create videos that he shares, and share videos he produces in return. One teen girl, Yuliya, posts photos of herself getting ready for and attending a Victory Day parade rehearsal, just as a Western teen might post photos before and after any big event they're attending. Yuliya, though, accompanies her post with a rote comment that repeats the state's—and Maksim's—speech: "Russia is my life. I can breathe here. Russia means home. Family. Love. Peace."

Another "young soldier" repeats the trick, posting a TikTok-style short clip showing off his acrobatic firing routines with an army-issue rifle in a school gym. He has overlaid a blue-and-white text box with the comment, "I'm here to save people!" An even younger child stands to attention in combat trousers and the Youth Army's relaxed red T-shirt to record an awkward recital of a Soviet-era war poem. An older teen who's attended a series of summer camps boasts in a video of becoming so adept at knife throwing that he now gets to teach the younger kids.

Maksim's young recruits are emulating role models like Nikita Nagornyy and Veronika Stepanova by projecting their association with the movement online. Groups and individuals are doing the same all over Russia. Log onto Instagram; VK; and, above all, TikTok, and it's easy to find videos with the hashtag #youtharmy viewed hundreds of thousands of times. The top Youth Army influencers have follower counts in the tens of thousands and beyond.

The young soldiers' short videos, just like Maria's, borrow the familiar forms of TikTok virality. They are accompanied by a soundtrack of electronic and hip hop beats—sometimes American, but often Russian. Text overlays provide an ironic commentary on the video. The most popular users are fresh-faced, beautiful, and cloyingly upbeat.

But the content of Youth Army TikTok videos reflects the group's tenets of discipline, militarism, and patriotic preparation. Tutorials teach viewers how to remove creases from a beret (dip it in hot water, squeeze it out, and smooth it around your head) or subvert Western memes.[20] Users take foreign forms, subverting them and capturing them for patriotic ends. One video, for example, borrows the popular meme showing Canadian rapper Drake shaking a finger—no—and smiling smugly—yes. The meme is projected onto scenes of a day's marching: "Forty-five-minute class? No!"; "Three hours of parade? Yes!" Attached to ironic internet memes, the warmongering world of the Youth Army is transformed into something familiar, fun, and even fascinating.

Sometimes, producing these videos is even part of organized Youth Army activities. Detachments from across Russia are uploading quirky material showing what their young charges are up to. In one video from a regional group in Novosibirsk, four uniformed teens gaze into the camera as the screen displays the questions, "What's the point of your Youth Army? What do you do there? Will it help you in the future?" Pumping music kicks in, and the camera cuts to the teens dancing wildly: "We've formed a friendly collective. We develop our military skills. We enjoy activities together. We train our bodies. We participate in civil society." The teens who created the clip hope to catch the attention of Nikita Nagornyy himself by tagging the leader's account. This is the language of fascist youth groups—collectivity, physicality, war, and the future—delivered using the aesthetic forms and fandoms of twenty-first-century social media.

But the Novosibirsk group is also creating much more violent material. A video of a violent military combat-skill display given by special forces troops to Youth Army "soldiers" has become one of the most viewed #youtharmy clips and garnered almost 30,000 likes. Men in camouflage and balaclavas move beyond sparring to engaging in real, MMA-style punching and kicking. They demonstrate how to strike an opponent with the butt of a gun and how to pin down and shoot an enemy soldier.

In the background, a gaggle of children gaze on, filming the action with their smartphones, ready to disseminate it through their own social media feeds.[21] Young users lapped up the violence: "Mad skills. I'm in Youth Army too!; "Yeeeeah! [strong arm emojis]"; "Absolute machines"; "With guys like that we'll fuck up any army." What is painted as military training and physical discipline rapidly spills into projection onto the current conflict: "any army" really means the armies of Ukraine and Western nations.

Youth Army groups emulate this sort of online violence across the country. One group from Sakhalin uploaded a clip of armed tactical training in a forest. Young soldiers throw themselves to the ground, take up firing positions, and move along a wooded track in response to their commander's barked instructions. Of the 1,000 comments left on the video, most are part of an intense argument about the "young soldiers'" technique. One side charges, "you're not doing it right" and "that's more like the Great Patriotic War approach!" The other responds: "Our guys are the best," and "we've got the strongest guys!"[22] Users, many of whom proclaim themselves to be Youth Army members, engage in Soviet-style internal competition, challenging each other to better their skills. However, they are united by a common thread—the sense that war is on the horizon. "Me and the other young soldiers are ready!!" proclaims one user. Another tries to cool tensions, directing his peers' attention to the bigger task at hand: "Everyone's arguing about who's better than who, but the army is better than everything!" And the target of the war? The ever-present "UkroNazis."

These Youth Army members have found a site of community, belonging, and wholeness on TikTok. Like social media Stakhanovites, they urge each other on to greater physical and military heights, impervious to the world of Ukrainian suffering or the effects of the destruction being wrought by their military abroad. This is the only language and the only culture they know.

Maksim, well into his sixties, doesn't really understand quite how to manipulate TikTok's algorithm. He's reticent to set foot on such a fast-paced, attention-sapping platform. He's pleased, however, that his young charges are taking their military education seriously. After all, it's preparing them for war—and war preparation, for the Youth Army, is becoming all-consuming.

Summer camp and sainthood

This year, as money floods into the Youth Army's coffers and the need for bodies to fuel the state's war machine becomes more pressing, the organization's military preparation activities are growing more overt.

Maksim shares photos of a teen girl clad in Red Army uniform. Against the crumbling asphalt and grimy brickwork of a local school, she bends over a boy of eight or nine. He stares down the barrel of a replica automatic rifle, elbows awkwardly akimbo as he tries to balance the oversized weapon. Children gather around their uniformed peers, framed by the fluttering flags of Donetsk, Luhansk, and Russia. A fourth flag is emblazoned with a black-and-orange World War II memorial ribbon curlicued into a giant "Z." Guns, training, belonging, war. This was Maksim's big spring recruitment day. It worked. He's been flooded with applications since February.

A new cohort of young boys and girls were soon packing out yards and gymnasiums. Thousands in Maksim's region even got the chance to spend part of the summer holiday at Youth Army training camps. Encouraged by the state's advertising rubles and parents who have a long-held nostalgia for Soviet Pioneer-style activities, attendance has boomed this year.

Maksim sends me a video documenting life at one of this year's two-week "shifts"—Russian parents are always keen to hoover up saccharine video and photo summaries of life at summer camps, even if they're of the military variety.

The kids spend their weeks away in Russia's deep forest, sleeping in spartan but well-appointed barracks. They wear their uniforms from dawn until dusk, occasionally swapping parade uniform of beige pants and red T-shirt for lighter, branded sportswear or for camouflage for firing and tactical exercises. There's no running or chaotic fun. There's very little laughter. These kids aren't here for fun and games. They're here for the serious business of honing bodies and minds. They march everywhere.

Maksim is the star of the video. "This year," he says, "the bosses asked the instructors to give the kids *special* preparation to make sure they could take over as senior young soldiers and enter the army." The video's voiceover echoes Maksim's comment: "Not every young soldier will go to military college, but they will become teachers, doctors, good citizens. And that's a feather in the cap of the Youth Army!"

Not every attendee wanted to go. Whether there from choice or at their parents' insistence, though, Maksim is confident in the summer camp program. All the attendees, he barks, are sure to learn to love the "exercise and friendship" the Youth Army camp provides. The promo video shows one teen girl who confesses that, "My mom forced me to participate. Probably because my behavior wasn't good! But everything here's so organized and disciplined." The interviewer asks, "So things are better now?" The interviewee responds without hesitation, "Absolutely. Yes!" Glorious transformation from unwilling outsider to smiling insider—all thanks to a spot of military training.

The Youth Army camp culminates in two visits that provoke waves of excitement among the children. The first visitor is a decrepit World War II veteran, who totters into the camp to lecture the children on the importance of remembering what happened to people like him in the 1940s. The young soldiers pose for selfies with the veteran. They ask him to sign their patriotic history textbooks. They listen attentively—just as if they had been visited by any other celebrity.

The second visit caused even more of a storm. The arrival of real "veterans" from the war in Ukraine was heavily trailed in advertising for the summer camps. The children race to embrace their idols. In a wave of selfies, videos, and captioned snippets shared on personal accounts and re-shared by Maksim and his colleagues, the sense of excitement races around the young attendees' social media feeds. A dash of the stardust that Nikita Nagornyy and Veronika Stepanova shower down on the Youth Army's activities from on high seems to have reached the forests of rural Russia as saintly warriors of past and present descend from on high.

The Youth Army camps reprise the Soviet summer camp tradition. But today, the Russian state makes no bones about the Youth Army's purpose as a military recruitment tool.[23] However, since enlisting might mean following in the footsteps of the grandfathers' generation to make the ultimate sacrifice, the state and its proxies are using the religion of messianic sacrifice to sell the possibility of death to the TikTok generation.

Using the stock language and visual forms of Russian, Soviet, and Orthodox iconography, the young men who die at the front are elevated to the pantheon of saints from Russia's mythical military past. The Youth Army showcases former members who died in fighting in Ukraine on a webpage, "The Alley of Memory."[24] The faces of young men who have died in battle stare from the screen. Each portrait is accompanied by a brief summary of the martyr's heroism, highlighting their service in the Youth Army and how and where they died in Ukraine. Text and portrait create miniature Orthodox hagiographies—tales for believers to emulate—for the internet age. In videos spread on social media, the trick is repeated. The images of heroic young men who've completed awesome spiritual feats—the *podvigi* of the great heroes of the past—flash constantly by.

By dying for the motherland, Youth Army boys can become saintly figures. They can enter the world of heroism embodied in the images, stories, films, and memes the government has conjured up over the last two decades. The Ukraine war might seem violent, senseless, and hateful, but in the logic of this fascist political religion, to fight against and be killed by the non-Russian, the Other, is a path to instant sainthood. The young can live up to the impossible sacrifice of their heavenly grandparents who fought the Nazis to resurrect Russia.

The martyrs' images are ready to be wielded, their stories of heroism retold, as new objects of veneration everywhere from Youth Army summer camps to school classrooms, Victory Day celebrations, and the funerals of fallen former members. And it's all wrapped ever deeper into the world of faith, destruction, propaganda, and influencers.

At camps, online, and in the Youth Army's regular activities, young soldiers are equipped with ideological and military skills. They are encouraged to imagine using those skills in the conflict against a mythical, supra-historical enemy—the West, fascism, and the non-Russian—in Ukraine. And as they photograph themselves, they show off their dreamy camp life, their belonging on the parade ground, their slices of military Elysium, for their friends online.

Maria takes it all in. She loads TikTok and hails her paramilitary heroes: "Guys, you've chosen a difficult but noble path!" Keep on beating the protestors.

Volunteers, new Pioneers, and beyond

Olga Zanko is, unsurprisingly, more zealous than ever. She continually pops up alongside Youth Army soldiers online. She's meeting veterans in droves. She learns to shoot a handgun, wearing a "Z"

T-shirt.[25] Next to a selfie with a Youth Army member, she declares, "I *believe*, like he does!"[26] She plans to take the ideological re-education of the upcoming generation out of the classroom and the youth group and into day-to-day life.[27] After all, patriotism—faith in the logic of young people's martyrdom—"can't be taught. Children must be brought up into patriotism." And social media is helping Zanko achieve her goal.

Led from the front by Zanko, the Victory Volunteers group has gone into overdrive in response to the Ukraine invasion. Like their younger brothers and sisters in the Youth Army, Victory Volunteers have written letters in support of troops at the front. They're collecting food and equipment for refugees from Donetsk.

And, of course, they're producing Instagrammable propaganda material. In their biggest summer hit, members clad in Russian and ethnic-minority costumes and in military uniforms past and present wave "Z" and Soviet-era banners and national flags. Splashes of blue and white twist around the frame, dragging the young crowd into a mythical war: "We are working for the good of Russia. Our fathers and grandfathers were victorious against fascism. We won't let anyone rewrite our history." A blond, ethnic Russian youth marches forward: "Ours is a single heroic history. It was here that fascism's back was broken!" Yet another rally—another moment of ecstatic, mythic togetherness—is launched into the eye of the internet storm.

The state isn't going to stop at promoting the Youth Army and Victory Volunteers. It's creating more new youth groups to further its grasp on childhood. Putin has signed off on plans to create an organization provisionally called "The Movement of the First," which is widely being labeled the "new Pioneer" movement. Many of the goals are similar to the Youth Army's, but with the aspect of military preparation stripped out. According to the government's press release, the "Movement of the First" will promote "traditional values, love and respect for the fatherland, a love of work, a respect for nature, and a sense of personal responsibility." Participants will take part in sports, music, history lessons, and creative enterprises.[28]

While the Youth Army might be too militarized for some cosmopolitan parents, who are still more attached to European ideals or worried about their children potentially entering the armed forces, the "new Pioneers" looks to be more palatable. Polling conducted in May 2022 suggested that 92 percent of today's parents thought positively about the Soviet Pioneer movement, so the state's plan to have 6 million children enrolled in an entirely new group by 2030 isn't as far-fetched as it sounds.[29]

The group won't simply be roleplaying Soviet-era Pioneering. Led by figures like Zanko and Nagornyy, it will presumably deploy all the social media savvy the state has displayed in recent years to create a TikTok and Instagram-friendly branded experience that delivers Putinist nationalist-religious patriotism to the next generation. Indeed, the project's launch was marked with a glitzy youth conference, "New Horizons." The conference was attended by leading politicians like Foreign Minister Sergey Lavrov, internet stars like the pranksters Vovan and Lexus, and young representatives from the Victory Volunteers and Youth Army.[30] While Lavrov delivered a dreary stump speech about the dangers of America and NATO, the pizzazz brought by young volunteers and internet stars hitched the state's bandwagon to something much more fun. Dozens more initiatives are in the pipeline.[31]

Nikolay, the provincial civil servant who believes his younger colleagues know nothing more than how to shout "hurrah" the loudest, has a long track record working with such youth groups. He says he won't be surprised if many of the new organizations fold quickly: "I know the kind of people who work with them. Back [when I was a Soviet Pioneer] there were real believers, but there were a lot of petty functionaries who made their careers out of these organizations." He says that in the past decade or so, he's seen similar groups "come and go. There was Walking Together. There was Nashi. But today they've sunk without trace. Many of these organizations exist for a couple of years then collapse."

However, Nikolay is more worried today than he has been in the past about the radicalization of children: "The careerists make a whole lot of noise, march around, and shout a bit, but most of them aren't fanatics. Their children, though, might become fanatics. They're not being taught properly. There are gaps in their education. They don't see the other side."

Nikolay gulps and pauses. Thanks to the amount of money and official support flooding into groups coordinated by the Kremlin, he is "very afraid that the future of Russian children might be to live in a giant barracks."

And today, the state is keen that volunteering into youth groups won't be the only route into the barracks. The first barrack that many children will encounter is the schoolroom.

A barrage in the schoolroom barrack

At 8 am on the first Monday of the school year in September, the children of a school just outside St Petersburg line up in their classes. They smile in the fall warmth as their shadows fall onto the crumbling brickwork and flaking paint of a squat school building.

"Raise the flag!" commands their principal, a canescent, portly man approaching retirement. You should be proud of the flag. Take delight in it, he tells them. The words to the national anthem sound from the children's mouth: "Russia is our sacred state, Russia is our most beloved country!" The children, uncertain and out of practice, fray rhythm and melody.

The pupils file inside for the first of their "Conversations about Important Things," a class every schoolchild in Russia will be taking this year. Each "Conversation" is to teach them about patriotism, conservative values, tradition, and love for the motherland. Through interactive games, videos, and slideshows—all produced by the state and distributed online—every child is getting a taste of what it means to be a good Russian. They're learning about why Russia is the most beautiful country in the world, why its scientists are the greatest in history, and why a family with one mother and one father is best.[32]

Their new patriotism lessons above all, though, teach children about war. Shocking elementary school kids with the brutal reality of sacrifice and war isn't a regrettable drawback of the new lessons. It's one of the desired outcomes. During the first "Conversation," one teacher frightened her elementary school class in Moscow with a tale of monstrous enemies:

> [The Ukrainians] ran toward the Russians. Then what do you think happened? One of the nationalists shot the mom from inside the building. The little boy stood up next to his mom—he was about four years old [the teacher starts to cry]. They shot him right in the head. I'll never understand it.[33]

Every child will learn—according to the model answers provided by the state in that week's lengthy teacher-instruction booklet—that "the motherland is dearer than life." That means "it's not scary to die for the motherland."[34] The unlucky few would soon be treated to visits from members of the Wagner Group, the state's arm's-length and brutal frontline force.[35] The state whipped up a whole classroom program paving the way from kindergarten to command-ant's office in Ukraine in mere weeks.

The changes are coming thick and fast in every part of school life in response to the war of 2022. Sometimes, the differences are almost incidental: the "Z" symbol is added to illustrations in an IT skills book, bringing the war into what might seem like it would be an apolitical subject.[36] On other occasions, the additions and adjustments are more significant. In a new middle-grade history textbook, the name of "Kievan Rus'"—the "cradle of Russian civilization" centered on Kyiv that existed between the ninth and thirteenth centuries before the rise of Muscovite power—has simply become *Rus'*. Ukraine's historical significance is erased from children's education in favor of a Muscovite, imperial myth, told as if it were a reality.

The "special military operation" is already being added to the school-leaving Unified State Exam syllabus.[37] Pupils sitting the exams next summer will, if the state's plans come good, learn about the links between the Ukraine war and "the rebirth of the Russian Federation as a major power." The West's economic sanctions are to be explained as a necessary struggle to ensure the reorientation of the world economy away from the West and towards Russian power.[38] And, better yet, even if students flunk the exam, those in some regions will still have learned all about why joining the army makes for a great career.

It doesn't stop outside of lesson time. Walking through the corridors, students are already coming across memorial plaques to the fallen. Members of their school's Youth Army detachment stand guard in honor of these modern-day saints. During the lunch hour, pupils might find themselves roped into participating in a "Z" photo shoot, or waving flags in a low-budget recreation of a viral video. Perhaps, on a class field trip, they might have already visited the Russian armed forces' annual expo, where they could dress up as a soldier or step inside a "Ukrainian classroom" filled with Nazi paraphernalia.

Minister of Education Sergey Kravtsov revealed plans to introduce mandatory military training into schools nationwide starting in September 2023.[39] Some schools in the provinces have already instituted such training. They display their patriotic credentials in public by videoing and sharing images of their "recruits" circling the schoolyard in cut-price fatigues, "Z" symbols scrawled on their backs.

Teachers like Sveta, Olga, and Lera are trying to keep their heads down. Lera, who teaches music, ignored her school administration's suggestion to play an absurd classroom trivia game about Russia's military achievements. But, she tells me, when directives come down from regional administrators or ministries, there's nothing she can do to stop the militarization of childhood. Every school leaver in the coming years will enter the adult world with a keen sense of why war is so important to Russia's strength and future.

And some are ready to fight today by imitating the aggressive behavior on display in their communities. As their elders have fifth graders arrested for the whisper of transgression, so children are cleaning their own communities of Putin's "scum and traitors" by denouncing their own teachers for supposed misdoings.[40] Growing up in a world of aggression, patriotism, religion, and paranoia—and potentially equipped with serious military skills—should we expect these young Russians to embrace humanitarian values or accept their nation's misdoings in Ukraine?

Saint Alyosha, Russia's boy hero

Veselaya Lopan is a tiny, dusty place on the road from Belgorod to Kharkiv, in Ukraine. Little more than a dilapidated rail station and a trickle of ramshackle rural homes flanked by vegetable plots it may be, but Veselaya Lopan has come to national attention in recent months as the home of a saintly young hope for Russia's future.

When a Ukrainian helicopter attacked a Belgorod fuel depot in April 2022, panic broke out on Russian Telegram groups. Was Kyiv launching an all-out assault on Russian territory? Were residents living in border regions in real danger? For the first time in the Ukraine conflict, the "Z" fanatics were confronted by the thought that they might be in danger at home.

The state's propagandists quickly unearthed the perfect tonic to calm the nerves.

In early May, grainy video of a cherubic blonde boy clad in tank commander's cap and baby military fatigues was uploaded to VK and Telegram groups. The boy merrily dashes, half running, half bouncing, along a dusty track from his home to the main road to Kharkiv. He waves boldly at troop columns making their way to the front. This is eight-year-old Alyosha, a resident of Veselaya Lopan.

Captions claimed that little Alyosha was performing his ritual of greeting every day. Social media users went into raptures at this exemplary display of patriotism: "This is going to warm your heart!" Likes and shares went through the roof. Alyosha became an overnight hero.

Journalists from the national media turned up in Veselaya Lopan to conduct interviews with the boy and his parents. Within days, leading politicians like former Chairman of the Federation Council and Duma Deputy Sergey Mironov were sharing news of the boy, describing him as a soldier of the future: "He is the future of OUR Russia! ... Our warriors won't let you down! We shall be victorious!"

More videos were released. Kindly soldiers stopped off on their way to Ukraine to give Alyosha gifts. The uniformed Alyosha bounded out to the road, smiling with euphoric delight. Alyosha appeared at the Belgorod regional traffic police headquarters, where he was presented with a specially tailored miniature parade uniform. Visiting a group of local cadets, he was invited to become a member. He met World War II veterans. He was even welcomed into the ranks of the Youth Army. Flanked by a gurning Nikita Nagornyy at a glitzy PR shoot, Alyosha stood in Youth Army uniform and read confidently from his lines: "I just want the soldiers to be happy. They're so far from home. They get sad."[41] Alyosha was everywhere.

Alyosha's saintly visage adorns everything from T-shirts to school notepads, tins of soup, and even internet fan art. The eighteen-year-old artist Vindemiatrix, for instance, produced a viral pen and ink piece depicting the youthful Alyosha dressed in his distinctive cap, gazing off into a hopeful future. The iconic Alenka chocolate bar was even briefly renamed in his honor, its packaging redesigned to feature a Sovietized painting of young Alyosha.

In this transfigured form, Alyosha was presented to Putin by Belgorod Governor Vyacheslav Gladkov in August 2022. Putin calmly nodded and accepted the "Alenka/Alyosha" chocolate as Gladkov explained that the boy's antics were not staged for the cameras: Alyosha was a real patriot who had started his ritual greeting of his own accord. In turn, state media sycophantically reported the boy's vicarious encounter with the president using a ritual language of praise: "The little boy's image has conquered people's hearts and become a reminder of why Russia is fighting in Ukraine!"[42] Touched by holiness from birth, little Alyosha recalls the Orthodox saints and Soviet child soldier heroes of the past.

Wrapped up in virality—a story of spontaneous patriotism, a tale of the Russian nation's inner spark—Alyosha is a Putinist ideal. He diligently performs his role as a soldier of the future; his parents are keen to show off their enthusiasm for his "heroics"; and his twinkle-eyed cuteness makes him an eye-catching internet star. His videos and pictures are wrapped into the state's language of war. Ordinary Russians like, share, comment, reproduce more and more stylized—and idealized—images of this boy soldier.

Subsumed in this process, the real Alyosha is lost. Who knows who he is, what he really thinks about all of this, or whether he understands anything about war, let alone the reality of the war in Ukraine? For the faithful, Alyosha is the perfect little soldier: emptied of his self, he exists as pure ideal. Millennial Russian parents on VK mothers' groups watch on, wild with gooey-eyed adoration: "Lyosha, you are Russia's hope, Russia's future!!!"; "You are the future of Russia! Here is Russia in one child!!"[43] Many clearly wish their own children would be filled up by the state's military myths as Alyosha has been.

Even in the Soviet era, Russia mourned over and again the children lost during World War II. Andrey Tarkovsky's 1962 film masterpiece *Ivan's Childhood* explores the trauma of the hero, a blonde-haired cherub just a shade older than Alyosha. Ivan finds foster parents in a frontline regiment but he loses something human, something essential, as he endures war. The 1985 Belarusian epic movie *Come and See* tears apart its young protagonist, Flyora, after his village is destroyed by Nazis and he has joined partisan fighters. Flyora ends the movie shaking, broken, and visibly aged. His wild eyes tear at the camera, his sobs silently shrieking through the film's conclusion, as war is rendered futile.

Today, village boys like Alyosha are reduced to playing out the Russian military ideal. Perfectly dressed, perfectly rehearsed lines, the perfect performer. Saint Alyosha waves the troops, under-equipped and doomed on the battlefield, off to war. The perfect model for imitation.

Am I Russian enough?

The Russian state might lack the widespread trust to make people consent to patriotism when given alternate, democratic options. Through youth groups, education, and social media, the authorities force the young to perform so constantly and intensely that "non-Russian" aspects of identity are being extinguished before they mature.[44] The political opposition performs its protests into ever narrower spaces. Many young Russians will never stumble across them. They either won't know where to look or they'll be unaware of the very possibility of their existence.[45] The many voices, identities, and outcomes that might emerge from a country as vast and diverse as Russia are being, to use George Orwell's term from *1984*, "vaporized."

Surrounded by models of fascist excellence, however, the young can fill up their emptied identities with the state's ideology of war. They can watch their peers singing, dancing, and miming their way to military expertise on Youth Army TikTok. From Vladivostok to St Petersburg, they'll learn the correct answers to questions of patriotism and belief in schools. They'll be taught to denounce and decry the enemy on the outside and the enemy within: the Ukrainian, the queer, the liberal, the non-Russian, even their own teachers.

The youngest Russians are being brought up in a war cult that ritually celebrates the wars of the past, the war of the present, and the eternal war between Russia and its Other. Theirs is an isolated, parallel existence fueled by domestic industry and social media platforms, state surveillance and education, and perpetuated by their social media-using peers and parents. It's a world of fairy tale, myth, messianism, latent rage, resentment, and racial and ethnic hatred built on layers of illusion: the illusion of a real, functioning state; the illusion of a successful war; the illusion that the war imitates a holy war of the past; the illusion that Russia's World War II actually was holy.

It's not an isolated few who are living in that world. It may not feel like it when we watch gray-haired gerontocrats deliver spittle-flecked rants on state TV or furious anti-Western invectives at political meetings, but Russia is a young country. Today, almost 19 percent of the population is under fourteen years of age. They are increasingly proud of their nation's military, and an overwhelming majority of children call themselves "Russian patriots."[46]

Their older peers might question state narratives, but the younger the demographic, the more children speak the language of the state fluently—reciting tales of fascist Ukrainians and World War II heroes unprompted.[47] These are the ideologically vetted children who will follow in the footsteps of Nikita Nagornyy and Olga Zanko. They will take up positions in schools, universities, and government at all levels. They will shape, through the popular culture they produce and the mythical worlds they inhabit, Russia's policies and actions in the real world. And, flooding the Russian cultural space with the rhetoric of violence and war, they will make it ever harder for the apathetic to find paths away from participating in those policies

* * *

Today's Russian children can look away from the state's twilight specter of a decaying, degenerate West. They can turn away from the victims of Russia's violence. And if they do, their eyes might briefly grasp a luminous fantasy—glittering away in endless social media reflections, gaudy memes, and viral popularity—of a vibrant national future.

The Young Soldier app blinks red and white into life on the phone screen. The state sits in thousands of children's pockets, nestled in the device they are using to create their reality. The state is watching.

Anybody can apply to join up, there and then. One click to belonging. But filling out the application form is a moment of dangerous, perhaps paralyzing, choices: am I Russian enough? Am

I giving the correct, patriotic answers? Millions of Vasily Grossman's Viktor Shtrums—fractured, listless—are logging on. They know exactly the person they should be. They'd like to join the crowd. They'd like to come into the light. They'd like to live in a mythical Russia.

The Z Generation is not here yet. But it's coming. And it's going to be ready for war—online and offline.

CONCLUSION

DEPROGRAMMING A FASCIST

"What does progress toward a brighter future mean?"
"It means we live better today than tomorrow."

"Even Putin," as Anton jokingly tells me, "has to die some day ... *probably*." Aging fast, isolated from his country and the world, and enduring a humiliating beating at the hands of the Ukrainian army, Vladimir Putin is approaching the end. Perhaps he'll soldier on, his reputation tarnished by military impotence, for a few years. Perhaps he'll be removed in a bloody palace coup tomorrow. Perhaps, as improbable as it feels, the Russian public will become so angry at the failure of the promised fascist utopia to materialize that they'll march on the Kremlin.

Pundits rifle through the Kremlin tea leaves, trying to picture who might replace Putin. Most likely another authoritarian leader. Maybe Yevgeny Prigozhin and his army of Wagner mercenaries. Perhaps Nikolay Patrushev, Putin's old friend, or even Patrushev's son, Dmitry. Or a coalition of nationalists, furious that today's president won't pursue an even more violent genocide in Ukraine.[1] A social media idol in the mold of Olga Zanko might even slip under the radar and into the cockpit.

And the war in Ukraine will end. Perhaps it will come to a screeching, sudden halt as Ukraine advances. Perhaps there'll be a drawn-out, years-long quagmire of "frozen" conflict. Perhaps Russia will yet strike back with a fearsome, obliterative strike on its enemy. Nobody yet knows.

But one thing is for certain. The quasi-religious concoction of nationalism, war, martyrdom, and rebirth being poured down the throats of Russia's young today will leave its mark. Everything tainted with the influence of the West—democracy, homosexuality, difference, the non-Russian—is suspicious. Everything Russian is praiseworthy, and everything Russian is under threat.

Even when Putin is long gone, this "Frankenstein" identity toolkit will live on. The president is idolized but he is not worshipped, like Joseph Stalin and Adolf Hitler were, as a demi-god. "Ukraine" as Russia's Other in 2022 could just as easily be replaced by Belarus, by Moldova, by the Baltic states, or by a new internal enemy—just as Ukraine replaced Chechnya and Georgia in the 2010s. Without major democratic reform in Russia, an increasingly fascist nation won't be content with a peaceful status quo. Stasis is the natural enemy of an ideology that seeks to rejuvenate society through destruction.[2] It's impossible to say where the next war will come. But, internal or external, the war will come. It must, if the fairy tale of the glorious future is to keep being told.

Indeed, despite the flashes of protest that have broken out since February 2022, the country doesn't seem much interested in moving past Putinism, even if some are falling out of love with Putin himself. When asked, most slavishly agree that the president would be right either to stop the war immediately or to turn up the heat and go on the offensive in Ukraine. They follow the leader. They ignore their moral compass and look to the environment around them to learn that what's happening is right.

Anyway, the death or deposition of an aging authoritarian doesn't always produce a stampede toward democracy. The memory of the 1990s means that few Russians are ready to spring for a Western-style democracy: justice for corrupt kleptocrats, liberalization in education, free and fair elections, and freedom of speech. Even if a widespread desire for democracy took hold and was realized, the post-fascist experiences of Germany—where denazification was deeply troubled and perhaps, even, a failure—and Italy—where today's far-right parties are sweeping to power on fever dreams of the Mussolini era—suggest that the path would be rocky.[3]

Those at the most extreme end of Russia's political spectrum have constructed an absurd reality. Yet, in the middle, few are embracing liberal democracy or know where to look for alternatives. Instead, queer children grow up suicidal, fighting inner battles of shame and trauma. Potential protestors see the state's vengeful eye everywhere. They quiet themselves. They drown in the noise of internal debates with the state's imagined voice.

CONCLUSION

The marginalized and the masses alike can choose to seek comfort in remaking themselves under the state's protective umbrella. The imagined mythical past—the past of tsarist and Soviet glory—is warm, welcoming. Putin's neo-fascism might not be perfect, but beyond the digital curtain that is closing around Russia's borders lie only moral depravity and fearsome military threats. It's better to be on the inside, in *nasha* Russia. In *our* Russia.

When Putin goes, the Youth Army might cease to exist. Victory Volunteers could collapse tomorrow. Perhaps there'll be no more mass rallies, and no more child soldier's uniforms sold online. But the social media reality will persist. The connections between Maksim and his young soldiers, between Zanko and her followers, between Nagornyy and his fans, won't disappear. The TikTok communities where young Russians out-compete each other with tales of military belonging and self-sacrifice won't evaporate. The culture might fragment, and perhaps split into fractious internal animosity, but it will perpetuate itself for years to come.[4]

The government in Kyiv has known that Russia won't back down since 2014, when it began undertaking mammoth preparations for a full-scale war with its belligerent neighbor. Now we must recognize it too. We ignore Russia's militarized youth at our own peril. Russia's fascism problem won't go away on its own.

So what can we do about a problem like the Z Generation, before yet more wars are wrought in and beyond Russia? I've spoken to politicians and experts to find out. They all agree. The time to act is now. Neo-fascism is embedding itself deeply in Russia's young. And its tentacles are reaching into our young people's smartphones and minds too.

Bob Rae, Canada's ambassador to the United Nations and special envoy to Myanmar when the Rohingya ethnic cleansing crisis unfolded in 2017, says, "This is going to be the battle that will define the world that our children and grandchildren will inherit." This is a battle worth fighting.

Lock them up?

Toomas Hendrik Ilves, the President of Estonia from 2006 to 2016, isn't a man to mince his words. The West has wasted thirty years, he tells me, trying to be "a psychological counseling service for a bunch of sick fucks. We tried the hand-holding bit. It didn't work. Instead what we get is the horrors of Bucha. On top of that, people are cheering it on." Ilves reminds me that Soviet Russia invaded and occupied Estonia, Latvia, and Lithuania, murdering and deporting thousands.[5] And today, he says, "nothing's changed. They're still as brutal and barbaric as they were back then."

Ilves recalls meeting Russian graduates from leading American business schools at a party after the 2014 invasion of Crimea. They were, he says, "all in" on "Crimea is ours." He's fed up of seeing "smart [Russians], who go study in Western universities, go home, and see how great the gap is between [their society] and the West." Driven by jealousy, explains Ilves, "the result is a turn to fundamentalism and a radical rejection of the West." He notes that Islamic extremists took the same path before 9/11: study abroad, adopt Western customs, then become radicalized. Promoting links between Russia and the West, he believes, won't help at all.

Ilves' solution is simple: "We need to arm ourselves, strengthen NATO, and contain them." That means massive investment in arms and military equipment and taking a hard line on cultural exchanges. For Ilves, there ought to be no more student and tourist visas for Russians, no more goodwill visits, and certainly no more economic links. He calls this a policy of "benign neglect": "The envy plus the hatred is something we don't want to deal with. They can deal with it over there. But don't come back into our yard, please."

Ilves isn't alone. Sweden and Finland have raced to join NATO in response to Moscow's latest war. Kaja Kallas' and Sanna Marin's governments in Estonia and Finland respectively have already introduced visa bans for Russian tourists. Zelenskyy is encouraging more nations to follow their lead. The task is made much easier when radical Russian bloggers travel abroad to provoke and hector their neighbors in the pursuit of social media likes in nationalist online communities. With the Russians locked away in Russia—so the thinking goes—there can't be another Bucha, even if the country collapses into extreme internal violence.

And the conditions for re-engagement? According to Ilves, simple: reparations for destruction; free, democratic elections; and, above all, "they need to get rid of the death cult known as *pobeda* [victory]. It's insane." Ilves' goals are noble. But will an isolationist approach really contain a nuclear power like Russia when many of its people are motivated by an irrational drive to wage destructive war within and around its borders? And when its fascist rallies go on night and day on social media groups and in shared memes and videos? The state could collapse almightily and the parades would just go on, luring in children and teens.

Isolating Russia might secure Europe's borders. It might, though, also bring us a bigger, more powerful, and even more unpredictable North Korea, full of zealots driven by revanchism against the "traitors" at home and abroad who've betrayed them. Wouldn't it be better to address the root cause of the problem by intervening in the sociopolitical development of the Z Generation?

Ukraine's social media-savvy info war teams have proven to be adept at countering the threat from their neighbor in cyberspace. They understand how important the long view is when it comes to defending themselves from their neighbor. Oleksandra Tsekhanovska is head of the Hybrid Warfare Analytical Group at the Ukraine Crisis Media Center. Her team develops policies and solutions to counter global threats, especially from Russia, and works with Western nations to nullify Russia's influence abroad. Few know the Ukrainian and Russian information security field better.

Will the "containment plan" work? "I love the idea," says Tsekhanovska, "but I live in the real world." Tsekhanovska explains that there's a growing Ukrainian interest in conducting influence operations within Russia: "This is something, regardless of whether we like it or not, we will have to do. Because when the war ends, however it ends, Russia in one form or another will still be there." She concurs that "we will have to take action ... if we don't want to have another big problem in ten or twenty years." Today, Ukraine has to focus its limited resources on fighting a hot war. But tomorrow, it's going to be ready to take action to prevent the next invasion.

Part of that pre-emptive defense preparation must be intervening in Russia to interrupt the training of a generation of fascist youth. That doesn't mean providing a "counseling service" for Russian teens. It's a way to head off a serious military threat. And the good news? There are plenty of proactive ways to shape Russian attitudes without risking a repeat of the 1990s, being tarred as Western provocateurs, or—worse—risking a nuclear war. Even better, we don't have to wait for the Putin regime to end. The work can start now.

Words are our bullets

Speaking to Canadian university students via video-link in June 2022, Volodymyr Zelenskyy explained that under Russia's dictatorship, "[f]or us, the internet is a weapon. We can [use it to] show what's going on in Ukraine, who conquered us, who are the victims and the casualties. It's a powerful instrument."

Zelenskyy is right. He and his predecessor as president, Petro Poroshenko, recognized the risk of Russian escalation years before the rest of the world. What's more, they knew that conflict doesn't end on the battlefield. Nor does it begin and end with political declarations of war (or even of "special operations"). In the twenty-first century, the information space is just as important as guns and bullets.[6] "Information," Zelenskyy told his Canadian audience, "the word—can sometimes strike a greater blow than a weapon. Just like real shells and bullets, we can't let words run out." Russian propagandists know it today, just as their Soviet forebears knew it a century ago.[7]

The Kremlin's digital curtain is made from gossamer-thin scraps, not great iron walls. Russia's citizens remain open to digital influence. The Kremlin knows it: 2021's new national-security strategy highlighted the importance of increased cyber defense against "the spread of false information" by external powers.[8] The dyed-in-the-wool Kremlin supporters and the young who've never known a world beyond Putinism are not looking to reach out to the West. But we can reach out to them.

Telegram, the country's most popular social app, is not beholden to the Russian state. Millions are still accessing banned Western social media using VPNs. The state's attempts to cut off access to Instagram in 2022 have been widely ignored: usage has barely fallen. And, with Western expertise, running undetected influence operations even on Russian networks like VK and Odnoklassniki—"Classmates"—isn't impossible. From offices in Europe and America, we can interrupt Russia's glittering bubbles of fascist reality.

Before intervening, we have to be certain that our approaches won't provoke a backlash. Russians like Alina, Vladislav, and Ivan Kondakov dismiss anybody who disagrees with them as a "traitor." Any criticism of any part of their identity—their Orthodoxy, their community, their leaders, their Russianness—must be driven by Western lies. Even moderates like Anton and Kostya have a knee-jerk dislike of terms like "liberal democracy."

Promises of the "American dream" or "Western values" aren't going to gain much traction when anything tainted with the West means lies, perversion, economic failures, and corruption. The slightest drop of counterevidence causes those deeply entrenched in the fantasy reality of Putin's Russia to reach for their toolkit of slogans and images, shoring up the damage to their harmonious world by piling it ever higher with fairy tale. Tell them that Russians have committed war crimes in Ukraine and they will wave away reality as a staged "provocation"—a CIA or Ukrainian psychological operation—and send you a stream of videos or posts about heroic Russian soldiers saving children. Fascism simply isn't a rational force.

What is often termed "counter propaganda"—providing the "real" news through, for example, Russian-language radio broadcasts or websites—isn't likely to convince those raised on a diet of myth. The snappy social media videos created by Navalny's team that expose regime leaders' corruption might rack up millions of views, but they're probably not winning over many regime supporters. When I ask him about Navalny, Kostya chuckles and waves his hands: "He's not a serious man." Telling Russians that they're brainwashed, that they've been abused, or that they've been lied to won't be effective. In fact, such efforts are more likely to be counterproductive.

The dangers of the confrontational approach are made clear in attempts to engage the citizens of a country even more distanced from reality than the Russian Federation: North Korea. Sokeel Park is country director at Liberty in North Korea, an NGO that assists refugees who have left their homeland. For years, Park has been guiding North Koreans as they rethink reality.

When they arrive in South Korea, North Korean refugees often hear stories that expose the corruption and hypocrisy of their leaders or that challenge the military myths underpinning the state's foundation (North Korea is as attached to tales of the Korean War as Russia is to those of World War II). But, says Park, all too often, even those who've chosen to risk their lives by leaving refuse to believe the truth in South Korea. Many even grow angry at challenges to the foundations their realities rest on—a response known as the "backfire effect."[9] The clash between their mythical world and empirical reality is simply too dissonant to process.

Indeed, forceful "counter propaganda" doesn't make people "wake up." It is more likely either to lead to doubling down or—equally dangerously—to the adoption of another illusory mindset.[10] The psychologically fragmented simply choose to seek out another fairy-tale reality. That's what's happened to many in the post-Soviet era. Men like Maksim ditched the Soviet illusion in favor of another fairy-tale reality. Fractured and fragmented after the fall of the USSR, they sought out simple versions of reality that seemed to provide a way to rebuild their sense of self. Like all those who experience trauma, they sought wholeness and harmony. If the attack on their new reality is too severe, they will snatch at anything that promises to repudiate renewed trauma.

Thus, former Soviet soldier Maksim, distressed at the loss of authority and identity the Red Army's slow descent at the end of the Cold War created, leapt at Putin's promises of military strength and at the chance to create the soldiers of tomorrow in the Youth Army. And howling the truth—that the Youth Army is a dangerous indoctrination program to feed the state with sacrificial bodies—at fourteen-year-old Maria won't help. She'll just retreat into the safety of her TikTok world. She'll resent the West even more than she already does. Perhaps she might be tempted down even more dangerous, revanchist paths offered by new, yet more radical online groups that promise to defend Russia.

The parasitic social media culture of Russia's fascism makes the task even harder. One of the most effective ways to deradicalize a cult member is to separate the individual from their group.[11] Indeed, research shows that the more personal links Russians have with positive role models and identities abroad, the less likely they are to support Putinism.[12] We've already seen that process work for Ilya Fedotov-Fedorov. Once he was able to live in Europe, Ilya recognized his own internal battles and his internalized homophobia. Living abroad gave him a new language to describe his experiences.

The Russian state emptied him of language and identity; life on the outside filled him back up. However, the effect is not always the same. Some North Korean refugees, for example, find the experience of living in a world at odds with their state's imagined propaganda reality deeply psychologically jarring; some even dream of returning to the comfortable psychological reality of the brutal regime.[13] When social media can constantly recycle infinite permutations of nationalist myth, the temptation to return to the "cult" will never go away.

Even when Russians do live or travel abroad, they can still be in contact with the culture of Russian fascism thanks to social media. Brute force—banning one community or Telegram channel—will see a dozen others pop up instead. Russia's web of fake-news networks, paid influencers, and bloggers living in Europe and North America, meanwhile, continues to spew dangerous pro-Kremlin content. Moscow's hand is inescapable. The most radicalized can never truly be separated from their networks in the twenty-first century.

If confrontation and isolation won't have much impact, what can we do instead? "Cults don't last forever," explains Rae: "They have to confront reality." But Rae doesn't have in mind a *clash* with reality, volleys of facts fired into worlds of myth. He suggests we target "deeper human emotions and aspirations. The notion of people wanting to live a decent life and get along with their neighbors, to provide for their children, to want to respect each other, and to live a dignified life? I don't think those are Western ideas."

Rae is right. Even the most radicalized individuals I have spoken to—Maksim, Kondakov, Vladislav—care deeply for their families and communities. They are convinced that they are motivated by human goodness. The moderate patriots, like Kostya and Anton, are drawn more to visions of family and home than to fantasies of butchering Ukrainians. And the youngest, like Maria and Alina, seem to seek belonging in familiar narratives and online communities. They are drawn to the fantasies of youthful rejuvenation the state has produced over the past twenty-two years, they revel in the always-available media rally: the movie scenes of joyous dancing and dreams come true; the downtown youth parades; the speeches, the fanfare, the triumph; the peers who profess that they belong to some or other group.

The task, then, is to use our access to Russia's social media world to recreate the atmosphere of those spaces—but shorn of the state's militaristic, destructive content. In its place, we must provide alternative language, images, and models of behavior. Tomorrow's young Alyoshas should be able to fill themselves up from a range of positive examples, not find themselves being turned into model young martyrs. Young Russians should be able to find a path from the present and toward the values of respect and dignity they share with their neighbors in Russia, in Ukraine, and beyond. As it happens, this is the same tonic Vasily Grossman suggests for his characters, who have been fragmented by totalitarianism, in *Life and Fate*. Embracing small acts of human kindness—like nursing an enemy soldier or altruistically helping a neighbor—rebuilds individual identities and communal bonds.

Staging the real world

Arnold Schwarzenegger sits at a desk in a well-appointed study. He addresses the camera as scenes from his youthful body-building career and shots of the Soviet past scroll by. Schwarzenegger remembers meeting Soviet weightlifting idol Yury Vlasov, a hero to bodybuilders everywhere, as a teen.

He speaks in English, but Russian subtitles explain Schwarzenegger's words: "He reached out to shake my hand. He had this powerful hand that swallowed mine. But he was kind, and he smiled at me." Schwarzenegger explains how much he admires his fans in Russia, where bodybuilding and powerlifting remain popular hobbies. Those young Russian fans watching Schwarzenegger speak could imagine, perhaps, looking up to this Austrian-American role model—even though the West is meant to be the enemy—and wanting, too, to reach out to the other side. To admire the other side.

An almost perfect counter-narrative. Until Schwarzenegger ends his personal story and attacks the Russian state's lies. "I know that your government has told you this is a war to denazify Ukraine. Denazify Ukraine? This is not true." Russia, explained Schwarzenegger, was the real villain. Russia, not Ukraine, was killing innocents. The knee-jerk reaction on Russian-language social media groups was all too predictable. Days after Schwarzenegger's video appeared, twenty-two-year-old Russian powerlifter Maryana Naumova released a response. The mise-en-scene and narrative arc of the clip imitate Arnie's: Naumova too speaks directly to the camera to address the "enemy" audience, relating a story of positivity then attacking American hypocrisy. Naumova recalls meeting her "kind" and "good" hero, Schwarzenegger, as a teen, just as he had met Vlasov decades earlier. Naumova claimed she had given Schwarzenegger letters detailing the plight of children in Donbas in 2015, and that he had broken a promise to help with the situation:[14] "*Your* message," she explains, "is based on some kind of an invented reality." We know. We understand. You do not. You cannot. The familiar breath of conspiratorial unlogic.

The clip, which saw this young, photogenic athlete tip Schwarzenegger's message on its head, went viral on Russian-language Telegram and VK groups. It could have been delivered by any one of the Kremlin's army of young social media-friendly sports heroes: by Veronika Stepanova, by Nikita Nagornyy, or by one of the Averina twins. Arnie's message of alternative masculinity sunk without trace. Instead, social media users tore into Schwarzenegger for shilling for America, attacking him with the same litany of homophobic and nationalist insults that have become all too familiar. They didn't accept his message. They bonded around rejecting it.

Dr Bruce White, director of the Organization for Identity and Cultural Development, highlights the clip as a nearly ideal example of the kind of material that might influence young Russians. But the direct attack on the state's reality from outside shrank its chances of changing minds. Whenever material like this appears, says White, "the powers that be can simply turn it around and say, 'But America's done all these terrible things!'"

White and his team have developed a smarter, data-driven approach to intervening in conflict scenarios around the globe. White's team sidesteps the idea of creating "counter narratives" at all. Instead, they crunch vast data sets from publicly available materials to see how entities like the Russian state have manipulated identity. Then, White explains, they "break down the components of identity into their constituent parts so that you can see the manipulation visualized."

He and his team then map out visual pathways showing, for example, how a Russian might associate being "Russian" with being

Orthodox, with messianism, and then move further into violent beliefs: war, violence, and anti-Ukrainian hatred. White's team is, in effect, using big data to map the counterpoints of Russia's fascist myth: the alternating modes of destruction and regeneration that the state and its allies have cultivated since Putin's ascent to power.

Analyzing thousands of examples, they can ascertain how alternate pathways might lead not from Orthodoxy to messianism and violence but to—hypothetically—the construction of churches and Christian community work. Using this approach, they can pinpoint where identity construction leads from positive or neutral beliefs to dangerous ends and vice versa. Then, they can design interventions that offer alternatives: videos, social media campaigns, texts, classroom materials, and so on.[15] The approach has already been tested in several post-conflict settings.

Following this method, Russians don't need to stop being "Russian" to be deradicalized. "We need to find a way," explains White,

> to celebrate the things that people want to celebrate to fulfill their needs. We need to ask, "How does my alternative narrative check the same boxes as the existing pathway?" If the current propaganda allows young men to feel valued, then we need to ensure that the alternate pathway checks the same boxes.

The chances of "backfire effect" are minimized; the appeal of alternative forms of nationalism reduced.

The approach doesn't rely on ramming a uniform, or even a Western, way of life down young Russians' throats. It's about methodically constructing different architectures of reality on the few positive foundations that Russian extremism has left behind. Then, it's up to individuals to take small steps towards inhabiting one of myriad different, non-violent realities. The evidence suggests that many will follow the same paths of extremism. But others, when faced with a branch in the road, will elect to move towards peace—even if they do so unknowingly.[16]

The situation in Russia may seem hopeless, the extremists' heads buried too deep in the sand. Even amateur efforts to make an impact, though, have met with some success. When the war broke out in February 2022, Paulius Senuta knew he wanted to do something to help. From his home in Riga, Latvia, he and a group of others founded Call Russia. Consulting with psychologists and policy experts, Senuta and his team developed an approach that resembles Bruce White's and that anybody could learn in a few minutes.

The group recruits volunteers to make calls to randomly generated Russian numbers using internet phone technology. Russians who pick up the phone are invited to speak about themselves and their views on the war. For the first five to seven minutes of the call, volunteers are instructed just to listen. Then, they are permitted to share their own views, to simply provide a flip side of the Russian's story. The aim is not to decimate Russians' beliefs with facts, but to provide alternate readings of the world, and to do so in a friendly way.[17]

The results of the more than half a million calls that Senuta's volunteers made in the first six months of the war were striking. More than half of the phone calls lead to lengthy conversations. Senuta says that he can often be lost in an hour-long conversation; sometimes his interlocutor even invites him to call back again. Of the hundreds of phone calls he's personally made, only two have led to furious responses or threats. Russians, when they're not angrily confronted, are ready to listen to other human beings.

Indeed, Sokeel Park notes that the most powerful messages North Koreans encounter are films and videos "showing Americans and South Koreans being friendly. Some of the simplest messages can erode threat narratives." Elaborate psychological warfare, outlandish promises of wealth, and mountains of lies aren't needed to win people over. Rae's simple truths of shared humanity will prove effective if delivered at scale. The scale, though, has to be vast.

Call Russia is an amateur effort. With the aid of state money, much more ambitious projects could be born. The Russian state and its allies have been staging a fake reality for their citizens for years. Using social media and approaches based on data like White's, we can show them an alternative, more positive reality. As the state's dazzling imperial edifices lure Russians in, we can shine our own beams of light into their fairy tales.

Imagine Alina logging onto VK. She comes across a new group with an appropriately military title: "RuZZia Proud." A few hundred others have already joined. The moderator has shared daily posts. A few quotes from Putin and neo-fascist thinkers. Images of fireworks in Moscow. A painting of Orthodox saint Aleksandr Nevsky riding into battle against European invaders. Photos of troops in Ukraine. An image of a dying "Russian" child in Donbas. Alina joins. She likes and shares the content. Slowly, the group's feed begins to be interrupted by more positive stories. Mere drops in the ocean of nationalist material. A story about a Ukrainian soldier who helped a Russian prisoner of war. A photograph of a modern-day priest helping Ukrainians. Alina likes and shares some of these posts. A hundred other Alinas see the same material.

Maria opens TikTok. Up pops a new account. A teen girl has joined the Youth Army. She posts all about her life in the Army. The usual bedroom selfies. Parade-ground snapshots. #RealMeWishList. A few weeks in, she issues a gentle complaint. An aging veteran who spoke at that day's meeting is going hungry. She decides to volunteer in the community. Over time, Youth Army content gradually recedes from view. She records videos describing how she's helping her community. She even starts attending church services. She quotes from the Bible: "Love thy neighbor." Maria decides she'll spend less time in the Youth Army. She'd like to be a part of a humanitarian volunteer group instead.

With a little coordination, it could all be staged from Europe or America with Russian-speaking actors and internet users, the content guided by research on identity pathways. The moments of belonging, the moments of shared enterprise, of shared values feel just as real as those staged by the Putin regime. Their reach and audience boosted by tech experts, the posts could find themselves influencing real Russians.

Perhaps the wisest starting point for identity reconstruction could be to turn to Putin's Valdai speech from the fall of 2013. How could "Russian language, Russian culture, the Russian Orthodox Church" be recast as positive starting points for identity? Can subtle social media campaigns seemingly delivered by other Russians convince the young that the Russian language belongs to its speakers, not the Russian state? That Russian culture does not exist independent of a mix of Tchaikovsky's homosexuality, the Russian ballet's French roots, Tolstoy's pacifism, and the contributions of countless ethnic-minority writers, poets, and musicians?

Young users could begin to build their own world around this reality of life outside of militarism. They will not have been lied to.

They will never realize they have been confronted, nor do they have to actively choose to leave the herd. They will have simply been provided with alternate models of living. Not all, but some, will choose them over extremism.

Within this web, it may only take a small pin prick to deeply affect an individual. Seohyun Lee, one of very few North Koreans able to study abroad in China, had an awakening in her early twenties in a taxicab. When the taxi driver asked her why North Korea's leaders left their people to starve, she says, "I couldn't reply to him." She was wordless—just like the many Russians who cannot explain the nature of reality beyond their fairy-tale lives. That moment of realization, explains Lee, "burst my bubble." Later, when her roommate was arrested, she realized that "we are all disposable, expendable ... the hope that I had for the future under the Kim regime vanished."[18] The Chinese taxi driver's question opened Lee to the possibility of an "alternate pathway," priming her to reject the regime totally and, eventually, flee abroad.

In new images, new groups, and new hashtags—just as patriotic and appealing as the state's—identities can be rebuilt. Totalitarianism, the renowned thinker Hannah Arendt wrote, feeds on bodies. It needs war. It demands sacrifice. Human materiel must be pushed through its mangle to keep the cogs of conflict turning. Starve Russia of bodies—the young conscripts who wage genocidal wars, the violent young thugs who attack the state's latest enemy on the streets—and its fascism will grow weaker. Young Russians need to rediscover that they can be patriotic without being violent. That they can refuse to take part in the state's wars at home and abroad.

Repluralizing identity, giving Russians the tools and language that they need so that they can identify as both proudly Russian and non-violent, is going to be hard work. Success won't come overnight. But a thousand pin pricks, delivered in online communities through carefully constructed interventions, might just have an effect.

We have already seen how such small moments can play out in Russia. Anna Veduta read a blog and discovered a vibrant, youthful language distinct from the state's; Ilya Fedotov-Fedorov recognized a queerness shared with a music star; Lera met peers who invited her into the world of Navalny and the opposition. Seemingly insignificant moments, embedded in popular and youth culture, open up individuals to change. But all too often, we have seen the inverse: Ivan Kondakov, Vladislav, and Alina all deepened their patriotism due to the state's memes and spectacles. As the Kremlin slams the door on pluralism for good, it's up to us to provide counterbalancing material.

We must set aside polarized political discussion in the West and agree that acting to stave off the threat of an increasingly radical generation of young Russians is a vital, long-term project. That does not mean launching a war or imposing our will on the Russian population. Nor are these "information warfare" approaches that need to be associated with or overseen by a country's military or intelligence agencies. All we need to do is add pluralism back into the Russian mix.

Between them, the United States, the UK, and Germany have already spent over 60 billion euros on the war in Ukraine in just eight months.[19] One HIMARS rocket launcher alone costs over $3 million. These vast expenditures do not count the global economic damage of the war. Leaving aside the human and economic cost of the war to Ukraine itself, even the most hard-nosed accountant would agree that influence operations are a bargain.

While Russia remains connected to global internet networks and social media, flooding its online space with positive examples of identity creation is a cinch—and far cheaper and less risky than preparing for or conducting hot wars for the next few decades. So play the Russians at their own game: give their young a social media reality of belonging and harmony that leads them away from their state's messages of violence and sacrifice. We can show Russians a reality in which Russia's "greatness" lies in human kindness, not imaginary worlds of lost imperial grandeur.

Born to be killed

"What do you make of groups like the Youth Army? And the new school classes? Will you sign your kids up?" I ask.

"Finally"—Ivan Kondakov looks me in the eye, pausing for effect—the state's education programs, both in and out of schools, are going to shake degeneracy out of the next generation. They will train children to, he says, overcome "the Western desire to eat, drink, and fuck." Children will at last, he says, have "examples of mass heroism" in the form of today's soldiers, the soldiers of the past, and neo-fascist messianic internet warriors (like Kondakov himself). Kondakov hopes that his children will have the "will" to transform themselves, to rise above the "base instincts" of the West, and to acquire enough "willpower" to resist the onslaught of American psychological warfare. Kondakov speaks fluently in the language of a fascism that subjugates the individual will to the national spirit.[20]

Like and comment, watch and share, consume and reproduce. Bathe in the glamour of the rally. Become whole. Purify yourself. Purify the nation. Purify the world. Destroy to save. Frightened of the shadowy West, some of Russia's young are already being drawn by these promises of a better, purer future.

Russia's apocalyptic messianism is inescapable, but it is built on fragile myths. A shoddy, incompetent government struggles to sell its war in Ukraine to millennials. People are dying. The economy is drying up. Soldiers are mutinying, fleeing, and refusing to serve. Living standards are falling. The hallowed reality of the war in Ukraine, spread by state propagandists on TV and thousands of memes, is a sham. People aren't reaping the benefits of the promised utopia.

Things might come tumbling down quickly. In the 1980s, plenty of Soviets blindly engaged in the daily rituals of communist life— joining the Communist Youth League, attending parades, "volunteering" for community work—even though they could see the state falling apart before their very eyes.[21] Perhaps, then, Russia in 2022 is closer to the USSR of 1989 than the Germany of 1939.

Indeed, as Bob Rae tells me, fascism cannot withstand contact with reality forever: "If you live in a society of war of all against all, life becomes brutish and nasty and short. It can't last very long." He's right. Fascist regimes can't last forever. But extinguishing a fascist mindset that spreads and exists beyond the bounds of state and party institutions is a new challenge.

* * *

Across the world, political movements are becoming detached from reality as their adherents succumb to the same tactics of online division and attack that Putin's regime has piloted. Extremists in America, Britain, and the European Union sell tales of imaginary threats and fairy-tale solutions, attack education, and use social media to build harmonious communities for their supporters.

They're not as violent as Russian fascists. Nor are they as war-mongering. But our worlds are built online. Many are losing their grip on what is real and what is not. And that leaves everybody vulnerable to being pushed towards a desire to cleanse their society of "enemies." Russia is already reaching into our spaces to ease that transition, flooding our political landscape with bots, trolls, diversions, and paid influencers.[22] I am vulnerable. So are you.

For all the brave talk of unity against Russian expansionism and violence in 2022, little is being done to build up our defenses. "The corruptibility of Western societies may do us in," says Toomas Hendrik Ilves, giving Russia "the ultimate victory." He laments the pervasiveness of Russian money in Western politics, especially in Britain and the United States; the timidity of European politicians; and our continued attempts to strike compromises with a government that will never be willing to make peace. Fascism can't and won't be beaten at the negotiating table, and Putin's money and social media armies are still on the march. Unless they're stopped, we're all at risk of succumbing to Russia's fascism.

If we cannot resolve the divisions and rage bubbling away within our own society, we may not be able to convince a generation of Russians that views us with total suspicion that we mean it when we say we do care about humanity and humans. "We have," says Rae, "to be prepared to fight for our views, for our concept of what it means to be a decent human being in a decent, humane society."

"We're at an existential moment," says Rae. "We're going through a period of great violence. How can we fight in the most intelligent and consequential way that will have the least damaging effect on our own society?" Rae is right. We must use all the tools at our disposal to go on the offensive; to reframe our thinking around Russia; and to realize that, as Zelenskyy knows, we are already fighting an information war. If we do not, there is nothing to stop Western democracies following in Russia's fascist path.

"Whither, then, are you speeding, o Russia of mine?" asked the author Nikolay Gogol at the end of his nineteenth-century Russian-language epic *Dead Souls*. Gogol's Russia is a whirl of arabesque sentences that wanders aimlessly through a corrupt, empty country; his novel's protagonist meanders around the landscape buying up dead serfs as a tax scam. Russia in the 2020s is speeding nowhere. The Russian world is a place of monolithic expression and stock language, of militarized performance and regimented life, and of perpetual violence. Russia is spiraling, collapsing in on itself, repeating its performances of grandeur and militarism in ever smaller concentric circles as it promises itself—and its youngest generation—a utopian future. But the promise, like the promise of the dead serf in Gogol, is empty.

I try to check in with Alina in Nizhny Tagil. She doesn't return my messages. She has, however, kept up her hectic VK posting schedule.

Alina's latest post is a photograph of a nuclear explosion. The caption is simple: "Your children were born to be killed by Russians. And nothing more."

NOTES

1. GOD IS WITH OUR BOYS

1. Russians identified by just their forename have been anonymized. Those with a surname are either public figures or have agreed to be identified.
2. In general, Russia's public has widely supported the war in Ukraine. Jade McGlynn argues that the population is as complicit as the Kremlin in manufacturing and conducting the conflict. See Jade McGlynn, *Russia's War* (Cambridge: Polity, 2023).
3. Vladimir Putin, "Obrashchenie prezidenta Rossiiskoi Federatsii," 24 February 2022, http://kremlin.ru/events/president/news/67843
4. I refer to the Ukrainian capital as Kyiv, the transliteration from Ukrainian and preference of the Ukrainian government and majority of Ukrainians. Where Russian speakers call it "Kiev," the Russian name, I have preserved their choice of language.
5. Sandro Bellassai, "The Masculine Mystique: Antimodernism and Virility in Fascist Italy," *Journal of Modern Italian Studies* 10, no. 3 (1 September 2005): 314–35.
6. Elizaveta Gaufman, "Religion, the Russian–Ukrainian War, and Social Media," Talk About: Law and Religion (blog), 3 March 2022, https://talkabout.iclrs.org/2022/03/03/religion-the-war-and-social-media
7. "Russia Adds Prominent Journalists, LGBT Activists to Registry of 'Foreign Agents,'" Radio Free Europe/Radio Liberty, 16 April 2022, https://www.rferl.org/a/russia-foreign-agents-journalists-lgbt/31805529.html
8. Polling in authoritarian countries is always riven with controversy. In Russia, the state conducts polls, explains Greg Yudin, as much to manufacture the semblance of a democracy as to actually create one. Those who respond to polls—often only a tiny minority—may give answers they think the pollster wishes to hear or the responses they believe the state expects. In this sense, Russia's pollling is a reflection of the performative state I describe throughout this work: a pantomime of speaking and listening designed to enact a totalitarian will. See Greg Yudin, "Governing Through Polls: Politics of Representation and Presidential Support in Putin's Russia," *Javnost: The Public* 27, no.1 (2020): 2–16.

9. Ian Garner and Jade McGlynn, "Russia's War Crime Denials Are Fuel for More Atrocities," *Foreign Policy* (blog), 23 April 2022, https://foreignpolicy.com/2022/04/23/propaganda-russia-atrocity-bucha

10. Ian Garner, "'We've Got to Kill Them': Responses to Bucha on Russian Social Media Groups," *Journal of Genocide Research* (9 May 2022): 1–8.

11. Vladimir Putin, "Meeting on Socioeconomic Support for Regions," 16 March 2022, http://en.kremlin.ru/events/president/news/67996

12. Jochen Hellbeck, *Revolution on My Mind: Writing a Diary under Stalin* (Cambridge, MA: Harvard University Press, 2009); Catriona Kelly, *Comrade Pavlik: The Rise and Fall of a Soviet Boy Hero* (London: Granta, 2005), 32; Ian Garner, *Stalingrad Lives: Stories of Combat and Survival* (Montreal: McGill-Queen's University Press, 2022).

13. Klaus Wiegrefe, "Bonn–Moscow Ties: Newly Released Documents Shed Fresh Light on NATO's Eastward Expansion," *Spiegel International*, 3 May 2022, https://www.spiegel.de/international/germany/bonn-moscow-ties-newly-released-documents-shed-fresh-light-on-nato-s-eastward-expansion-a-5a362292-dfe6-4355-b90f-10d635d7d664

14. "Vecher s Vladimirom Solovyevym," Rossiia 1, 5 May 2022.

15. There are two words for "Russian" in the Russian language. *Rossiskiy* refers to the administrative state of post-Soviet Russia, as in the "Russian" Federation. *Russkiy*—as it is here—refers to anything deemed ethnically or culturally Russian, which for the state and its supporters includes Ukrainians, Belarusians, Russian-speaking Balts, and so on.

16. This cultural genocide resembles the colonizing genocides carried out by other European powers, for example in Canada. See Robert Cohen, *Canada's First Nations and Cultural Genocide* (New York: Rosen, 2016).

17. For a summary of the many definitions of fascism, see Roger Griffin, *The Nature of Fascism* (London: Pinter, 1991), 4–7. Some experts were in the mid-2010s singling out militarism and the cult of a charismatic totalitarian leader like Putin as evidence of Russia's growing fascism (Alexander J. Motyl, "Putin's Russia as a Fascist Political System," *Communist and Post-Communist Studies* 49, no. 1 (2016): 25–36). More recently, a slew of experts have published comparisons between Russia's actions today and the behavior of the irredentist Nazi state in the 1930s, arguing that history is repeating itself or that Putin's regime is a fascist "cult of irrationality" or a death cult (Francine Hirsch, "Putin's Russia Has Crossed a Threshold," *Boston Globe*, 28 April 2022; Timothy Snyder, "We Should Say It: Russia Is Fascist," *The New York Times*, 19 May 2022).

18. Umberto Eco, *How to Spot a Fascist* (New York: Random House, 2020).

19. Griffin, *The Nature of Fascism*, 18, 45.

20. Mikkel Bolt Rasmussen, *Late Capitalist Fascism* (Cambridge: Polity, 2022), 8.

21. Ibid., 9.
22. Ibid., 15, 19.
23. Judith Butler, *Gender Trouble: Feminism and the Subversion of Identity* (New York: Routledge, 1990).
24. Bolt Rasmussen, Late Capitalist Fascism, 66.
25. J. Furman Daniel III and Paul Musgrave, "Synthetic Experiences: How Popular Culture Matters for Images of International Relations," *International Studies Quarterly* 61, no. 3 (1 September 2017): 503–16.
26. Academics will continue debating the nature of this new fascism. They may term it "para fascism," "neo-fasccism," or "quasi-fascism." Perhaps they'll coin an entirely new term. But for now, we'll stick with the best word available, despite its limitations: Russia is a fascist nation.
27. For example, see Mark Galeotti, *We Need to Talk about Putin: How the West Gets Him Wrong* (New York: Random House, 2019); Mikhail Zygar, *All the Kremlin's Men: Inside the Court of Vladimir Putin* (New York: PublicAffairs, 2016).
28. Marlène Laruelle, *Is Russia Fascist? Unraveling Propaganda East and West* (Ithaca, NY: Cornell University Press, 2021).
29. Håvard Baekken, "The Return to Patriotic Education in Post-Soviet Russia: How, When, and Why the Russian Military Engaged in Civilian Nation Building," *Journal of Soviet and Post-Soviet Politics and Society* 5, no. 1 (2019).
30. Julia Davis (@JuliaDavisNews), tweet, September 14, 2022, https://twitter.com/JuliaDavisNews/status/1569870269191229440
31. See Eliot Borenstein, *Meanwhile, in Russia…: Russian Internet Memes and Viral Video* (London: Bloomsbury, 2022), and Christina Cottiero et al., "War of Words: The Impact of Russian State Television on the Russian Internet," *Nationalities Papers* 43, no. 4 (4 July 2015): 533–55, on how state TV and media influenced the development of the Russian internet and meme culture.
32. Yanina Sorokina, "Who Is the Author of Russia's 'Blueprint for Genocide' Essay?," *The Moscow Times*, 7 April 2022.
33. S.A. Karaganov, "From Constructive Destruction to Gathering," *Russia in Global Affairs* 20, no. 1 (2022).
34. Sergei Karaganov, "Vozobnovlenie dialoga Rossiia-NATO budet oshib-koi," *Rossiiskaia gazeta*, 15 January 2017, https://rg.ru/2017/01/15/sergej-karaganov-vozobnovlenie-dialoga-rossiia-nato-oshibka.html
35. Serge Schmemann, "Why Russia Believes It Cannot Lose the War in Ukraine," *The New York Times*, 19 July 2022.
36. Petr Akopov, "Rossiia budushchego—vpered, v SSSR," RIA, 22 March 2022, https://ria.ru/20220322/rossiya-1779337226.html
37. For example, Telegram, @nasha_stranaZ, https://t.me/nasha_stranaZ/17360

38. For a summary of the complex definitions and arguments over the term 'totalitarianism,' see Emilio Gentile, "Total and Totalitarian Ideologies," in The Oxford Handbook of Political Ideologies, ed. Michael Freeden and Marc Stears (Oxford: Oxford University Press, 2013).

39. Vasilii Semenovich Grossman, *Life and Fate* (London: Vintage Classic, 2011).

40. For a copy of the video, see Tadeusz Giczan (@TadeuszGiczan), tweet, 10 April 2022, https://twitter.com/TadeuszGiczan/status/15130808 37117517825?s=20&t=KuURbjD59Z7Z1LMEE28Iyg

41. Telegram, @novnew, https://t.me/novnew/11135

42. Griffin, *The Nature of Fascism*, 15.

2. A FAIRY-TALE REBIRTH

1. Larisa Popovich et al., "Russian Federation: Health System Review," *Health Systems in Transition* 13, no. 7 (2011).

2. Clementine Fujimura, *Russia's Abandoned Children: An Intimate Understanding* (Westport, CT: Praeger, 2005), 5, 53, 124.

3. Cathy Caruth, *Trauma: Explorations in Memory* (Baltimore: Johns Hopkins University Press, 1995); Caruth, *Unclaimed Experience: Trauma, Narrative, and History* (Baltimore: Johns Hopkins University Press, 1996).

4. Stephen Shenfield, *Russian Fascism: Traditions, Tendencies, Movements* (New York: M.E. Sharpe, 2001).

5. *Putin: The New Tsar*, BBC, 2018.

6. Putin was reiterating points he had already made in an article, "Russia at the Turn of the Millennium," in a national newspaper the previous day, where he laid out the threat of Russia losing its great-power status and suggested "traditional Russian values" as the solution. See Fiona Hill and Clifford Gaddy, "Putin and the Uses of History," *The National Interest* 117 (2012): 21–31.

7. Vladimir Putin, "Novogodnee obrashchenie i.o. Prezidenta Putina," 31 December 1999, http://kremlin.ru/events/president/transcripts/ 22280

8. Benedict Anderson notes the importance of creating national communities out of "deliberately empty" monuments. Today's "monuments" exist in mediatized spaces: as pop songs, TV shows, memes, and so on (Benedict Anderson, *Imagined Communities: Reflections on the Origins and Spread of Nationalism* (London: Verso, 2016)).

9. Peter Pomerantsev, *Nothing Is True and Everything Is Possible: The Surreal Heart of the New Russia* (New York: Public Affairs, 2014), 6–7.

10. This is often termed "managed democracy." See Zygar, *All the Kremlin's Men*, 20.

11. Nikolay Petrov, "The Essence of Putin's Managed Democracy," Carnegie

Endowment for International Peace, 18 October 2005, https://carnegieendowment.org/2005/10/18/essence-of-putin-s-managed-democracy-event-819

12. Jade McGlynn, *The Kremlin's Memory Makers: The Politics of the Past in Putin's Russia* (London: Bloomsbury, 2023).

13. Serguei Alex Oushakine, *The Patriotism of Despair: Nation, War, and Loss in Russia* (Ithaca, NY: Cornell University Press, 2011).

14. The great Canadian theorist Northrop Frye argues that myth functions through a series of alternating oppositions: summer and winter, light and dark, day and night, life and death. See Northrop Frye, *Anatomy of Criticism* (Princeton, NJ: Princeton University Press, 1957).

15. Vladimir Putin, "Annual Address to the Federal Assembly of the Russian Federation," 25 April 2005, http://en.kremlin.ru/events/president/transcripts/22931

16. Ilya Yablokov, *Fortress Russia: Conspiracy Theories in the Post-Soviet World* (Cambridge: Polity, 2018), 83.

17. Katherine Graney, *Russia, the Former Soviet Republics, and Europe since 1989: Transformation and Tragedy* (Oxford: Oxford University Press, 2019), 151.

18. Bruce Berglund, *The Fastest Game in the World: Hockey and the Globalization of Sports* (Oakland: University of California Press, 2020), 226.

19. Guzel Sabirova and Alexey Zinoviev, "Urban Local Sport Clubs, Migrant Children and Youth in Russia," *Community Development Journal* 51, no. 4 (4 October 2016): 482–98; Marina G. Kolosnitsyna, Natalia A. Khorkina, and Marina V. Lopatina, "The Factors of Physical Activities in Russian Youth: Evidence from Micro-Data," HSE Working Papers, National Research University Higher School of Economics, 2018, https://ideas.repec.org/p/hig/wpaper/21-psp-2018.html

20. Katerina Clark, *Moscow, the Fourth Rome: Stalinism, Cosmopolitanism, and the Evolution of Soviet Culture, 1931–1941* (Cambridge, MA: Harvard University Press, 2011).

21. Birgit Beumers, *World Film Locations: Moscow* (Bristol: Intellect Books, 2014), 6–7.

22. Tobias Köllner, "Patriotism, Orthodox Religion and Education: Empirical Findings from Contemporary Russia," *Religion, State and Society* 44, no. 4 (1 October 2016): 366–86.

23. Thanos Pagonis and Andy Thornley, "Urban Development Projects in Moscow: Market/State Relations in the New Russia," *European Planning Studies* 8, no. 6 (1 December 2000): 751–66; Vladimir Kolossov and John O'Loughlin, "How Moscow Is Becoming a Capitalist Mega-City," *International Social Science Journal* 56, no. 181 (2004): 413–27.

24. Robert Argenbright, "Moscow on the Rise: From Primate City to Megaregion," *Geographical Review* 103, no. 1 (2013): 20–36.

25. See, for instance, "Flesh-mob 'Stilyagi' tanets," YouTube, 20 May 2012, https://youtu.be/80dI9Eoc_jY

26. The owner of vast industrial holdings and, when *Stilyagi* was produced, the 185th richest man in Russia, Lebedev sponsored several similar projects designed to boost Russia's reputation at home and abroad in the 2000s (including, for example, an exhibition of Russian art at the Guggenheim in New York).

27. Peter Pomerantsev, "Putin's Rasputin," *London Review of Books*, October 2011, https://www.lrb.co.uk/the-paper/v33/n20/peter-pomerant-sev/putin-s-rasputin

28. Marit Sundet, Per-Anders Forstorp, and Anders Örtenblad, *Higher Education in the High North: Academic Exchanges between Norway and Russia* (Cham: Springer, 2017), 38.

29. For a summary of youth responses to the "wild nineties" myth, see Allyson Edwards and Roberto Rabbia, "The 'Wild Nineties': Youth Engagement, Memory and Continuities between Yeltsin's and Putin's Russia," in *Youth and Memory in Europe: Defining the Past, Shaping the Future*, eds. Félix Krawatzek and Nina Friess (Berlin: De Gruyter, 2022).

30. "Vospriiatie devianostykh," Levada Centre, 6 April 2020, https://www.levada.ru/2020/04/06/vospriyatie-devyanostyh

31. Yuri Lobunov, "Putin's 150 Promises," Riddle Russia, 18 April 2018, https://ridl.io/560-2/ [note the type of dash here, which has been altered in typesetting]

32. Lara Ryazanova-Clarke, "Russian Linguistic Culture in the Age of Globalization: A Turn to Linguistic Violence," in *Russian Culture in the Age of Globalization*, eds. Vlad Strukov and Sarah Hudspith (Abingdon: Routledge, 2018).

33. Patrick Cockburn, "Russian Warplanes Kill Dozens of Villagers," *The Independent*, 11 October 1999.

34. Arkady Babchenko, *One Soldier's War* (New York: Open Road + Grove/Atlantic, 2009), 172.

35. Anna Politkovskaya, *Putin's Russia: Life in a Failing Democracy* (New York: Henry Holt & Company, 2007).

36. Jim Headley, "War on Terror or Pretext for Power? Putin, Chechnya, and the 'Terrorist International,'" *The Australasian Journal of Human Security* 1, no. 2 (January 2005): 13–35.

37. Paul Kolbe, "The Global War on Chechnya: What Does 9/11 Teach Us about Counterterrorism Cooperation with Russia?," Russia Matters, 13 October 2021, https://www.russiamatters.org/analysis/global-war-chechnya-what-does-911-teach-us-about-counterterrorism-cooper-ation-russia

38. The return of the Cult of Victory to prominence, though, was not all

Putin's doing. Boris Yeltsin had also used parades and militarization for political effect in the 1990s. See Allyson Edwards, "Russia on a Throne of Bayonets: Militarisation without the Military in Yeltsin's Russia, 1990–2000" (PhD thesis, Swansea University, 2021).

39. Garner, *Stalingrad Lives*, 1.
40. Elizabeth A. Wood, "Performing Memory: Vladimir Putin and the Celebration of World War II in Russia," *The Soviet and Post-Soviet Review* 38, no. 2 (1 January 2011): 172–200.
41. Aleksey Ekart, as quoted in Oushakine, *The Patriotism of Despair*, 36.
42. V.I. Lutovinov, "Grazhdansko–patrioticheskoe vospitanie segodnia," *Pedagogika* 5 (2006); Håvard Baekken, "Patriotic Disunity: Limits to Popular Support for Militaristic Policy in Russia," *Post-Soviet Affairs* 37, no. 3 (4 May 2021): 261–75.
43. Jason B. Hood, *Imitating God in Christ: Recapturing a Biblical Pattern* (Downers Grove, IL: InterVarsity Press, 2013), 195.
44. The phrase "we can do it again"—*mozhem povtorit*—began to spread widely after appearing at a parade in 2014. Anna Borshchevskaya, "The Role of the Military in Russian Politics and Foreign Policy over the Past 20 Years," *Orbis* 64, no. 3 (1 January 2020): 434–46.
45. Ingo Schröder and Asta Vonderau, *Changing Economies and Changing Identities in Postsocialist Eastern Europe* (Münster: LIT Verlag, 2008).
46. As quoted in Roland Dannreuther and Luke March, "Chechnya: Has Moscow Won?," *Survival* 50, no. 4 (1 September 2008): 97–112.
47. The state also funded "historical patriotic" productions about tsarist heroes such as 2008's *Admiral*, a biography of the anti-Bolshevik Civil War leader Aleksandr Kolchak. Regardless of the historical setting, the plot of the heroic tale always follows the same arc: a masculine hero lays down his life for the greater (that is, the Russian) good.
48. Richard Paddock, "Russians Confirm Troop Deaths 84 Fatalities in Worst Battle of War with Chechen Rebels," *Chicago Sun Times*, 12 March 2000.
49. *Ninth Company*, a 2005 film about the Soviet–Afghan war, repeats the same myth. By the end of the movie, only one of a company of young recruits is left alive. Mass heroism emerges through death, not survival. Vladimir Putin himself praised the hit movie as "a tragic story from the life of our country and our people. But people who fought there for their ideals did a good job" ("Putin Praise for Russian War Film," BBC, 8 November 2005, http://news.bbc.co.uk/2/hi/entertainment/4416774.stm).
50. Philipp Casula, "Between 'Ethnocide' and 'Genocide': Violence and Otherness in the Coverage of the Afghanistan and Chechnya Wars," *Nationalities Papers* 43, no. 5 (September 2015): 700–18.

51. For a discussion of mothers' and sons' sacrifices and identity in post-Soviet Russia, see Maya Eichler, *Militarizing Men: Gender, Conscription, and War in Post-Soviet Russia* (Stanford, CA: Stanford University Press, 2011).

52. Aurélie Lacassagne, "Controlling the Russian Soldiers' Mothers and Chechen Mothers: The Story of a Hidden War," *Journal of the Motherhood Initiative for Research and Community Involvement* 1, no. 1 (1 October 2010).

53. Pomerantsev, *Nothing Is True and Everything Is Possible*, 57.

54. Jim Nichol, "Bringing Peace to Chechnya?," in *Focus on Politics and Economics of Russia and Eastern Europe*, ed. Ulric Nichol (New York: Nova, 2007).

55. Andrei P. Tsygankov, "If Not by Tanks, Then by Banks? The Role of Soft Power in Putin's Foreign Policy," *Europe-Asia Studies* 58, no. 7 (1 November 2006): 1079–99.

56. Sarah Moser, "New Cities in the Muslim World: The Cultural Politics of Planning an 'Islamic' City," in *Religion and Place: Landscape, Politics and Piety*, ed. Peter Hopkins, Lily Kong, and Elizabeth Olson (Dordrecht: Springer Netherlands, 2013), 39–55.

57. Karina Arturovna Bagdasaryan, "Modern Directions of Socio-Economic Development of the North Caucasian Federal District," *Science and Technology* 1, no. 4 (2013). For a typical piece of imperial whitewashing, see a 2013 episode of the Ukrainian-produced travel show *Orel i reshka* ("Heads or Tails"), which was hugely popular among young Russians. In the episode, the presenters visit Grozny. The war is barely acknowledged. Instead, the young leads spend a weekend eating and dancing their way through the majestic palaces and hotels of the new Chechnya.

58. Ironically, Yulia Volkova, one half of Tatu, has gone on to make pointedly homophobic public remarks. She committed to Orthodoxy after a brief dalliance with Islam and even attempted to stand for United Russia in the Duma elections of 2021. Her bandmate, Lena Katina, has forcefully criticized Volkova. Leonie Cooper, "Tatu's Lena Katina Responds to Bandmate's Homophobia: 'People Should Be Free to Love Who They Love,'" *NME* (blog), 21 September 2014, https://www.nme.com/news/music/tatu-1229252

59. Francesca Stella, "Queer Space, Pride, and Shame in Moscow," *Slavic Review* 72, no. 3 (2013): 458–80.

60. Jamey Gambrell, "Russia's New Vigilantes," *New York Review of Books*, 16 January 2003, https://www.nybooks.com/articles/2003/01/16/russias-new-vigilantes

61. Donald Kursch, "Intolerance in Contemporary Russia," Washington, DC: Commission on Security and Cooperation in Europe, 2003, 9–10.

62. The policy of "managed nationalism" that the regime had instituted meant tolerating and even using violent youth groups while attempting to keep their behavior in hand. Dozens of radical nationalist and neo-Nazi political groups like Russky obraz ("The Russian Way") were not just tolerated but encouraged (Robert Horvath, *Putin's Fascists: Russkii Obraz and the Politics of Managed Nationalism in Russia* (Abingdon: Routledge, 2020)). Through tacit signals from the regime, they—and especially football-hooligan groups—were asked to intimidate and attack opponents—in particular LGBT and liberal youths (see "Time for Action: Incidents of Discrimination in Russian Football," Sova Center, 2015, https://www.farenet.org/wp-content/uploads/2015/02/SOVA-monitoring-report.pdf). At the same time, official rhetoric increasingly drew a line between the Russian, who was supposedly "particularly tolerant," and the non-Russian Other of fifth columnists; liberals; non-Orthodox Slavs; and, especially, Muslims from the Caucasus (Yablokov, *Fortress Russia*, 87).

63. Iuliia Taratuta and Aleksey Sobolev, "U 'Idushchikh vmeste' razoshlis' puti," *Kommersant*, 14 January 2005.

64. The "Vladimir Vladimirovich Putin Fan Club," an organic group co-opted by the state, carried out this "action" with support. The group still exists, plastering bedrooms in soapy teen Putin fan art, flags, and pictures. See Bela Doka, "Fan Club Putin," LensCulture, 2014, https://www.lensculture.com/articles/bela-doka-fan-club-putin

65. Yablokov, *Fortress Russia*, 93.

66. A. Ishkanian, "Nashi: Russia's Youth Counter-Movement," Open Democracy, 30 August 2007, https://www.opendemocracy.net/en/russia_nashi

67. Luke Harding, "Welcome to Putin's Summer Camp," *The Guardian*, 23 July 2008, https://www.theguardian.com/world/2008/jul/24/russia

68. Andrei Kozenko and Aleksandr Chernykh, "Moskva pokrasnela patruliami," *Kommersant*, 21 April 2011.

69. Julie Hemment explores many of the contradictions around the state's use of Nashi as an authoritarian participatory project in *Youth Politics in Putin's Russia: Producing Patriots and Entrepreneurs* (Bloomington: Indiana University Press, 2015).

70. Viacheslav Opakhin, "Ivan Katanaev: 'U bol'shinstva fanatov v strane kasha v golove,'" SpartakWorld (blog), 2015, https://www.spartak-world.ru/fans-spartak/18471-ivan-katanaev-u-bolshinstva-fanatov-v-strane-v-golove-kasha-s-odnoy-storony-ermak-s-drugoy-gitleryugend.html

71. Iurii Dud', "Chem zanimaetsia samyi izvestnyi fanat 'Spartaka,'" Sports.

ru, 23 July 2015, https://www.sports.ru/tribuna/blogs/dud/808057.html

72. For a good summary, see the VICE documentary *Putin's Secret Neo-Nazi Armies*, 2022, https://video.vice.com/en_uk/video/putins-secret-neo-nazi-armies/62f3d1b6e7ea5f6f67548ef1

73. Simon Parkin, "The Rise of Russia's Neo-Nazi Football Hooligans," *The Guardian*, 24 April 2018, https://www.theguardian.com/news/2018/apr/24/russia-neo-nazi-football-hooligans-world-cup

74. Aleksey Sidorenko, "Russia: 'Why Did They Kill Yuri Volkov?,'" Global Voices (blog), July 2010, https://globalvoices.org/2010/07/22/russia-why-did-they-kill-yuri-volkov; A. Savel'ev, *Rossiia i russofobiia* (Moscow: Russii informatsionnyi tsentr, 2010).

75. E. Kholmogorov, "Pochemu 'Rossiia dlia russkikh,'" *Russkii obozrevatel'*, 16 December 2010.

76. "Sovsem ofanateli,"? Interfax, 14 December 2010, https://www.interfax-russia.ru/view/sovsem-ofanateli; "Aktsiiu pamiati fanata 'Spartaka' vozglavila partiia 'Yabloko,'" NewsRU, 14 January 2011, https://www.newsru.com/russia/14jan2011/yabloko.html

77. See Oksana Dudko, "A Conceptual Limbo of Genocide: Russian Rhetoric, Mass Atrocities in Ukraine, and the Current Definition's Limits," *Canadian Slavonic Papers* 64, nos. 2–3 (15 September 2022): 133–45.

78. Clara Ferreira-Marques, "Russia: Moscow's Street Children Struggle to Survive," Reuters, 28 February 2002; "An Epidemic of Street Kids Overwhelms Russian Cities," *The Globe and Mail*, 16 April 2002, https://www.theglobeandmail.com/news/world/an-epidemic-of-street-kids-overwhelms-russian-cities/article4141933

3. THE ENEMY WITHIN

1. Not much has changed even today in the area where Egor Polyakov grew up. "I always carry a knife with me," said one local resident in 2019, "because a quarter of the people here are ex-cons" (Antonina Matveeva, "Moskvichi o zhizni v Golianove," Riamo, 2019, https://riamo.ru/article/396426/hozhu-s-nozhom-boyatsya-ne-sobirayus-moskvichi-o-zhizni-v-golyanove-xl).

2. See L. Trigos, *The Decembrist Myth in Russian Culture* (New York: Springer, 2009).

3. Philip Short, *Putin* (New York: Henry Holt & Company, 2022), 507–8.

4. *Rus* is the term for ancient Russia, often used by nationalists and here used mockingly. Video and comments of Putin's embarrassment are available at https://youtu.be/uNNdlobSIAc

5. For an exploration of the state's electoral cheating and the social responses to fraud, see Mischa Gabowitsch, *Protest in Putin's Russia* (Cambridge: Polity, 2017).

6. Andrei Soldatov and Irina Borogan, *The Red Web: The Struggle between Russia's Digital Dictators and the New Online Revolutionaries* (New York: PublicAffairs, 2015), 230–1.

7. "Russian Election: Biggest Protests since Fall of USSR," BBC News, 10 December 2011, https://www.bbc.com/news/world-europe-16122524

8. Megan Hauser, *Electoral Strategies under Authoritarianism: Evidence from the Former Soviet Union* (Lanham, MD: Lexington Books, 2019).

9. All of Navalny's old blog entries can be read in Russian at https://navalny.livejournal.com

10. See Jan Matti Dollbaum, Morvan Lallouet, and Ben Noble, *Navalny: Putin's Nemesis, Russia's Future?* (London: Hurst, 2021), 21–2.

11. "Miting na Chistykh Prudakh: Segodnia. 19–00," 5 December 2011, https://navalny.livejournal.com/656297.html?page=5

12. Dmitrii Zykov, "Manezhnaia pytaetsia otvetit' Bolotnoi," Radio Svoboda, 12 December 2011, https://www.svoboda.org/a/24419362.html; "Na Manezhnoi ploshchadi sostoialsia miting storonnikov 'Edinoi Rossii,'" Forbes.ru, 12 December 2011, https://www.forbes.ru/news/77428-na-manezhnoi-ploshchadi-sostoyalsya-miting-storonnikov-edinoi-rossii

13. Elena Shishkunova, "Surkov: 'Sistema uzhe izmenilas,'" *Izvestiia*, 22 December 2011.

14. "Russian Patriarch Says Punk Band 'Desecrated' Church," Radio Free Europe/Radio Liberty, 25 March 2012, https://www.rferl.org/a/russia_church_punk_band_pussy_riot_/24526352.html

15. Samuel A. Greene and Graeme B. Robertson, *Putin v. the People: The Perilous Politics of a Divided Russia* (New Haven: Yale University Press, 2019), 33.

16. It wasn't plain sailing all the way for the returning Putin, who had to deal with a brief and half-hearted bid from Medvedev to retain the presidency. See Zygar, *All the Kremlin's Men*, 204–6.

17. The "patriotic turn" of the early 2010s is well documented. See Petr Kratochvíl and Gaziza Shakhanova, "The Patriotic Turn and Re-Building Russia's Historical Memory: Resisting the West, Leading the Post-Soviet East?," *Problems of Post-Communism* 68, no. 5 (3 September 2021): 442–56; Gulnaz Sharafutdinova, "The Pussy Riot Affair and Putin's Démarche from Sovereign Democracy to Sovereign Morality," *Nationalities Papers* 42, no. 4 (July 2014): 615–21.

18. Vladimir Putin, "Rossiia: National'nyi vopros," *Nezavisimaia gazeta*, 23 January 2012.

19. "Putin Addresses Massive Moscow Rally," Radio Free Europe/Radio Liberty, 23 February 2012, https://www.rferl.org/a/russia_putin_rally_/24493191.html

20. Soviet culture was just as ill at ease with homosexuality, where hundreds of men were convicted of sodomy each year even under Mikhail Gorbachev.

21. Dan Healey, *Russian Homophobia from Stalin to Sochi* (New York: Bloomsbury Academic, 2017), 1–3.

22. Janet Elise Johnson, "Pussy Riot as a Feminist Project: Russia's Gendered Informal Politics," *Nationalities Papers* 42, no. 4 (July 2014): 583–90.

23. Frank Snowden, *The Fascist Revolution in Tuscany, 1919–22* (Cambridge: Cambridge University Press, 2004), 100.

24. Tiffany Jones, "Double-Use of LGBT Youth in Propaganda," *Journal of LGBT Youth* 17, no. 4 (1 October 2020): 408–31.

25. *Stephen Fry: Out There*, BBC, 2013.

26. The incident attracted worldwide attention. See, for example, Joseph Patrick McCormick, "Russian TV Host Denies Homophobia after Saying the Hearts of Gay Men Should Not Be Used for Organ Donation," PinkNews (blog), 12 August 2013, https://www.pinknews.co.uk/2013/08/12/russian-tv-host-denies-homophobia-after-saying-the-hearts-of-gay-men-should-not-be-used-for-organ-donation

27. Opakhin, "Ivan Katanaev."

28. "License to Harm: Violence and Harassment against LGBT People and Activists in Russia," Human Rights Watch, 15 December 2014, https://www.hrw.org/report/2014/12/15/license-harm/violence-and-harassment-against-lgbt-people-and-activists-russia

29. Ibid.

30. K. Guskov, O. Kucheryavenko, and M. Walker, "Cost of Indulgence: Rise in Violence and Suicides among LGBT Youth in Russia," *Health and Human Rights Journal* (blog), 2013, https://www.hhrjournal.org/2013/12/cost-of-indulgence-rise-in-violence-and-suicides-among-lgbt-youth-in-russia

31. "License to Harm."

32. Mark Gevisser, "Life under Russia's 'Gay Propaganda' Ban," *The New York Times*, 27 December 2013, sec. Opinion, https://www.nytimes.com/2013/12/28/opinion/life-under-russias-gay-propaganda-ban.html

33. "License to Harm."

34. Healey, *Russian Homophobia*, 2.

35. Irina V. Soboleva and Yaroslav A. Bakhmetjev, "Political Awareness and Self-Blame in the Explanatory Narratives of LGBT People amid the Anti-LGBT Campaign in Russia," *Sexuality & Culture* 19, no. 2 (June 2015): 275–96.

36. Nikolay Alekseyev, "Fighting the Gay Fight in Russia: How Gay Propaganda Laws Actually Only Help," RT International, accessed 13 October 2022, https://www.rt.com/op-ed/russia-gay-rights-sochi-945

37. Michael Lucas, "Nikolai Alexeyev: The Kremlin's New Pocket Gay," Out.Com, 28 August 2013, https://www.out.com/news-opinion/2013/08/28/nikolai-alexeyev-kremlin-new-pocket-gay

38. "License to Harm."

39. Guskov, Kucheryavenko, and Walker, "Cost of Indulgence."

40. Austin Charron, "Whose Is Crimea? Contested Sovereignty and Regional Identity," *Region* 5, no. 2 (2016): 225–56.

41. Vladimir Putin, "Obrashchenie prezidenta Rossiiskoi Federatsii," 18 March 2014, http://en.kremlin.ru/events/president/news/20603

42. Jekatyerina Dunajeva and Karrie J. Koesel, "'Us versus Them': The Politics of Religion in Contemporary Russia," *The Review of Faith & International Affairs* 15, no. 1 (2 January 2017): 56–67.

43. Sophia Kishkovsky, "Ukrainian Crisis May Split Russian Orthodox Church,"RISU, 27 March 2014, https://risu.ua/en/ukrainian-crisis-may-split-russian-orthodox-church_n68069

44. Mikhail D. Suslov, "'Crimea Is Ours!' Russian Popular Geopolitics in the New Media Age," *Eurasian Geography and Economics* 55, no. 6 (2 November 2014): 588–609.

45. Ol'ga Musafirova and Viktoriia Makarenko, "'Mal'chika' ne bylo, no on zhivet," *Novaia gazeta*, 15 July 2015.

46. The tale bore similarities to the most effective Soviet-era anti-Nazi stories in which the Nazis ritually slaughtered innocent youths, who were subsequently transformed into saintly idols.

47. As quoted in Andrew Roth, "Putin Opens 12-Mile Bridge between Crimea and Russian Mainland," *The Guardian*, 15 May 2018, https://www.theguardian.com/world/2018/may/15/putin-opens-bridge-between-crimea-and-russian-mainland

48. "MMP: Russian Imperial Movement," Stanford Centre for International Security and Cooperation, 2021, https://cisac.fsi.stanford.edu/mappingmilitants/profiles/russian-imperial-movement

49. Short, *Putin*, 633.

50. John Berryman, "Crimea: Geopolitics and Tourism," in *Tourism and Geopolitics: Issues and Concepts from Central and Eastern Europe*, ed. Derek R. Hall (Wallingford: CABI, 2017).

51. For a look at some of the ways in which liberals and the state continued to grapple with the memory of the 1990s online and in person, see Roberto Rabbia, "Russian Youth as Subject and Object of the 1990s' 'Memory War,'" in Krawatzek and Friess, *Youth and Memory in Europe*.

52. This "superfluous man," educated but at a loose end, dominated the Russian novel for several decades in the nineteenth century (Neil Cornwell and Nicole Christian, "The Classic Russian Novel," in *Reference Guide to Russian Literature* (London: Routledge, 1998)).

4. REMAKING THE YOUNG

1. Greene and Robertson, *Putin v. the People*, 19
2. Nyash Myash video, YouTube, 15 April 2014, https://www.youtube.com/watch?v=TBKN7_vx2xo
3. "Zasedanie mezhdunarodnogo diskussionogo kluba, 'Valdai,'" 19 September 2013, http://kremlin.ru/events/president/news/19243
4. The work, as it happened, was supervised by none other than Sergey Karaganov—the advocate of "constructive destruction" in the 2022 invasion of Ukraine. In a foreword, Karaganov lauds the authors' insights into "an idea that would bring the country together" and end "corruption and stagnation." See A. Likhacheva et al., "National Identity and the Future of Russia," Valdai Discussion Club, 2014, https://valdaiclub.com/files/11461/
5. For more on ethnocentric identity building, see Helge Blakkisrud, "Blurring the Boundary between Civic and Ethnic: The Kremlin's New Approach to National Identity under Putin's Third Term," in *The New Russian Nationalism*, ed. Pål Kolstø and Helge Blakkisrud, Imperialism, Ethnicity and Authoritarianism 2000–2015 (Edinburgh: Edinburgh University Press, 2016), 249–74, https://www.jstor.org/stable/10.3366/j.ctt1bh2kk5.16
6. Ben Judah, "A Day in the Life of Vladimir Putin: The Dictator in His Labyrinth," *The Independent*, 26 July 2014, https://www.independent.co.uk/news/world/europe/a-day-in-the-life-of-vladimir-putin-the-dictator-in-his-labyrinth-9629796.html
7. Filip Rudnik, "State Funding for Rappers," New Eastern Europe, 21 December 2018, https://neasterneurope.eu/2018/12/21/state-funding-rappers
8. Andrei Nedashkovskii, "Sasha Chest: 'Postupili kommentarii, chto prezidentu ponravilas' nasha s Timati pesnia,'" Flow (blog), 10 November 2015, https://the-flow.ru/features/moi-luchshiy-drug-sasha-chest-interview
9. Mikhail Nemtsev, "How Russia's Immortal Regiment Was Brought to Life," Riddle Russia, 8 May 2019, https://ridl.io/how-russia-s-immortal-regiment-was-brought-to-life; Ian Garner, "Russia's Youth Is Tired of Lavish Military Parades: Could Digital Culture Change the Country's Wartime Pageantry for Good?," The Calvert Journal, 9 May 2020, https://www.

calvertjournal.com/articles/show/11797/victory-day-digital-culture-remembrance-may-9-great-patriotic-war-personal-memory

10. See Introduction in Garner, *Stalingrad Lives*.

11. "Medinskii: 'Stalingrad' ne imel shansov na Oskar," RIA, 27 December 2013, https://ria.ru/20131227/986848356.html. For more on the production and reception of *Stalingrad*, see Stephen Norris, *Fedor Bondarchuk: "Stalingrad"* (Bristol: Intellect, 2022).

12. "VTsIOM: Ukhodiashchii god byl trudnym dlia trany?," Interfax, 24 December 2015, http://www.interfax.ru/presscenter/487104

13. For example, *Anna's War* (2018), *Little Sister* (2019), and *Alyosha* (2020). These films updated the formulaic Soviet pictures about children at war, which were still regularly shown on Russian television. The plots revolve around orphaned, lost, or traumatized children who, through their Soviet cunning and with the help of caring quasi-parents—usually soldiers—find new homes and outwit the monstrous Nazi invaders. Each film hammers home the same message: even children can become great warriors.

14. V. Karpov and E. Lisovskaya, "Educational Change in Time of Social Revolution: The Case of Post-Communist Russia in Comparative Perspective," in *Educational Reform in Post-Soviet Russia: Legacies and Prospects*, ed. B. Eklov, L. Holmes, and V. Kaplan (Abingdon: Routledge, 2014).

15. See, for example, a Voronezh State University newsletter from 2016: https://vovr.elpub.ru/jour/article/view/441/391

16. The group's official website is at http://юнкера-мхпи.рф

17. Most of the MAII Army's videos are available on their YouTube channel at https://www.youtube.com/channel/UCwC2G0qIKr1eY_Jd-TqxrDw

18. "Posviashchenie v Iunkera MkhPI," YouTube, 12 September 2012, https://youtu.be/jB2o_arXw3c

19. Samuel C. Woolley, "Digital Propaganda: The Power of Influencers," *Journal of Democracy* 33, no. 3 (2022): 115–29.

20. "Koeffitsient poleznosti deputatov gosdumy," KPDGD, 2022, https://vk.com/doc7898314_642671349?hash=vs5GVzrxwMy6EA7zK3joRakvFBuYEOj3ZC5YnAHwcCT&dl=LP3zuBaxyerii9BRltuZzabrzwITYcWvqatbTp7ikxo; "Zanko, Olga Nikolaevna," Putin's List: Database of Free Russia Forum, 2022, https://www.spisok-putina.org/en/personas/zanko/

21. "O dvizhenie," n.d., https://волонтёрыпобеды.рф/about; "Volontery Pobedy: Soobshchestvo neravnodushnykh liudei," n.d., https://vk.com/vsezapobedu

22. Zanko's public feeds are at https://vk.com/olga_zanko and https://t.me/o_zanko

23. VK, @olga_zanko, 25 March 2018, https://m.vk.com/wall7898314_4428

24. Ibid.

25. Juha Portaankorva, "11-letnii iunarmeets Demid," InoSMI, 8 October 2017, https://inosmi.ru/20171008/240428996.html

26. See the group's website at https://юнармейцы.рф

27. "Programma detskogo otdykha Voenno-patrioticheskogo lageria 'Iunarmeets,'" Iunarmiia RF, 2018, https://yunarmy.ru/upload/iblock/7e0/1.Voenno_patrioticheskiy_lager_YUNARMEETS.pdf

28. "'My nashli, chem interesovat' detei': glava Iunarmii," TASS, 29 March 2019, https://tass.ru/armiya-i-opk/6081524

29. The magazine, from December 2017, was inserted into *Ogonyok*, a popular lifestyle magazine.

30. "'My nashli, chem interesovat' detei': glava Iunarmii."

31. Alla Hurska, "Putin Seeks to Garner Support of Russian Youth Through Military-Patriotic Upbringing," Eurasia Daily Monitor (blog), 10 April 2019, https://jamestown.org/program/putin-seeks-to-garner-support-of-russian-youth-through-military-patriotic-upbringing-part-one

32. Baekken, "Patriotic Disunity."

33. The indoctrination efforts seem to have been successful. Even early participants were enthusiastic to join the real forces after spending time with the Youth Army: "I'm going to be a tank commander," declared one ninth grader to a Russian journalist in 2016. A sixteen-year-old explained that "military service and defending the motherland is my duty as a man." These young Russians fluently speak the language of the state, using rote forms they have seen and heard online and in person at Youth Army events to express their desire to serve. "Ot 'Iunarmii' do armii," *Komsomol'skaia Pravda*, 30 September 2016, https://www.spb.kp.ru/daily/26588.4/3604314/

34. Aleksey Tarasov, "Detstvo: Pod ruzh'e," *Novaia gazeta*, n.d., https://novayagazeta.ru/articles/2019/03/13/79863-detstvo-pod-ruzhie

35. Ibid.

36. "Andrei Kormukhin: 'Spasat'sia nuzhnoi 'Bandoi,'" Pravoslavie.ru, 17 June 2015, http://www.pravoslavie.ru/80033.html

37. Dud', "Chem zanimaetsia samyi izvestnyi fanat 'Spartaka.'"

38. Katanaev's blog posts from 2014–15 are available at https://archive.ph/https://i-k.livejournal.com/

39. On Russia's state capacity, see Brian D. Taylor, "Coercion and Capacity: Political Order and the Central State," in Taylor, *State Building in Putin's*

Russia: Policing and Coercion after Communism (Cambridge: Cambridge University Press, 2011), 71–111.

40. Jake Cordell, "Russia's Dwindling Middle Classes No Catalyst for Shift in Kremlin Foreign Policy," Russia Matters, 22 April 2021, https://www.russiamatters.org/blog/russias-dwindling-middle-classes-no-catalyst-shift-kremlin-foreign-policy

41. "Zoya" refers to a film about Zoya Kosmodemyanskaya, a sanctified wartime martyr. See Adrienne M. Harris, "Memorializations of a Martyr and Her Mutilated Bodies: Public Monuments to Soviet War Hero Zoya Kosmodemyanskaya, 1942 to the Present," *Journal of War & Culture Studies* 5, no. 1 (12 June 2012): 73–90.

42. Dariya Vyugina, "How McLuhan Would Have Talked to Us," in *Generations Z in Europe: Inputs, Insights and Implications*, ed. Christian Scholz and Anne Rennig (Bingley: Emerald, 2019).

43. I use Vasily Gatov's term the "censorship of noise" to describe the effect of Russia's always-on, omnipresent propaganda.

44. Maria Snegovaya, "Is It Time to Drop the F-Bomb on Russia? Why Putin Is Almost a Fascist," *World Policy Studies* 34, no. 1 (2017).

45. Catherine Shu, "Putin Passes Law That Will Ban VPNs in Russia," TechCrunch, 30 July 2017, https://techcrunch.com/2017/07/30/putin-passes-law-that-will-ban-vpns-in-russia/?guccounter=1&guce_referrer=aHR0cHM6Ly93d3cuZ29vZ2xlLmNvbS88guce_referrer_sig=AQAAABd8QgD7p5QddAu_akwPvdWY-qdNan7VYWMSQgZ-pzprCckIQPaT3Ra0OT2aHkBw_zg9qazJPP-M3VbHGeWr8oP_txeF7PkydB0Nclq0qV_6usds4Kv_60YuVl8T_4ZngPMhIA8Wh4QP6cYqtwdIlgzH9LB8RJ2etJ_HB_ykW0iIP

46. "Russia: Growing Internet Isolation, Control, Censorship," Human Rights Watch (blog), 18 June 2020, https://www.hrw.org/news/2020/06/18/russia-growing-internet-isolation-control-censorship

5. FASCISM UNLEASHED

1. "Opportunistic China Comes to Rescue of Russian Economy," *Le Monde*, 16 September 2022, https://www.lemonde.fr/en/international/article/2022/09/16/china-comes-to-rescue-of-russian-economy-with-pragmatic-and-opportunistic-support_5997183_4.html

2. Boris Grozovski, "Russian Youth against War," Wilson Center, 25 July 2022, https://www.wilsoncenter.org/blog-post/long-read-russian-youth-against-war

3. For more on the rhetorical preparation for genocide and historical roots of the phenomenon, see Alexander Etkind, "Ukraine, Russia, and Genocide of Minor Differences," *Journal of Genocide Research* (7 June 2022): 1–19.

4. "Minsk" refers to the protocols signed in 2014 and 2015 that aimed but failed to end the war in Eastern Ukraine.

5. I used tools available at tgstat.com to analyze all Telegram channel data cited in the text.

6. For example, see @novnew, @z_orator, @clubpravdy. Each of these relatively small channels has had moments of viral fame when bigger channels have highlighted their posts.

7. Vasily Grossman jokes about this phenomenon in *Life and Fate*. One character, a Red Army general, is perplexed to discover that Tolstoy did not fight in the war of 1812, even though he had so perfectly captured its essence in *War and Peace*: "He didn't take part in it—what do you mean? … He hadn't been born? What on earth?" (*Life and Fate*, 441).

8. Aleksey Morozov, "'My voiuem na storone dobra': Chto proiskhodilo na marafone 'Znanie,'" *Komsomol'skaia Pravda*, 1 September 2022, https://www.kp.ru/daily/27439/4641630

9. "Patriarch Kirill Congratulated Putin on Defender of the Fatherland Day," HRWF, 24 February 2022, https://hrwf.eu/russia-23-february-patriarch-kirill-wished-putin-peace-of-mind-on-defender-of-the-fatherland-day

10. Kateryna Tyshchenko, "Patriarch Kirill Says Occupiers in Ukraine 'Defend Russia on the Battlefield,'" Yahoo News, 19 June 2022, https://news.yahoo.com/patriarch-kirill-says-occupiers-ukraine-151846931.html

11. "Patriarkh Kirill obratilsia k voinam," Tsargrad, 23 September 2022, https://tsargrad.tv/news/patriarh-kirill-obratilsja-k-voinam-idite-smelo-ispolnjat-svoj-dolg_631218

12. Allyson Edwards, "Russia's Programme of Educational Indoctrination in Ukraine's Occupied Territories," ZOiS Berlin (blog), 29 June 2022, https://www.zois-berlin.de/en/publications/zois-spotlight/russias-programme-of-educational-indoctrination-in-ukraines-occupied-territories

13. Putin, "Meeting on Socioeconomic Support for Regions."

14. Russia, of course, has a sordid history with this phenomenon—in particular during World War II, when thousands of troops who had evaded capture were interrogated and even executed by Stalin's agents.

15. "Russian Journalist Detained for Reports on Mariupol Theater Bombing," Radio Free Europe/Radio Liberty, 27 April 2022, https://www.rferl.org/a/russian-journalist-mariupol-bombing/31823899.html

16. "Neizvestnye izbili zhurnalista Sota," Radio Svoboda, 31 May 2022, https://www.svoboda.org/a/v-peterburge-neizvestnye-izbili-zhurnalista-sota-petra-ivanova/31875760.html

17. Dugin's wartime writing is available at https://vk.com/duginag

18. See VK, @rossia3, 10 October 2022, https://vk.com/wall-23755 719_45703

19. Alya Ponomareva, "'V rai ikh nikto ne pustit'. Blogery ob ugroze Tret'ei mirovoi," Radio Svoboda, 29 April 2022, https://www.svoboda.org/ a/v-ray-ih-nikto-ne-vpustit-blogery-ob-ugroze-tretjey-mirovoy/ 31826902.html

20. Mark Galeotti, "At Home and on the Battlefield, Seven Self-Inflicted Traps Are Snaring Putin," *The Times*, 15 October 2022, https://www. thetimes.co.uk/article/at-home-and-on-the-battlefield-seven-self-inflicted-traps-are-snaring-putin-2sshjwx9d

21. VK, @publicsobor, 4 May 2022, https://m.vk.com/wall-167504204_ 10917

22. "Meeting with the Winners and Finalists of the Teacher of the Year Contest," Kremlin.ru, 5 October 2022, http://en.kremlin.ru/events/ president/transcripts/69519; "People's Choice: Together Forever Concert Rally," Kremlin.ru, 30 September 2022, http://en.kremlin. ru/events/president/transcripts/69519

23. Telegram, @sotaproject, https://t.me/sotaproject/37474

24. Telegram, @readovkanews, https://t.me/readovkanews/28636

25. Nonetheless, said Sergey Galanin, a sixty-one-year-old singer who performed at one of the events, the concerts are still useful. After all, such concerts "show people that they're not alone, that we are many, that we love the motherland, and that we aren't ashamed." Even if individual concerts weren't always well received, the overall project has been widely discussed, bringing yet more momentum to the sense of what was in the summer of 2022 a brutal, stagnant war as an exciting carnival. Not a bad return for a paltry $1.5m state investment (https://360tv. ru/news/tekst/lozhnyj-patsifizm).

26. Telegram, @partizanskayapravda, https://t.me/partizanskayapravda/ 10502

27. In the summer of 2022, only one of the top ten most shared Russian-language Telegram channels about politics was a non-state aligned outlet. The others featured three politicians (Ramzan Kadyrov, Dmitry Medvedev, and Duma Chairman Vyacheslav Volodin), a news channel, two TV journalists (Vladimir Solovyov and Margarita Simonyan), and four frontline war correspondents. War correspondent Aleksandr Kots, who ran the most popular channel, saw his stories reposted over 100,000 times in July alone.

28. M. Alyukov, M. Kunilovskaya, and A. Semenov, "Propaganda Setbacks and Appropriation of Anti-War Language: 'Special Military Operation' in Russian Mass Media and Social Networks," Russian Election Monitor, 2022, https://www.russian-election-monitor.org/Second-Front.html?

file=files/rem/pictures/Media%2008-2022/War%20Media%20 Monitoring%20Eng.%20v2.pdf

29. The contrast is so stark that Igor Girkin, who was instrumental in the 2014 invasion of Ukraine and has committed war crimes, joked that Russia should create two defense ministries: one for real work, and one for the "important tasks ... building and storming fake Reichstags, staging tank biathlons, making cartoons, and organizing military concerts." Telegram, @strelkovii, https://t.me/strelkovii/3093

30. Polnaia versiia nterv'iu Mikhail Onufrienko Ivanu Kondakovu, YouTube, September 16 2022, https://www.youtube.com/watch?v=YYKBJpv YAM4

31. "Immigratsiia v Evropy: Real'nost,'" YouTube, 31 May 2022, https:// www.youtube.com/shorts/dfSJP2YS3yM

32. Telegram, @OpenUkraine, https://t.me/OpenUkraine/14123

33. Telegram, @cyber_frontZ, https://t.me/cyber_frontZ/4611

34. Takhir Gareev, in his late twenties from the far-flung Siberian oil town of Nizhnevartovsk, is one of the dozens of amateur singers who are flaunting their patriotic credentials by releasing wartime tracks online. Working under the name *Zhelezny tigr* ("Iron Tiger"), Gareev uploads performative, shambolic demonstrations of his macho nationalist credentials, posting videos that imagine him traveling to the Ukrainian front to fight, telling local social media news sites that artists who've left Russia are "reptiles," and filming himself traveling to St Petersburg for the national Airborne Forces Day in 2022. Gareev's sole viral hit has been a track of abominable lyrical quality: "America, I'll give it to you, smack smack smack! Z Battalion gonna give it to you, smack smack smack!" Dressed in a cheap camouflage T-shirt and bandana, Gareev is flanked by two female friends, each also dressed up in symbolic militaria. The work is crude and poorly produced, but it's indicative of the outlets bored young Russian men find for themselves to create militarized identities full of anti-Western aggression. The track might have been widely derided after it was mocked by Navalny's social media team, but nationalist Telegram groups shared the video as an example of admirable, homegrown effort. In turn, the clip has become a viral sensation on Russian-language TikTok, where users film themselves or set footage of children dancing along: "Well then, Banderovites, you gonna get it now, smack smack smack!" VK, @edodowr, 16 October, 2022, https://www.tiktok.com/@edodowr/video/7154993108374 064390

35. Matthew Cullerne Bown and Brandon Taylor, eds, *Art of the Soviets: Painting, Sculpture, and Architecture in a One-Party State, 1917–1992* (Manchester: Manchester University Press, 1993), 76.

36. Yura refers to the "Ghost of Kyiv," a fictional Ukrainian fighter ace claimed to have tormented the Russian invaders in the first two weeks after the February 2022 invasion ("How Ukraine's 'Ghost of Kyiv' Legendary Pilot Was Born," BBC News, 1 May 2022, https://www.bbc.com/news/world-europe-61285833).

37. VK, @vindemiatrix_art, 18 June 2022, https://vk.com/wall707516 809_138?t2fs=721bde92e8bddab3f2_3

38. "RT, Apachev i pevitsa Dar'ia Frei sniali sovmestnyi videoklip."

39. For example, VK, @rusaesthetics, https://vk.com/rusaesthetics; @veneden, https://vk.com/veneden; and @krivoglazzz, https://vk.com/public173957939

40. VK, @vegchel, 9 May 2022, https://vk.com/vegchel?w=wall-6735 9347_5891577

41. "Obrashchenie 'Blood & Honour/Combat 18 Rossiia' ko vsem russkim natsional-sotsialistam," LiveJournal, 22 February 2007, https://sieben-star.livejournal.com/168664.html?ysclid=l4e88ly3gp355654052

42. "Ideologicheskaia propaganda v Rossiia vedetsia dostatochno slabo," *Pravda*, 30 August 2022, https://www.pravda.ru/news/world/1741395-kozyrev_propaganda_rossija

43. Mark Townsend, "Pro-Kremlin Neo-Nazi Militia Inciting the Torture and Murder of Ukrainian Prisoners," *The Guardian*, 2 October 2022.

44. Dmitrii Steshin, "Pochemu Bog ne dal nam bystroi pobedy," *Komsomol'skaia Pravda*, 5 October 2022, https://www.kp.ru/daily/27454/4657672

6. THE UNMEANING OF PROTEST

1. On silence and disengagement from politics, see Félix Krawatzek, "Adrift from Politics: Youth in Russia before the War," Friedrich-Ebert-Stiftung, July 2022, https://library.fes.de/pdf-files/bueros/wien/19388.pdf

2. See, for example, Maryana Prokop and Arleta Hrehorowicz, "Between Political Apathy and Political Passivity: The Case of Modern Russian Society," Torun International Studies 1, no. 12 (December 2019).

3. Juri Rescheto, "Russia: Tens of Thousands Flee 'Cold Civil War,'" DW, 13 July 2022, https://www.dw.com/en/russia-tens-of-thousands-flee-cold-civil-war/a-62462008; Karen Gilchrist, "A Second Wave of Russians Is Fleeing Putin's Regime," CNBC, 14 July 2022, https://www.cnbc.com/2022/07/14/russians-flee-putins-regime-after-ukraine-war-in-sec-ond-wave-of-migration.html

4. Brash young rappers like Face and Alisha Morgenshtern, who found himself in hot water for questioning the cult of World War II in 2021, have departed the country after speaking out. Others fled Russia to arrange anti-war concerts. Oxxxymiron, an Oxford-educated rapper with over

2 million Instagram followers, organized a London concert, "Russians Against War," attended by expats and emigres displaying Ukrainian colors. Noize MC, a hardcore rapper who had appeared at the Bolotnaya Square protests back in 2011, launched "Voices for Peace," a tour of Central Europe and the Baltics in collaboration with Monetochka, a twenty-three-year-old purveyor of whimsical Soviet-Russian pop.

5. I spoke with one young Moscow resident whose IT work evaporated in March: "I've applied for a new passport. I want to apply for repatriation to Israel (my mom has that magic last name, so she can take us all). We're not looking to live there," he continues. "We just need to become citizens so we can leave Russia." The queue of applications means that he has been waiting months to leave. Now he's worried that he might have to use money saved for his Tel Aviv flight to bribe recruiters if they try to conscript him.

6. Iuliia Pleskanovskaia, "Liudi udivilis' tomu, chto ia russkaia," Kholod Media (blog), 12 April 2022, https://holod.media/2022/04/12/humanitarian/

7. The popular LGBT network, lgbtnet.org, did not post on its social media feeds for several months after the war began.

8. Dilia Gafurova, "Russia Shuts Down Its Biggest LGBT+ Organisation," openDemocracy, 22 April 2022, https://www.opendemocracy.net/en/5050/cf-sphere-russia-lgbtqi-shut-down/

9. A video tour of Ilya's show is available at https://youtu.be/y1sRlkAaEbc

10. Dmitrii Sidorov, "Meet the Student Journalists Who Are Trying to Change Russia," openDemocracy, 14 April 2021, https://www.opendemocracy.net/en/odr/interview-with-doxa-russian-student-magazine

11. The "blank placard" arrests are not entirely new. The state has been engaging in this sort of absurd anti-performativity with protestors for years. "Russia: Activists Held over 'Invisible Posters,'" BBC News, 8 April 2014, https://www.bbc.com/news/blogs-news-from-elsewhere-26936770

12. Rachel Rodriguez, "Signed, a Foreign Agent," *Russian Life*, 25 April 2022, https://russianlife.com/the-russia-file/signed-a-foreign-agent/

13. Mischa Gabowitsch in the early 2010s showed how Russian protestors didn't always define themselves as political opposition, and sometimes refused to "identify themselves with a political movement." Noting the turn to aesthetics, slogan, and graphics-driven protest, Gabowitsch spotted the trend that would explode in the wartime social media ecosphere (Andrey Makarychev, "The Culture of Protest: Counter-Hegemonic Performances in Putin's Russia," *The Russian Review* 72, no. 4 (2013): 653–7).

14. Peter Reddaway, *Uncensored Russia: Protest and Dissent in the Soviet Union*

(New York: American Heritage, 1972), 95–100,https://soviethistory. msu.edu/1968-2/crisis-in-czechoslovakia/crisis-in-czechoslovakia-texts/red-square-demonstration/

15. Stas Iurasov, "Keeping Silent Kills You," Dev.Ua, 14 May 2022, https://dev.ua/news/lentaru

16. An archive of the defaced Lenta homepage is available at https://web.archive.org/web/20220509065825/https://lenta.ru

17. Telegram, @cyber_frontZ, https://t.me/cyber_frontZ/2185

18. VK, @kulinarnayashkola2018, 13 May 2022, https://vk.com/wall485207127_3499

19. Andrey Pertsev, "The Ministry of Happiness," Riddle Russia, 6 September 2022, https://ridl.io/the-ministry-of-happiness

20. Leyla Latypova, "NGO Helps Women Fleeing Ukraine War, Political Repression," The Moscow Times, 11 August 2022, https://www.the-moscowtimes.com/2022/08/11/ngo-helps-women-fleeing-ukraine-war-political-repression-a78538

21. Note that the Soviet Union also claimed the language of "activism" for itself, part of its hypocritical crusade against "imperialism" and "fascism."

22. Katyusha's campaigns and wares are available for viewing at http://возвращать-укреплять.рф

23. Telegram, @ukraina_ru, https://t.me/ukraina_ru/74257

24. Telegram, @SolovievLive, https://t.me/SolovievLive/120514

25. Telegram, @OpenUkraineChat, https://t.me/OpenUkraineChat/2072604

26. Mohiuddin Ahmed and Paul Haskell-Dowland, "Is Russia Really about to Cut Itself Off from the Internet? And What Can We Expect if It Does?," The Conversation (blog), 9 March 2022, http://theconversa-tion.com/is-russia-really-about-to-cut-itself-off-from-the-internet-and-what-can-we-expect-if-it-does-178894

27. Gregory Asmolov, "Russia, Ukraine, and the Emergence of 'Discon-nective Society,'" Riddle Russia, 21 April 2022, https://ridl.io/russia-ukraine-and-the-emergence-of-disconnective-society

28. "Deputat predlozhila sazhat' v tiur'mu roditelei," Lenta, 3 August 2022, https://lenta.ru/news/2022/08/03/butina

29. "Peskov priznalsia v ispol'zovanii VPN," RBC, 2 April 2022, https://www.rbc.ru/society/02/04/2022/62489abf9a79474f0fbfd249

30. Erik C. Nisbet, Olga Kamenchuk, and Aysenur Dal, "A Psychological Firewall? Risk Perceptions and Public Support for Online Censorship in Russia," *Social Science Quarterly* 98, no. 3 (2017): 958–75.

31. Gregory Asmolov, "The Disconnective Power of Disinformation Campaigns," *Journal of International Affairs* 71, no. 1.5 (2018): 69–76.

32. Valerii Gannenko, "Osnovatel' 'Lukomor'ia': Siloviki ne ponimaiut nichego," Sobesednik, n.d., https://sobesednik.ru/obshchestvo/201 61114-osnovatel-lurkomorya-siloviki-ne-ponimayut-v-internetah-sove

33. VK, @olga_zanko, 12 August 2022, https://vk.com/wall7898314_ 12879

34. VK, @olga_zanko, 4 October 2022, https://vk.com/wall7898314_ 14053

7. THE Z GENERATION

1. Will Oremus, "TikTok Created an Alternate Universe Just for Russia," *Washington Post*, 13 April 2022, https://www.washingtonpost.com/ technology/2022/04/13/tiktok-russia-censorship-propaganda-track-ing-exposed/

2. "Kazhdogo piatogo rossiiskogo shkol'nika pod ruzh'e," Finanz.ru, August 2022, https://www.webcitation.org/query?url=https://www.finanz. ru/novosti/aktsii/kazhdogo-pyatogo-rossiyskogo-shkolnika-postavyat-pod-ruzhe-1030224248

3. Other efforts included a massive Communist Party recruitment drive on Red Square on the weekend of 21–22 May. Between 5,000 and 6,000 children were inducted. The event was widely covered in the media.

4. "V Korsakove proshel fleshmob," BezFormata, 28 January 2022, https:// ujnosahalinsk.bezformata.com/listnews/podderzhku-rossiyskih-olimpi-ytcev/101947002

5. Telegram, @nasha_stranaZ, https://t.me/c/1400700658/86643

6. Telegram, @RKadyrov_95, https://t.me/RKadyrov_95/2599

7. Nicholas Laznovsky, "The Mutated Chechen Identity: 'Akhmat Sila!' The Significance of a Slogan and Its Proliferation in the Digital and Physical Space" (PhD, University of Texas at Austin, 2021).

8. "Iunarmeitsy Krasnodara uchastvovali v otkrytii murala," 2022, https:// yunarmy.ru/press-center/news/yunarmeytsy-krasnodara-uchastvovali-v-otkrytii-murala-geroyu-spetsialnoy-voennoy-operatsii. The poem's author references Stepan Bandera, a Ukrainian nationalist leader during World War II who collaborated with the Axis invaders. Bandera is reg-ularly invoked by Russian propaganda as evidence of Ukraine's innately fascist nature.

9. VK, @yunarmy175, 15 August 2022, https://vk.com/video-191596 332_456239047

10. H. Coynash, "29 Thousand Crimean 'Youth Army' Recruits Taught to Hate Ukraine and Be Ready to Die for Russia," Kharkiv Human Rights Protection (blog), 9 February 2022, https://khpg.org/en/1608810007

11. Sergey Mokrushin, "'Iunarmiia' dlia Krymchan," Krym.Realii, 13 August 2021, https://ru.krymr.com/a/yunarmiya-dla-krymchan-plany-rosiii-po-voenno-patrioticheskomu-vospitaniyu/31418125.html

12. Facebook, @denisovaombudsman, 9 April 2022, https://www.facebook.com/100044138451142/posts/518112373003373/?d=n

13. Dmitrii Novikov, "Popadanie 'Iunarmii' pod sanktsii ob'iasnili strakhom Zapada," News.ru, 22 July 2022, https://news.ru/society/popadanie-yunarmii-pod-sankcii-obyasnili-strahom-zapada-pered-detmi-iz-rf

14. Nagornyy's social media profiles are available at https://www.tiktok.com/@nikitagym; https://www.instagram.com/nikushkarus

15. VK, @nikushkarus, 9 May 2022, https://vk.com/wall-211042971_1559

16. "MGER, 'Edinaiia Rossiia' i 'Iunarmiia' zapuskaiut aktsiiu 'Komanda druzhby,'" Molodaia gvardiia, 19 March 2022, https://mger.ru/novosti/glavnoe/17724-mger-obshchestvennye-priemnye-edinoy-rossii-i-yunarmiya-zapuskayut-aktsiyu-komanda-druzhby-dlya-shko/

17. Stepanova's developed a reputation as something of a social media attack dog, laying into skiers from abroad who've criticized Russia by telling them that "only we, Russians, will choose our leader" and to "go learn history." Sprinkling her comments with acerbic and personal remarks—one Norwegian skier is "over the hill"—and threats—"go have a look at what happened in Oslo last time [there was a fascist invasion]"—Stepanova doesn't hold back. Unlike Nagornyy, who stays above the fray, Stepanova throws herself right into the online fight, responding to fans positively and assailing opponents unrelentingly. See Elena Grigor'eva, "Lyzhnitsa ili blogger?," SportBox, 25 March 2022, https://news.sportbox.ru/Vidy_sporta/cross_country/spbnews_NI1556808_Lyzhnica_ili_bloger_Stepanova_pochti_ne_vystupajet_no_vyskazyvajetsa_po_lubomu_povodu; "Lyzhnitsa Stepanova posovetovala kritikovavshemu rossiian norvezhtsu izuchit' istoriiu," SportBox, 26 April 2022, https://news.sportbox.ru/Vidy_sporta/cross_country/spbnews_NI1577588_Lyzhnica_Stepanova_posovetovala_kritikovavshemu_rossijan_norvezhcu_Iversenu_izuchit_istoriju

18. Telegram, @SolovievLive, https://t.me/SolovievLive/103238; https://t.me/SolovievLive/104121

19. The idea of fighting "for a just cause" refers to a line from Soviet minister Vyacheslav Molotov's radio speech from the day after Germany invaded the USSR in 1941.

20. TikTok, @unarmy_ast, 27 January 2022, https://www.tiktok.com/@unarmy_ast/video/7057851763155553538

21. TikTok, @unarmia_nso, November 2021, https://www.tiktok.com/@unarmia_nso/video/7033057460994723073

22. The Sakhalin Youth Army group's TikTok feed is available at https://www.tiktok.com/@sakh_unarmy_ys/

23. See, for example, "Ot 'Iunarmii' do armii." The state does not, however, release statistics revealing how many former Youth Army have entered active military service, let alone the numbers serving in Ukraine today. But several of Maksim's former charges have been at the front in recent months. Back in Saratov, Nikita, who had joined the Youth Army as a twelve-year-old soon after the group's foundation, is still contemplating signing up after he graduates high school.

24. "Alleia pamiati," https://yunarmy.ru/for-you/alley-memory

25. VK, @olga_zanko, 18 August 2022, https://vk.com/wall7898314_12961

26. VK, @olga_zanko, 17 June 2022, https://vk.com/wall7898314_11585

27. Oleg Mel'nik, "Patriotizm mozhno tol'ko vospitat'," Vzgliad, 18 May 2022, https://vz.ru/politics/2022/5/18/1150056.html

28. Telegram, @SolovievLive, https://t.me/SolovievLive/107806

29. "Vozvrat pionerii podderzhan starshimi," 19 May 2022, https://pobedarf.ru/2022/05/19/rossiyane-vyskazalis-o-vozrozhdenii-pionerii/; Marc Bennetts, "How Vladimir Putin Is Turning Russia's Children into Propaganda Pioneers," *The Times*, 17 July 2022, https://www.thetimes.co.uk/article/how-vladimir-putin-is-turning-russias-children-into-propaganda-pioneers-xxxbh5w3q

30. Mel'nik, "Patriotizm mozhno tol'ko vospitat'."

31. Newer groups include the "Navigators of Childhood," which seeks to find young leaders to "support" classroom teaching with patriotism and morality and pumps out soft-focus inspirational videos about assisting children to "make their dreams come true," and the "Healthy Way of Life Generation," whose "healthy" life includes both Instagram-style clean living and healthy patriotism. Both have been heavily promoted in young people's media spaces in recent months.

32. Each lesson's videos, quizzes, and teaching materials are available at https://razgovor.edsoo.ru

33. "'Nobody Faced Persecution in the Soviet Union': An Excerpt from a Student-Made Recording of One of Russia's New 'Patriotism' Lessons," Meduza, 6 September 2022, https://meduza.io/en/feature/2022/09/06/nobody-faced-persecution-in-the-soviet-union

34. Alesia Marokhovskaia and Irina Dolinina, "Schast'e Rodiny dorozhe zhizni," iStories, 26 August 2022, https://istories.media/investigations/2022/08/26/schaste-rodini-dorozhe-zhizni/?utm_source=twitter&utm_medium=mainpage&utm_campaign=schaste-rodini-dorozhe-zhizni

35. See, for example, Francis Scarr (@francis_scarr), tweet, 8 October

2022, https://twitter.com/francis_scarr/status/157871999997564
9280/photo/1

36. Sasha Vasilyuk (@SashaVasilyuk), tweet, 25 April 2022, https://twitter.com/sashavasilyuk/status/1518697956303507456?s=21&t=vcjCt
eHF27fPYbGDyR_DXg

37. Liliia Pashkova, "V shkol'nyi kurs istorii predlozhili vkliuchit' voennuiu
operatsiiu na Ukraine," RBC, 23 June 2022, https://www.rbc.ru/soc
iety/23/06/2022/62b47b5a9a794735c31d52fb

38. Anatasiia Stognei, "Shkol'naia metodika o 'pol'ze' sanktsii," BBC News,
8 April 2022, https://www.bbc.com/russian/features-61001133?
fbclid=IwAR30B9RTK47WIX-GLYrbJjaivP—1uVXD1R-nyOFFAE-
4f1uOCE06nXBNjvs

39. Anna Luk'ianova, "Nachal'naia voennaia podgotovka dlia detei vvedena
v shkolakh Rossii," 10 November 2022, https://www.kp.ru/daily/
27469/4675324

40. Jeanne Whalen, "Russian School Children Dobbing in Teachers Who
Don't Back Putin's War on Ukraine," *The Sydney Morning Herald*,
10 April 2022, https://www.smh.com.au/world/europe/russian-
school-children-dobbing-in-teachers-who-don-t-back-putin-s-war-on-
ukraine-20220411-p5achh.html

41. "Mal'chika Aleshu iz Belgorodskoi oblasti posviatili v iunarmeitsy,"
28 May 2022, https://aif.ru/society/army/malchika_aleshu_iz_bel-
gorodskoy_oblasti_posvyatili_v_yunarmeycy

42. Sergey Bolotov, "Putin pokazal novyi simvol spetsoperatsii," Ura.ru,
8 August 2022, https://ura.news/articles/1036285156

43. VK, @vegchel, 12 May 2022, https://vk.com/feed?w=wall-69628799_
1783405

44. Baekken, "Patriotic Disunity."

45. In this sense, Russia is returning to the Soviet era. Soviet children might
have been ahead of American schoolchildren in knowledge, but thanks
to an emphasis on rote learning they struggled to think for themselves
or voice their own opinions.

46. "Molodye prikinuli zadachi na budushchee," 1 July 2022, https://pobe-
darf.ru/2022/07/01/molodye-prikinuli-zadachi-na-budushhee/
?doing_wp_cron=1661620206.4858419895172119140625

47. Krawatzek, "Adrift from Politics: Youth in Russia before the War."

CONCLUSION: DEPROGRAMMING A FASCIST

1. Telegram, @strelkovii, https://t.me/strelkovii/2625

2. Griffin, *The Nature of Fascism.*

3. Timothy R. Vogt, *Denazification in Soviet-Occupied Germany: Brandenburg, 1945–1948* (Cambridge, MA: Harvard University Press, 2000).

4. Petter Törnberg, "How Digital Media Drive Affective Polarization through Partisan Sorting," *Proceedings of the National Academy of Sciences* 119, no. 42 (18 October 2022).

5. For a survey of Moscow's Soviet-era deportations, see Nikolai Bugai, *The Deportation of Peoples in the Soviet Union* (New York: Nova, 1996).

6. For the importance of social media and information on the twenty-first-century battlefield, see Matthew Ford and Andrew Hoskins, *Radical War: Data, Attention, Control* (London: Hurst, 2022).

7. Peter Kenez, *The Birth of the Propaganda State: Soviet Methods of Mass Mobilization, 1917–1929* (Cambridge: Cambridge University Press, 1985).

8. "Ukaz Prezidenta Rossiiskoi Federatsii: O Strategii national'noi bezopasnosti," 2 July 2021, http://publication.pravo.gov.ru/Document/View/0001202107030001

9. Thomas Wood and Ethan Porter, "The Elusive Backfire Effect: Mass Attitudes' Steadfast Factual Adherence," *Political Behavior* 41, no. 1 (1 March 2019): 135–63; "Police Arrest Fifth Grader during a Class," Meduza, 9 October 2022, https://meduza.io/en/feature/2022/10/09/police-arrest-fifth-grader-during-class

10. Leon Festinger and Stanley Schachter, *When Prophecy Fails* (London: Simon & Schuster, 2013); Steven Hassan, *The Cult of Trump: A Leading Cult Expert Explains How the President Uses Mind Control* (London: Simon & Schuster, 2020), 304.

11. Hassan, *The Cult of Trump*, 304.

12. Félix Krawatzek and Gwendolyn Sasse, "Transnational Links and Political Attitudes: Young People in Russia," *Europe-Asia Studies* 74, no. 7 (9 August 2022): 1278–99.

13. Sung Kyung Kim, "'I Am Well-Cooked Food': Survival Strategies of North Korean Female Border-Crossers and Possibilities for Empowerment," *Inter-Asia Cultural Studies* 15, no. 4 (2 October 2014): 553–71.

14. Telegram, @zrussia_1, https://t.me/zarussia_1/897

15. Academic evidence to support this "alternative pathway" approach is plentiful. See, for example, Tobias Borck and Jonathan Githens-Mazer, "Countering Islamic State's Propaganda: Challenges and Opportunities," in *ISIS Propaganda: A Full-Spectrum Extremist Message*, ed. Stephane J. Baele, Katharine A. Boyd, and Travis G. Coan (Oxford: Oxford University Press, 2020); Sara Monaci, "Social Media Campaigns against Violent Extremism: A New Approach to Evaluating Video Storytelling," *International Journal of Communication* 14 (2020): 980–1003.

16. The effects of such counter-propaganda have been shown on extremists in the Middle East, where actors can slowly shift from one group to another without ever really realizing they're doing it. See Robin Burda, "PsyOps of Non-State Armed Actors in the Middle East: Vanishing Borders?" (PhD, Masarykova University, 2021).

17. Research from conflict and post-conflict zones suggests that sharing stories and dialogue is an effective way to have the radicalized recognize the values they share with their enemy. In Northern Ireland, which experienced brutal civil strife in the late twentieth century, Chris Reynolds has observed that simply by listening to the other side's experiences of trauma, tragedy, and war, participants in classroom, museum, and other educational projects became more sympathetic (Chris Reynolds, "Beneath the Troubles, the Cobblestones: Recovering the 'Buried' Memory of Northern Ireland's 1968," *The American Historical Review* 123, no. 3 (1 June 2018): 744–8). Likewise, after the 1994 genocide in Rwanda, which left some half a million ethnic Tutsis dead, programs that mandated dialogue between victims and perpetrators proved effective. Some who had committed genocidal acts became more willing to pay reparations and face penal justice as a result of such activities. Activities such as speaking clubs for young people from different sides of a conflict and healing programs that involved collaboration from across the community towards common goals have proved particularly effective (https://www.peaceinsight.org/en/organisations/ami).

18. *Our Bubbles of Certainty: A Perspective from My Life in North Korea*, YouTube, 2022, https://www.youtube.com/watch?v=Qh25Zo58UQY

19. "Ukraine Support Tracker," Kiel Institute, https://www.ifw-kiel.de/topics/war-against-ukraine/ukraine-support-tracker

20. Russian extremists' language of will, spirit, individualism, and collectivism resembles the mythical speech of Nazi culture (see Vicki O'Donnell Stupp, "Myth, Meaning, and Message in 'The Triumph of the Will,'" *Film Criticism* 2, no. 2/3 (1978): 40–9).

21. See Alexei Yurchak, *Everything Was Forever, until It Was No More: The Last Soviet Generation* (Princeton, NJ: Princeton University Press, 2006).

22. For an examination of how intensely information war can be waged not just against nations and communities but against individuals, see Jessikka Aro, *Putin's Trolls: On the Frontlines of Russia's Information War against the World* (New York: Ig Publishing, 2022).

SELECT BIBLIOGRAPHY

Anderson, Benedict. *Imagined Communities: Reflections on the Origins and Spread of Nationalism*. London: Verso, 2016.

Aro, Jessikka. *Putin's Trolls: On the Frontlines of Russia's Information War against the World*. New York: Ig Publishing, 2022.

Asmolov, Gregory. "The Disconnective Power of Disinformation Campaigns." *Journal of International Affairs* 71, no. 1.5 (2018): 69–76.

Babchenko, Arkady. *One Soldier's War*. New York: Open Road + Grove/Atlantic, 2009.

Baekken, Håvard. "Patriotic Disunity: Limits to Popular Support for Militaristic Policy in Russia." *Post-Soviet Affairs* 37, no. 3 (4 May 2021): 261–75.

Beumers, Birgit. *World Film Locations: Moscow*. Bristol: Intellect Books, 2014.

Blakkisrud, Helge. "Blurring the Boundary between Civic and Ethnic: The Kremlin's New Approach to National Identity under Putin's Third Term." In *The New Russian Nationalism: Imperialism, Ethnicity and Authoritarianism 2000–2015*, edited by Pål Kolstø and Helge Blakkisrud, 249–74. Edinburgh: University Press, 2016. https://www.jstor.org/stable/10.3366/j.ctt1bh2kk5.16.

Bolt Rasmussen, Mikkel. *Late Capitalist Fascism*. Cambridge: Polity, 2022.

Borenstein, Eliot. *Meanwhile, in Russia ...: Russian Internet Memes and Viral Video*. London: Bloomsbury Publishing, 2022.

Butler, Judith. *Gender Trouble: Feminism and the Subversion of Identity*. New York: Routledge, 1990.

Caruth, Cathy. *Trauma: Explorations in Memory*. Baltimore: Johns Hopkins University Press, 1995.

———. *Unclaimed Experience: Trauma, Narrative, and History*. Baltimore: Johns Hopkins University Press, 1996.

Casula, Philipp. "Between 'Ethnocide' and 'Genocide': Violence and Otherness in the Coverage of the Afghanistan and Chechnya Wars." *Nationalities Papers* 43, no. 5 (September 2015): 700–18.

251

Clark, Katerina. *Moscow, the Fourth Rome: Stalinism, Cosmopolitanism, and the Evolution of Soviet Culture, 1931–1941*. Cambridge, MA: Harvard University Press, 2011.

Cottiero, Christina, Katherine Kucharski, Evgenia Olimpieva, and Robert W. Orttung. "War of Words: The Impact of Russian State Television on the Russian Internet." *Nationalities Papers* 43, no. 4 (4 July 2015): 533–55.

Daniel, J. Furman, III, and Paul Musgrave. "Synthetic Experiences: How Popular Culture Matters for Images of International Relations." *International Studies Quarterly* 61, no. 3 (1 September 2017): 503–16.

Dollbaum, Matti Jan, Morvan Lallouet, and Ben Noble. *Navalny: Putin's Nemesis, Russia's Future?* London: Hurst, 2021.

Dudko, Oksana. "A Conceptual Limbo of Genocide: Russian Rhetoric, Mass Atrocities in Ukraine, and the Current Definition's Limits." *Canadian Slavonic Papers* 64, nos. 2–3 (15 September 2022): 133–45.

Eco, Umberto. *How to Spot a Fascist*. New York: Random House, 2020.

Edwards, Allyson. "Russia on a Throne of Bayonets: Militarisation without the Military in Yeltsin's Russia, 1990–2000." PhD thesis, Swansea University.

NB: Are you sure this shouldn't be Swansea University?, 2021.

Eichler, Maya. *Militarizing Men: Gender, Conscription, and War in Post-Soviet Russia*. Stanford, CA: Stanford University Press, 2011.

Etkind, Alexander. "Ukraine, Russia, and Genocide of Minor Differences." *Journal of Genocide Research* (7 June 2022): 1–19.

Ford, Matthew, and Andrew Hoskins. *Radical War: Data, Attention, Control*. London: Hurst, 2022.

Frye, Northrop. *Anatomy of Criticism*. Princeton, NJ: Princeton University Press, 1957.

Fujimura, Clementine. *Russia's Abandoned Children: An Intimate Understanding*. Westport, CT: Praeger, 2005.

Gabowitsch, Mischa. *Protest in Putin's Russia*. Cambridge: Polity, 2017.

Galeotti, Mark. *We Need to Talk About Putin: How the West Gets Him Wrong*. New York: Random House, 2019.

Garner, Ian. *Stalingrad Lives: Stories of Combat and Survival*. Montreal: McGill-Queen's University Press, 2022.

———. "'We've Got to Kill Them': Responses to Bucha on Russian Social Media Groups." *Journal of Genocide Research* (9 May 2022): 1–8.

Graney, Katherine. *Russia, the Former Soviet Republics, and Europe since*

1989: Transformation and Tragedy. Oxford: Oxford University Press, 2019.

Greene, Samuel A., and Graeme B. Robertson. *Putin v. the People: The Perilous Politics of a Divided Russia*. New Haven: Yale University Press, 2019.

Griffin, Roger. *The Nature of Fascism*. London: Pinter, 1991.

Grossman, Vasilii Semenovich. *Life and Fate*. London: Vintage Classic, 2011.

Hauser, Megan. *Electoral Strategies under Authoritarianism: Evidence from the Former Soviet Union*. Lanham, MD: Lexington Books, 2019.

Healey, Dan. *Russian Homophobia from Stalin to Sochi*. New York: Bloomsbury Publishing, 2017.

Hellbeck, Jochen. *Revolution on My Mind: Writing a Diary under Stalin*. Cambridge, MA: Harvard University Press, 2009.

Hemment, Julie. *Youth Politics in Putin's Russia: Producing Patriots and Entrepreneurs*. Bloomington: Indiana University Press, 2015.

Horvath, Robert. *Putin's Fascists: Russkii Obraz and the Politics of Managed Nationalism in Russia*. Abingdon: Routledge, 2020.

Johnson, Janet Elise. "Pussy Riot as a Feminist Project: Russia's Gendered Informal Politics." *Nationalities Papers* 42, no. 4 (July 2014): 583–90.

Kelly, Catriona. *Comrade Pavlik: The Rise and Fall of a Soviet Boy Hero*. London: Granta, 2005.

Kenez, Peter. *The Birth of the Propaganda State: Soviet Methods of Mass Mobilization, 1917–1929*. Cambridge: Cambridge University Press, 1985.

Kratochvíl, Petr, and Gaziza Shakhanova. "The Patriotic Turn and Re-Building Russia's Historical Memory: Resisting the West, Leading the Post-Soviet East?" *Problems of Post-Communism* 68, no. 5 (3 September 2021): 442–56.

Krawatzek, Félix. "Adrift from Politics: Youth in Russia before the War." Friedrich-Ebert-Stiftung, July 2022. https://library.fes.de/pdf-files/bueros/wien/19388.pdf.

Krawatzek, Félix, and Nina Friess, eds. *Youth and Memory in Europe: Defining the Past, Shaping the Future*. Berlin: De Gruyter, 2022.

Krawatzek, Félix, and Gwendolyn Sasse. "Transnational Links and Political Attitudes: Young People in Russia." *Europe-Asia Studies* 74, no. 7 (9 August 2022): 1278–99.

Laruelle, Marlène. *Is Russia Fascist? Unraveling Propaganda East and West*. Ithaca, NY: Cornell University Press, 2021.

Makarychev, Andrey. "The Culture of Protest: Counter-Hegemonic Performances in Putin's Russia." *The Russian Review* 72, no. 4 (2013): 653–7.

McGlynn, Jade. *The Kremlin's Memory Makers: The Politics of the Past in Putin's Russia*. London: Bloomsbury, 2023.

————. *Russia's War*. Cambridge: Polity, 2023.

Motyl, Alexander J. "Putin's Russia as a Fascist Political System." *Communist and Post-Communist Studies* 49, no. 1 (2016): 25–36.

Oushakine, Serguei Alex. *The Patriotism of Despair: Nation, War, and Loss in Russia*. Ithaca, NY: Cornell University Press, 2011.

Politkovskaya, Anna. *Putin's Russia: Life in a Failing Democracy*. New York: Henry Holt & Company, 2007.

Pomerantsev, Peter. *Nothing Is True and Everything Is Possible: The Surreal Heart of the New Russia*. New York: Public Affairs, 2014.

Schröder, Ingo, and Asta Vonderau. *Changing Economies and Changing Identities in Postsocialist Eastern Europe*. Münster: LIT Verlag, 2008.

Sharafutdinova, Gulnaz. "The Pussy Riot Affair and Putin's Démarche from Sovereign Democracy to Sovereign Morality." *Nationalities Papers* 42, no. 4 (July 2014): 615–21.

Shenfield, Stephen. *Russian Fascism: Traditions, Tendencies, Movements*. New York: M.E. Sharpe, 2001.

Short, Philip. *Putin*. New York: Henry Holt & Company, 2022.

Snegovaya, Maria. "Is It Time to Drop the F-Bomb on Russia? Why Putin Is Almost a Fascist." *World Policy Studies* 34, no. 1 (2017): 48–53.

Snyder, Timothy. "We Should Say It: Russia Is Fascist." *The New York Times*, 19 May 2022.

Soboleva, Irina V., and Yaroslav A. Bakhmetjev. "Political Awareness and Self-Blame in the Explanatory Narratives of LGBT People amid the Anti-LGBT Campaign in Russia." *Sexuality & Culture* 19, no. 2 (June 2015): 275–96.

Soldatov, Andrei, and Irina Borogan. *The Red Web: The Struggle between Russia's Digital Dictators and the New Online Revolutionaries*. New York: PublicAffairs, 2015.

Stella, Francesca. "Queer Space, Pride, and Shame in Moscow." *Slavic Review* 72, no. 3 (2013): 458–80.

Strukov, Vlad, and Sarah Hudspith, eds. *Russian Culture in the Age of Globalization*. Abingdon: Routledge, 2018.

Suslov, Mikhail D. "'Crimea Is Ours!' Russian Popular Geopolitics in the

New Media Age." *Eurasian Geography and Economics* 55, no. 6 (2 November 2014): 588–609.

Wood, Elizabeth A. "Performing Memory: Vladimir Putin and the Celebration of World War II in Russia." *The Soviet and Post-Soviet Review* 38, no. 2 (1 January 2011): 172–200.

Yablokov, Ilya. *Fortress Russia: Conspiracy Theories in the Post-Soviet World.* Cambridge: Polity, 2018.

Yurchak, Alexei. *Everything Was Forever, until It Was No More: The Last Soviet Generation.* Princeton, NJ: Princeton University Press, 2006.

Zygar, Mikhail. *All the Kremlin's Men: Inside the Court of Vladimir Putin.* New York: PublicAffairs, 2016.

INDEX

INDEX